RESEARCH METHODS IN SERVICE INDUSTRY MANAGEMENT

NICK JOHNS *and* DARREN LEE-ROSS

CASSELL
LONDON AND NEW YORK

Cassell
Wellington House
125 Strand
London WC2R 0BB

370 Lexington Avenue
New York
NY 10017-6550

www.cassell.co.uk

First published 1998

British Library Cataloguing-in-Publication Data
A catalogue record for this book is available from the British Library.

ISBN 0–304–33513–4 (hardback)
       0–304–33512–6 (paperback)

Typeset by Fakenham Photosetting Limited, Fakenham, Norfolk
Printed and bound in Great Britain by Redwood Books, Trowbridge, Wiltshire

Research Methods in Service Industry Management

Mountbatten Library
Tel: (01703) 319249 Fax: (01703) 319697
Please return this book on or before the last date stamped.
Loans may be renewed on application to the Library Staff.

Contents

Introduction

Research is increasingly significant at all levels of service industry management, particularly in the hotel, tourism, leisure, retail and banking sectors. There is heavy pressure upon academic departments in these subject areas to produce and publish research, and increasing numbers of faculty members are turning their attention to research studies. Support for postgraduate researchers is increasing, and modules in research methods are increasingly becoming an integral part of undergraduate curricula.

This book provides a fairly simply constructed, straightforward text which describes the whys and wherefores of research and puts different methodologies, paradigms and styles of research into a comprehensible perspective. Thus it will give undergraduates in research methods modules a good basic grounding and provide a springboard for further reading and study in this subject. The book will also be very useful to students preparing themselves to undertake a dissertation: both undergraduates and masters level candidates (e.g. MBA). It will provide a valuable overview for individuals considering research for a higher degree. In order to achieve these aims, the scope is set as wide as possible, and research theory and methodology are treated in a general way. We feel that this is necessary, in order to fill many of the gaps that we have identified in students' understanding when we have been supervising dissertations or starting potential PhD candidates on their initial programmes of reading.

In traditional academic subjects, it is taken largely for granted that research is a beneficial activity. Research is the source of most of the knowledge on which curricula are based, and it also provides an ideal learning opportunity for students who are ready to take the major responsibility for their own learning. In our experience, the value of research is not always appreciated by those engaged in vocationally oriented studies. For instance, it is often harder to convince practising service industry managers of the value of research, despite the fact that marketing, business strategy and training provision, for example, all demand a good understanding of an existing situation before any informed decision can be made. Sometimes the scepticism of practitioners carries over to students in this field, who have to be convinced of the value of research before they will give their full attention to the subject. It can be still more difficult to persuade students of the value of methodological theory or the philosophy of knowledge. Without these things it is impossible to appreciate the precise contribution made by any study. Yet they tend to complicate and mystify the academic study of research.

For these reasons, this book presents the activity of researching as a life skill, an extension of everyday experience, which is itself often a continuous process of gathering and sifting information, in the hope of coming to a clear decision. The following excerpt from John Wyndham's *The Day of the Triffids* illustrates the main features of the process. It draws its strength of course from the fact that our awareness is heightened by a change in our surroundings, and directs this 'everyday research' process at novel and puzzling occurrences. Yet the process itself occurs all the time at some level of our consciousness.

> I left the pub door swinging behind me as I made my way to the corner of the main road. There I hesitated.
>
> To the left, through miles of suburban streets, lay the open country; to the right, the West End of London, with the City beyond. I was feeling somewhat restored, but curiously detached now, and rudderless. I had no glimmering of a plan, and in the face of what I had at last begun to perceive as a vast and not merely local catastrophe, I was still too stunned to begin to reason one out. What plan could there be to deal with such a thing? I felt forlorn, cast into desolation, and yet not quite real, not quite myself here and now.
>
> In no direction was there any traffic, nor any sound of it. The only signs of life were a few people here and there cautiously groping their ways along the shop-fronts.
>
> The day was perfect for early summer. The sun poured down from a deep blue sky set with tufts of white woolly clouds. All of it was clean and fresh, except for a smear made by a single column of greasy smoke coming from somewhere behind the houses to the north.
>
> I stood there indecisively for a few minutes. Then I turned east, Londonwards.

This brief scene includes an initial, interest-catching anecdote which may lead to further enquiry (the plume of smoke). There are also observations which support previous experience (the streets almost emptied by a catastrophe which has blinded the population). The excerpt illustrates the 'wondering' quality of research, the continual taking stock and the constant need to formulate and evaluate plans. There is also theory (the author has begun to see the situation as a 'vast and not merely local catastrophe'). John Wyndham adds a final decision, related to his hero's observations (the hero turns towards London for the next part of the adventure).

In the present textbook we have simplified this 'natural research' process into the three stages – anecdote, observation and theory – which are used to explain inductive and hypothetico-deductive approaches to research. These in turn are integrated into a discussion of positivism, phenomenology and the nature of 'reality'. We believe that by doing this we have demystified some of the problems which beset students when they are faced with planning a programme of research and first begin to consider methodology in detail. In order to gain a thorough grasp of the theory and philosophy of research, it is necessary to read widely and to cover each part of the topic in much greater depth than can be provided in a single volume of this kind. We believe that this book fills an important gap, by providing an overview, which is at once suitable for undergraduates on research methods courses and for postgraduates seeking to identify and position their own reading needs. At the end of each chapter we include examples of suitable further reading to assist this process.

We have sought as far as possible to present the scope of research in an open way without a bias towards (for example) quantitative or qualitative investigations. Indeed, we feel that the best way to research is to consider every methodological option, and as far as possible to use a variety of approaches, in order to obtain the best possible understanding of the situation being studied. This view is also reflected in Chapter 6, which considers how quantitative and qualitative methodology may be effectively integrated.

We have slanted our treatment of analysis towards a systems view, both of business problems and of the research process itself. We recognize that this is not the only approach that can be taken toward interpreting data, but feel that it is often the most appropriate way to understand business organizations and the sub-units from which they are derived. The systems paradigm is also the one in which organizations tend to think of themselves. 'Scientific management' and Taylorism are no longer in favour, but the changes that continue to occur within organizations (particularly in service industries) – downsizing, re-profiling, re-structuring, cultural engineering, empowerment and so on – all seem to spring from a systems view of the world. Besides this, soft systems methodology is a powerful general purpose tool for structuring problems and ideas, and its use represents a widely applicable skill for aspiring managers. Even individuals who take no further interest in research after their course has ended will find these aspects of systems theory a useful window on the world of management practice.

Much service industry research regards itself as interdisciplinary in nature. Indeed, journals and conferences sometimes reject papers on the grounds that they lack this quality. We feel that far too often 'interdisciplinarity' is really interpreted as multidisciplinarity, in which accepted approaches from established disciplines are brought to bear upon problems identified within service industries. We believe that this is a cause for regret, since almost by definition, new situations generate new problems, which in turn have the potential to stimulate new solutions. We would like to see service industries develop their own self-awareness, to the point where service industry research can develop as an independent area, rather than, as at present, being overshadowed by longer-established academic sectors. We feel that by providing a background grounded in the service sector, this text will facilitate the disentanglement of service industry management from other fields of knowledge, so that it can develop its own research approaches, methods and techniques.

REFERENCE

Wyndham, John (1954) *The Day of the Triffids*, Penguin Books, London.

1

The Nature of Research

INTRODUCTION

Research is about discovering and understanding the human environment. In its simplest terms it is a fundamental activity, since all individuals must be aware of their world and understand it sufficiently to adapt to its changes and survive. Understanding the environment and making sense of it are also important management skills, essential to decision-making and control. Yet the word 'research' seems to indicate a highly specialized, abstract activity, divorced from everyday life. This is partly explained by the difference between personal experience and organizational activity. The informal, common-sense 'research' by which we form our individual, day-to-day perceptions of the environment is usually integrated into a whole range of other functions and activities, which do not need to be formulated into words, or subjected to conscious analysis. Environmental observations often *do* need to be reported or recorded in management situations, but here again they tend to be only one component of management activity, seldom undertaken solely for their own sake.

'Formal' research activities are undertaken in response to a specific objective, i.e. observing and analysing a stated problem or situation. They therefore require a level of conscious organization which is not shared by less formal processes. It is necessary to be aware of the advantages and drawbacks of the research methods used. Communication, which seems so simple in personal, or informal, 'research' processes, becomes all-important when a group of individuals must share complex activities such as observation, analysis and conclusion and impart the results meaningfully to a third party: the instigator and sponsor of the research.

Research activities can be thought of as having four identifiable but interdependent phases: preparation, planning, process and product. These can be described broadly as follows.

- *Preparation* is about identifying the purpose at the heart of every research exercise. The preparation of research includes the objectives of the sponsor and the way the work is funded. In a vocational subject such as service industry management, research should aspire to a practical purpose and ultimately to the improvement of management practice in the industry. 'Formal' research also includes practical and philosophical issues, e.g. of the methods employed and the use to which the results will be put. A research exercise usually contributes to subject knowledge and must therefore often consider previous groundwork by other researchers. Another important aspect of the purpose of research may be the agenda, interests and even the personality of the researcher. Purpose implies an understanding of the basic process of research: the interplay between researchers, disciplines and techniques. There may well be tension between preparation and methodology, between preparation and the outcomes of the programme, and even between different purposes, such as those of the sponsor and the individual researcher.

- *Planning* is essential to all research, whether it is conceived as an exercise, a programme or an ongoing organizational activity. Planning involves rationalizing and integrating the various purposes of the research. It includes balancing the needs of the study itself with the techniques and philosophy to be used, the requirements of the research team and the way the research outcomes are to be managed. Once these decisions have been made, the planning process involves setting time scales and managing the contingencies which tend to be an inevitable part of investigative work.

- *Process* is about method and methodology, two distinct but related considerations. 'Method' refers to the methods and techniques which are to be used in a given research study. 'Methodology' is a wider term indicating the whole approach that is to be used and including the underlying philosophy or rationale. Methodological considerations reflect the personal preferences of the researchers and research sponsors. They may also dictate the way the research is conducted and the order in which techniques are used. Method and methodology are therefore also functions of the planning phase. In addition, the research process almost always involves integrating the study with previous work by other researchers – another aspect of the planning phase. The 'method' phase requires the integration of different techniques and team members and, increasingly, demands the integration of specialists from different fields into interdisciplinary programmes.

- *Product* represents the outcomes of a research project or programme. These should relate to the objectives and may include a statement or restatement of the problem. The products of research are wide in scope, but generally involve some kind of written report. Other possible manifestations of research programmes are presentations, static and multimedia displays. However, the outcomes of research do not stop at its exposition. Often the research information is employed for some strategic purpose, such as the production of a management plan (e.g. for marketing a product, managing personnel or increasing productivity). Research may also be used to justify itself (as, for example, in some academic institutions) and the intended outcome may be to attract more funding so that more research may go ahead.

The relationship between the four phases is shown diagrammatically in Figure 1.1. Although these phases are common to all research, every project, programme or activity will differ in the way it is conducted. The phases are always likely to be interrelated to some extent. For example, preparation and product tend to be particularly interdependent, as do planning and process. Subtle interactions also

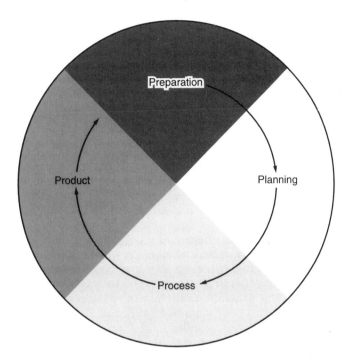

Figure 1.1　Model of a typical research programme

occur between the other two pairs. Thus the phases are distinct, but their boundaries tend to be blurred.

This chapter examines the nature of the research process and of the philosophical considerations underlying research methodology. In doing so it contributes to the 'preparation' phase. 'Preparation' is, of course, highly specific to the particular research programme in hand. It is also a very personal area, which can vary widely in style and content, depending upon the skills and attitudes of the individuals sponsoring and undertaking the work. Nevertheless, an understanding of the principles which underlie the research process will enable the individual to choose an appropriate topic and methodology and to undertake the planning of the research programme in a purposeful way.

THE NATURE OF RESEARCH

The *Oxford English Dictionary* gives three basic definitions of 'research'. It is (a) 'the act of searching, closely or carefully for or after a specified thing' or (b) 'an investigation directed to the discovery of some fact by careful study of a subject [i.e. a course of critical or scientific inquiry]'. The third definition (c) is '(without article): investigation, inquiry into things [or the] habitude of carrying out such investigation'. All three definitions are relevant within a vocational academic field such as service industry management. Academics and students in the field must have a general appreciation of research (definition c) because it is the source of knowledge and the means by which the curriculum is built and maintained. However, the practice of management frequently involves initiating research investigations (definition b) into a range of aspects, such as the activities of competitors, the perceptions of customers or the behaviour of employees. Therefore, it is important that management students learn the skills of 'searching, closely or carefully for or after a specified thing' (definition a).

Three elements – *anecdote, observation* and *hypothesis* – can be regarded as making up all research processes. These are discussed below.

- The word *anecdote* is derived from the Greek word for gossip, and means a short, noteworthy and usually unsubstantiated story. For example, it can refer to an amusing story told at a social gathering. Research studies do not have to start with an anecdote in this strict sense, but practically all research programmes start with what may be called an *anecdotal stage*. This may take the form of a casual observation which prompts a question, or perhaps two specialists get talking at a social event and an idea emerges. Another possibility is a 'hunch' or inspiration. Someone then wonders whether the observation, idea or hunch (the 'anecdote') is representative of the world as a whole. For example, the original hunch might be the idea that organizations tend to resist change. The next question is whether this generally applies, i.e. do all organizations resist processes of change? This question may be widened: if all organizations in fact resist change, do they do so in a similar way? *Why* do they resist change? And so on. The anecdotal stage itself is by definition unsubstantiated and cannot provide answers to these questions. In order to do so, a research programme will have to identify suitable methods of questioning or observation which are likely to provide a more dependable answer. Anecdotes are widespread in management situations, where they are frequently used to support decisions without further evaluation or analysis. There may of course be good reasons of cost or timing why this is so, but generally a worthwhile question is worthy of further study.
- For the purposes of research, an *observation* includes any fact learned during the detailed study of a problem or situation. For example, observations made of the way organizations respond to change could include details of the organizational structures and the way they change over time. Interviews or surveys could be conducted, providing information ('observations') about employee attitudes to change. Other relevant information might include descriptions of how communication processes take place, the range of products or services offered, accounting information and so on. Thus all aspects of organizations which are likely to be relevant to their function and to the area under study should be considered. The principal difference between an observation and an anecdote is that a research observation must be able to satisfy other researchers that it is valid, and to some extent substantiated. Thus, the observation stage of a research programme must be carefully planned. For example, accepted research observations may be made in a precisely structured way, under specially controlled conditions.
- A *hypothesis* (plural *hypotheses*) attempts to explain observations, usually by linking one set of facts with another. For example, analysis of the data obtained from observing organizations may enable the researcher to put forward generalizations about the way organizations behave when confronted by change. These might lead to hypotheses about employee attitudes, motivation and group

behaviour in similar situations. It might be possible to link attitudes further to other aspects of the organization: for example, to an observed drop in productivity or profitability caused by reaction to an environmental change. Further hypotheses may associate the stimulus of change with management responses, such as alterations in the organizational structure or the way work is scheduled. A hypothesis thus enables the researcher to understand, explain and model the environment. In general, the more aspects the hypothesis can explain, the more useful and persuasive it is.

Anecdote, observation and hypothesis are thought to underlie (in modified form) the way in which all human individuals set about making sense of their world. The psychologist George Kelly argues that people identify areas of interest more or less randomly according to their personality and the nature of their environment. This is the anecdotal stage of the process. Next comes a stage of focused observation, and finally individuals develop what Kelly calls 'personal constructs', associating ideas with the reality around them and drawing parallels and generalizations. For example, 'mother' might come to be associated with 'loving'. Personal perceptions are very complex, and 'mother' may also come to be associated with a range of ideas, each of which will be associated with a range of other objects. In this way individuals build up a 'personal space' in which constructs form a basis for making sense of their perceptions and understanding their world.

Kelly (1969) uses the phrase 'every man his own scientist', likening the formation of personal constructs to the research known as scientific method. He says:

> A scientist's inventions [i.e. theories about observations] assist him in two ways: they tell him what to expect and they help him to see it when it happens. Those that tell him what to expect are theoretical inventions and those that enable him to observe outcomes are instrumental inventions. The two types are never wholly independent of each other, and they usually stem from the same assumptions. This is unavoidable. Moreover, without his inventions, both theoretical and instrumental, man would be both disoriented and blind. He would not know where to look or how to see.

For the purposes of this book it is more appropriate to use the word 'research', rather than 'science'. Kelly uses the terms 'science' and 'scientist' because he regarded scientific method as the most valid approach to research observation in the field of psychology. Scientific method also suited him as a model for personal construct theory, because it allowed him to account for both theoretical and instrumental constructs in his subjects. Other workers would disagree; there are several objections to using scientific method as the model, two of which follow. In the first place, personal constructs are primarily non-verbal. Indeed, Kelly devoted most of his life to developing a non-verbal technique (Kelly's repertory grid) for studying them. In the second place, individuals tend to view their world not as scattered entities, but as a whole which is generally more than the sum of its parts.

TWO RESEARCH MODELS

Anecdote, observation and hypothesis are used in research in two recognizably different ways. These are characterized respectively as the *inductive* and *hypothetico-deductive* processes, and the difference between them is chiefly concerned with the sequence in which they occur during the research activity.

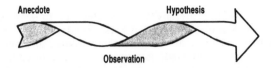

Figure 1.2   Inductive model of the research process

The inductive model of research processes is shown diagrammatically in Figure 1.2. The anecdote alerts the researcher to the field of interest, after which careful observations are made. The data are examined and analysis enables the researcher to extract hypotheses. The model of science is called inductive reasoning, because the observations are supposed to lead naturally to the hypothesis. Another way of putting this is that the facts *induce* the conclusion. The word 'induce' is defined (*Oxford English Dictionary*) as 'to lead to ... a conclusion or inference'.

The inductivist's job is one of meticulous observation and careful data-gathering. Once the data have been gathered, they are subjected to scrutiny, whereupon natural, inescapable inferences emerge.

Example 2.1   A classical view of the inductive process

Sir Arthur Conan Doyle (1974) makes his hero Sherlock Holmes rely almost exclusively upon the inductive model for unravelling puzzles and solving crimes:

'I'll tell you one thing which may help you in the case', he said '... the murderer was a man. He was more than six feet high, was in the prime of life, had small feet for his height, wore coarse, square-toed boots and smoked a Trichinopoly cigar. He came here with his victim in a four-wheeled cab, which was drawn by a horse with three old shoes and one new on his off foreleg. In all probability the murderer had a florid face and the finger nails of his right hand were remarkably long ...'

'You amaze me, Holmes', said I. 'Surely you are not as sure as you pretend to be of all those particulars which you gave.'

'There's no room for mistake', he answered. 'The very first thing which I observed on arriving there was that a cab had made two ruts with its wheels close to the kerb. Now, up to last night, we have had no rain for a week, so that those wheels, which left such a deep depression must have been there during the night. There were the marks of the horse's hooves too, the outline of one of which was far more clearly cut than that of the other three, showing that that was a new shoe ...'

'That seems simple enough', said I; 'but how about the ... man's height?'

'Why ... from the length of his stride. It is a simple calculation enough.'

'And his age?' I asked.

'Well, if a man can stride four and a half feet without the smallest effort, he can't be quite in the sere and yellow. That was the breadth of the puddle on the garden walk which he had evidently walked across ... Is there anything else that puzzles you?'

'The finger nails and the Trichinopoly,' I suggested.

'The writing on the wall was done with a man's forefinger dipped in blood. My glass allowed me to observe that the plaster was slightly scratched in doing it, which would not have been the case if the man's nail had been trimmed. I gathered up some scattered ash from the floor. It was dark and flakey – such an ash as is only made by a Trichinopoly ...'

'And the florid face?' I asked.

'Ah, that was a more daring shot, though I have no doubt that I was right. You must not ask me that at the present state of the affair.'

In Sherlock Holmes's case the carefully observed clues led to inescapable conclusions about the case ('elementary, my dear Watson') and eventually to the perpetrator of the crime. The 'art' of the inductivist consists of making minute, meaningful observations. Once these have been accurately made and analysed, the induced conclusions should automatically be correct. Sir Arthur Conan Doyle's genius is to make us believe in Sherlock Holmes's infallible powers of observation – his assumptions would be much more risky to make in practice.

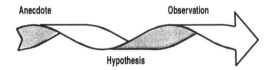

Figure 1.3   Hypothetico-deductive model of the research process

An important alternative to the inductive model of research is the *hypothetico-deductive* model, represented in Figure 1.3. According to this model, the anecdote provokes the researcher to put forward a hypothesis, which is then tested by experiment to see whether it is supported by practical experience. Thus, the observation stage of the process comes *after* the formulation of a hypothesis. The *Oxford English Dictionary* defines the word 'deduce' as 'to draw something as a conclusion from something known or assumed' or 'to derive by reasoning'.

Unlike the inductivist, who merely observes and analyses, the hypothetico-deductivist puts forward hypotheses, designs experiments to test them and from the results decides whether the original hypotheses still stand. An experiment cannot *prove* the validity of a hypothesis, but it can invalidate it. A positive experimental result does not confirm a hypothesis, but only allows it to persist until another experiment succeeds in falsifying it at a later date.

Inductive and hypothetico-deductive methodologies have both been put forward as suitable models for research in the management field. However, both are highly simplified representations; actual research programmes can be shown to proceed in a much more complex and integrated way. The best way to understand the complexities of the research process is to examine the philosophy of scientific method, probably the most widely studied area of research methodology in this respect. The term 'scientific method' can be a somewhat emotive one in the social sciences, and the reader should note that it is not being recommended as a model for the development of research in management, or any area of social study. However, it does provide a good example of the problems of modelling research processes in general.

SCIENTIFIC METHOD

The following is a much compressed and simplified synopsis of developments in the philosophy of science. The reader should note that it represents only sketchily the work of many eminent thinkers. For a more detailed picture the reader is recommended to read Alan Chalmers's (1982) excellent book on the subject. This provides a readable history of the development of thought about scientific method (and by extension about research methodologies in general). In the interests of brevity, references to the works of individual philosophers are not included in this text, but these are fully referenced in Chalmers's work.

Until the early twentieth century, scientific method was regarded as being an inductive process. The scientist's job was seen as one of meticulous observation and careful data-gathering, after which 'natural laws' (generalizations about the way the world works) were assumed to manifest themselves automatically. This view of scientific method was first proposed in the reign of Queen Elizabeth I by the philosopher Francis Bacon. Subsequent writers in the eighteenth and nineteenth centuries tended to accept without question that it was the way in which eminent workers such as Newton formulated the laws of the natural sciences. However, the inductive standpoint suffers from an important flaw as a model of scientific investigation. Scientific observations are nearly always made within the pre-planned framework of an *experiment*, designed to test the effect of changing just one environmental factor at a time. Its success depends upon holding all the others constant. For example, an experiment designed to discover the effect of a particular treatment upon rats would have to set up a 'control' group as well as the test group. Otherwise, any observed change might be due to some other aspect of the test, such as the temperature at which the animals were kept, or the food they were given.

Such experimental design depends upon producing a detailed hypothesis *before* the experiment takes place. Observations are then made in order to test it, as proposed by the hypothetico-deductive model. An experiment does not lead directly to natural laws, but merely enables the scientist to deduce whether the theory is true or false, or needs modification. In this model, scientific knowledge is built up piece by piece, each hypothesis being laboriously tested before it can be added to the jigsaw puzzle.

Although the hypothetico-deductive model provides a more accurate picture of what individual scientists do, it is not really representative of scientific development as a whole. The reason for this is that it ignores the social dimension of the research process. New hypotheses have to convince the scientific community of their truth before they can achieve general acceptance. However, individual hypotheses are usually only accepted if they can be related to existing ones. Thus, self-sustaining patterns of thought develop, and a new theory will only achieve acceptance if it fits the pattern. This is the reasoning of Thomas Kuhn, who called these patterns *paradigms* (pronounced 'paradymes'). A paradigm (literally a pattern or model) represents a generally accepted way of scientific thought; a scientific 'world view' rather than simply a theory.

Although paradigms are made up of a large number of separate, but compatible, theories and hypotheses, they are generally based upon one central view from which the subsidiary hypotheses are derived. For example, the principal paradigm of astronomy during the middle ages was *geocentricism*. The earth was considered the centre of the universe, circled by the sun, moon and stars. Planets (literally, 'wanderers') clearly did not perform regular rotations, and all sorts of complex models were constructed to try to make them fit the paradigm. Over the course of about two hundred years, Copernicus, Galileo, Kepler, Lorenz, Newton and others built up a new paradigm, the central tenet of which was that smaller heavenly bodies such as the Earth orbited larger ones such as the sun. It was also discovered that the same principles applied not only to the solar system, but also to the motion of material objects on the earth's surface. This paradigm is known as classical mechanics, and can be used to account for the motion of bullets, rockets and vehicles as well as the orbits of planets.

Kuhn proposed that people get used to explaining their world in terms of a particular paradigm. They tend to find a new paradigm shocking and unacceptable because they have much emotional security invested in the old one. The medieval establishment, which was strongly influenced by the Church, accepted the teachings of Aristotle and the 'common-sense' notions that the Earth was flat and formed the centre of the universe. Most scholars and teachers of the time strongly resisted the new paradigm. Copernicus and Galileo, for example, were persecuted and prevented from publishing their ideas. Experiments which contradicted established teachings were denounced on the grounds that the experimenters must have used witchcraft to achieve their results.

Entrenched paradigms are not easily changed. In order to do this, renowned 'experts' must admit they are wrong and public opinions must change. The more profound the paradigm, the greater the change it demands, and the greater the resistance incurred. Kuhn argues that paradigms generally arise from the combined work of a number of individuals, supported by mutual theory and experiment. When the new movement has reached sufficient momentum a *scientific revolution* occurs. The new paradigm then rapidly gains acceptance and many new converts are persuaded to accept it, on the grounds that it explains known facts better than the old one. However, there is also generally a residual 'old guard' and bitter recriminations occur between the old order and the new. Eventually the older generation dies out and resistance ceases, but in time another new paradigm appears and gradually gathers acceptance until a new scientific revolution can occur.

The job of science, indeed of all research, is to explain the nature and structure of the world. The better a paradigm does this, the more effective it is and the more likely it is to be accepted in the course of a 'scientific revolution'. Research represents mankind's reaching out for understanding and no paradigm is likely to provide a complete explanation of all our observations. By the same token, any observation can be explained on the basis of a number of different paradigms, many of which coexist simultaneously at any given moment. There is an 'ecology of ideas', some of which approximate to the establishment view more than others. In addition, all individuals are simultaneously seeking to develop personal constructs to understand their world. Some of these may develop their thinking into coherent scientific theories, a few of which may eventually become accepted paradigms. Underlying Kuhn's work is the assumption that despite the existence of an established paradigm, individuals are free to hold their own views. Indeed, unless they do so, no new paradigms can arise to further the development of scientific knowledge.

Kuhn's theory suggests that neither the inductive nor the hypothetico-deductive model adequately explains the way in which paradigms develop. In the first place, examination of scientific literature tends to show two kinds of scientist. Some seem mainly to be putting forward theories, setting up paradigms and (perhaps) initiating new revolutions. Others appear to concentrate upon testing the hypotheses of others. Thus it is not reasonable to assert that there is 'one scientific method', which is exclusively based upon the hypothetico-deductive model. Another consequence of Kuhn's theory is that three stages of research must exist side by side at any one time: the anecdotal, observational and hypothesis stages examined earlier in this chapter. All are being adopted, questioned or rejected by different scientific individuals and groups engaged upon the development of paradigms. Since Kuhn, other theorists have questioned the idea that scientific method follows one particular model (inductive or hypothetico-deductive) on a number of different grounds. It seems more likely that some sort of resonance occurs between the process of observation, the formulation of hypotheses, the design of experiments and the choice of new fields for study. What is inescapable, however, is the dependence of science upon experiment to test, falsify or confirm its hypotheses.

Some philosophers of science maintain that this ability to test theories pragmatically by experiment makes science a completely 'objective' approach to research. There is a view, known as 'scientism', that the methods of science are superior to other modes of investigation. As a result, the uncritical use of scientific methods has been advocated in a number of fields, including management and the social sciences. The error of this view can be understood by examining the way in which new paradigms gain general acceptance, i.e. the mechanism of scientific revolutions. Kuhn suggested that a new paradigm is accepted if it explains observations of the natural world more persuasively than the old one. However, there are two aspects to this: the proof itself and the credulity of the scientific community. Proof depends upon the design of an experiment carried out to confirm or refute some key aspect of the paradigm. As such, the design depends upon the paradigm itself, and upon the way in which the experimenters perceive it. This will represent only one way of looking at the test situation, because *the same experiment* will have to be able to support the next paradigm that comes along after the next scientific revolution.

In principle, the value of a paradigm depends upon the quality of the test experiment and the way it is presented to the scientific establishment. However, its real value depends only upon the fact of acceptance. In the real scientific world there are many anomalous observations over which experimenters argue, so that experimental method cannot be regarded as absolutely objective in the way the hypothetico-deductive model assumes. There are also examples of valid theories which for many years failed to gain acceptance for personal or social reasons. Two positions can therefore be argued on the objectivity of science. It may truly provide its hypotheses with an external frame of reference, and therefore endow them with objectivity. However, since the basis of the scientific process is the acceptance of paradigms by the majority, science can also be viewed as a subjective process in the same way as other types of research. This text does not attempt to favour one or the other of these two views; they are presented in order to explain the philosophical complexities of research methodology.

Although scientific method is a complex entity, with both individual and social dimensions, it nevertheless has one distinguishable feature: it is possible to test scientific theories by experiment. Other aspects of the scientific process are the development of paradigms and the occurrence of scientific revolutions, in which one paradigm displaces another. In order to illustrate these points, an example of the development of scientific theory is given below. It shows the interaction of anecdote, observation and hypothesis and the development of new paradigms. It also goes some way towards explaining the complex relationship between experimental design and the testing of hypothesis.

SCIENTIFIC METHOD IN ACTION

In medieval times the Greek philosopher Aristotle was regarded as the ultimate scientific authority, probably because fewer of his works than those of his contemporaries had been lost during the dark ages. Because of the fixed, hierarchical nature of ecclesiastical orders, Aristotle's writings tended to be accepted without

Figure 1.4   As Aristotle predicted it

question. Many of them did contain valuable knowledge, but some of his theory appears to have been based upon conjecture, or at best on very doubtful observation. For example, Aristotle is supposed to have noted that a heavy object falling from the masthead of a moving galley strikes the deck not at the foot of the mast, but some distance behind. This was supposed to be the product of the ship's forward motion, together with the downward movement of the falling object. Aristotle considered that these two motions made the object fall towards the stern, away from the direction in which the ship was moving (see Figure 1.4).

In fact, both the observation and the explanation are erroneous. A heavy object on board a moving vessel actually falls vertically downwards to the foot of the mast (see Figure 1.5). This happens irrespective of the speed at which the boat is moving, and is well known to sailors, who are careful not to stand near the bottom of the mast when items are being dropped from the masthead. (However, it *is* true that a light object such as a feather or a piece of string travels with the prevailing wind, and might be swept backward by the motion of a fast boat.) The way objects fall to earth is a crucial clue to understanding how moving objects – vehicles, bullets and the earth itself – behave. Yet Aristotle's theory was accepted for many centuries. When it could not be verified by experiment (i.e. the weight fell straight downwards), this was assumed to be owing to faulty experimental design. Perhaps the distance the weight travelled away from the mast was too small to measure accurately, or perhaps ships had moved more quickly in Aristotle's time.

Isaac Newton's laws of motion were developed at the beginning of the eighteenth century. They were part of a scientific revolution which ushered in a new paradigm, capable of explaining the movement of all material objects. Newton's laws also provided a plausible answer to the problem of objects falling to the deck of a moving

Figure 1.5   As the sailors saw (and felt) it

ship. Newton pointed out that just before it fell, an object at the masthead would have
the same speed as the ship. According to the laws of motion it would not lose this
momentum, so when it fell there were two components to its movement: one
downwards and one forwards (as shown in Figure 1.6). The forward motion continued

Figure 1.6   As Newton predicted it

to carry the falling object forwards at the same speed as the ship. It would then move in a curved path and hit the deck exactly at the foot of the mast.

An experiment to test this theory could put forward two hypotheses:

1. The heavy object falls vertically downwards overall, and lands on the deck directly below, as if the ship were stationary.
2. The object moves forward in a curve arriving at the deck at the precise spot below the point from which it was released.

Testing the first of these involves observing where the object falls. The second could not be tested in Newton's time, but it is now possible to set up an experiment using cameras. In order to show the object falling in a curve, the camera must be mounted on a fixed area, separate from the ship. The curve of the fall is then as shown in Figure 1.7, and the object strikes the deck precisely below the point where it was released. If the camera is mounted on the ship, it simply shows the object falling straight down (as in Figure 1.5). Newton's paradigm is fully supported by this experiment, but is still unable to tell us exactly what the heavy object does during its fall.

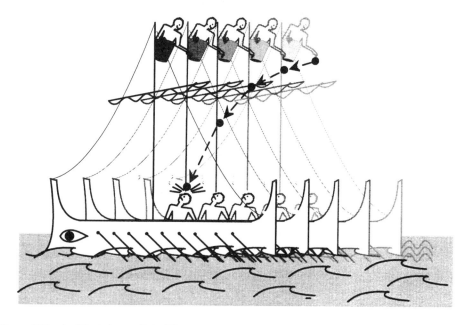

Figure 1.7   As Einstein predicted it

For many years, Newtonian mechanics constituted the only accepted theory of motion, but in the early twentieth century a new paradigm, Einstein's theory of relativity, emerged to challenge it. Relativity theory can account the motion of all bodies, including those for which classical mechanics has no explanation: for example, the behaviour of black holes in space or of light bending as it passes around galaxies and stars. The crux of Einstein's theory is that observations of the way matter behaves depend upon the relationship between the position and velocity of both the object being observed *and the observer*. Thus, Einstein's theory of relativity neatly explains the behaviour of an object dropped from the mast of a moving ship. For observers on the ship, the object falls straight downwards towards the pull of gravity, which is always below the ship. This is as expected, because observers, ship, masthead and falling object all have the same forward motion, so none will experience any forward motion relative to each other. Observers on the land will see the object falling forwards and downwards in a curve (as shown in Figure 1.7). The ship moves forward at the same rate and seems to the static observer neatly to 'catch' the falling object at a point on the deck directly beneath the place where it was released.

OBJECTIONS TO SCIENTIFIC METHOD

Some time has been devoted in this chapter to examining scientific method as a typical research process. Science does indeed have many features typical of research in general. It takes into account important phases of research, such as anecdote, observation and theory. In addition, it illustrates the process of thought revolution. The growth and general acceptance of paradigms were portrayed above as an aspect of science, but there are good grounds for regarding them as the model for all research development. However, there are also some serious objections to scientific method as a research model, particularly from the viewpoint of management studies and the social sciences. One source of such objections is the design and management of experiments, which are a key part of the scientific process. Others are concerned with the relationship between the observer and the individuals, organizations or situations which are being observed.

A scientific experiment seeks to narrow down its frame of reference until it can say something absolutely unequivocal about one very small aspect of a problem. It is usually designed to test the effect of just one factor, and its success depends upon holding all the others constant. Thus science typically breaks down observable reality into such small chunks that their significance becomes hard to see. The example discussed above, of a weight falling from the masthead of a ship, is a case in point. It is not easy to see the significance of such an observation, let alone its relevance to the motion of stars and planets. Yet much time would have to be spent on the elaborate detail of such an experiment. It should ideally be performed with weights of different size and at different rowing speeds, to see if these have any effect. It would also be necessary to rule out the effects of wind, by performing the experiment on a still day, or perhaps by carrying it out twice: once travelling into the wind and once away from it.

In a rigorous research style such as that of science, it is important to identify the point which will be tested in the form of a written hypothesis. For example, in the falling weights example the hypothesis is: 'a weight dropped from the masthead of a moving ship falls at an angle relative to the deck, which it hits at a point behind the mast'. A converse null hypothesis can also be stated: 'a weight dropped from the masthead of a moving ship falls vertically relative to the deck, which it hits immediately below its point of release'. The role of experiment is then to falsify either the hypothesis or the null hypothesis (i.e. to distinguish between them).

This level of focus is frequently counterproductive in management research. Within such situations, solutions to problems tend to be complex in nature, often involving a number of different aspects which act and react in a dependent way. Concentrating upon just one small area at a time may give a false impression of the nature of the problem and suggest an over-simplified solution. In addition, perfect experimental control is hardly ever practicable in a management situation. Yet managers frequently see themselves as carrying out 'experiments' in an effort to solve even day-to-day problems. For example, one aspect of a product's packaging may be changed in order to see the effect upon sales, or the speed of a production line may be altered in order to test the effect upon productivity. Such exercises appear to examine the effect of changing one factor, while holding the others constant. In practice they hardly ever actually do this, owing to the complexity of real management situations. Altering the packaging of a product may induce sales staff to sell it more efficiently, or it may make it appeal to a different market segment. There may also be other unrelated effects, such as a localized 'rush' on the product, or an economic boom or recession. All of these are likely to affect the outcome. Changing the speed of a production line may influence the rate at which people work, but it may also impact upon individuals and groups in unexpected ways (for example, by causing stress) and thus substantially affect the volume of output or the quality of the product.

This is not to say that such 'experiments' are useless. It is highly desirable to know the effects of packaging changes or productivity drives. An 'experiment' of this kind may shed valuable light on a problem, but is not bound to do so, and the results often need careful interpretation. Unlike the results of a scientific experiment, the results of such management experiments cannot necessarily be transferred from one situation to another. They might not be duplicated exactly if the experiment is carried out by a different individual. Because real-life situations are so complex, it is impossible to control all possible variables. Instead, allowances must be made, as far as possible, for contingencies – uncontrolled variables which may have affected the result, or which may affect it in future trials.

A scientific observer is expected to remain detached from the experimental observations. The clearest example of this in an applied research situation is the clinical trial, in which a treatment is administered to a set of patients in order to test whether a cure takes place. In case the act of just taking medicines should make patients imagine that they feel better, a control group receives a placebo. This is a pill or medicine which looks exactly like that received by the test group, but is made from inert materials, with no active ingredient. In order to remove experimenter bias, both groups are assigned code numbers, and these are not released to the workers who administer the medication or monitor the results. The only person who knows the full picture is the manager of the overall programme, who should not participate in any of the practical work. Such a procedure is called a *double blind trial*, because neither the patients nor the experimenters know who has received what.

Example 1.2   Problems with scientific method in a management study

In practical management situations, true scientific detachment is hardly ever possible. The experimenter is generally closely involved with the subjects of the study, must interview them and so on. Thus there is always a danger that the experimenter may influence the outcome. The best known example of such an effect is perhaps the Hawthorne study (Mayo, 1933), which sought to discover the 'ideal' working conditions (such as lighting levels) for workers. In practice, it was discovered that virtually any change seemed to motivate the workforce. Output went up no matter what new conditions were introduced; there was even an additional increase when they returned to their original level. Eventually the researchers realized that this was not because they were providing optimum physical conditions, but because workers perceived the change of conditions as a sign of management interest and approval, and were therefore motivated to work harder. However, the experimenter may also be shunned as an outsider by the work group, and may thus have a negative impact upon motivation or behaviour (see Bulmer, 1986).

There is also an ethical dimension to social experiments. This is commonly associated with the philosophy known as *positivism*, developed by the French author Auguste Compte from 1854 onwards. The positivist point of view only recognizes the existence of observable facts, and views abstract entities such as thoughts as having no existence. This may be unacceptable when experiments place the experimenter in an apparently superior position over human subjects. For example, it is ethically unacceptable for an experimenter to treat human experimental subjects as if they do not have thoughts or feelings. Because of its dependence upon objective observation, science tends to encourage a positivist view; in fact, many observers equate the scientific and positivist approaches with one another.

The scientific approach to management research was developed by a number of pioneer workers at the beginning of the twentieth century. Perhaps the most celebrated of these was Frederick Winslow Taylor (1856–1915); important contributions were also made by Henry Gantt, Frank B. Gilbreth and his wife Lillian Gilbreth. At that time there was some confusion about the actual nature of 'scientific method', and the main influences were inductivism and positivism. The early years of the twentieth century saw extensive, uncritical use of scientific methodology in management and the social sciences. By the 1940s, when the hypothetico-deductive model had established itself as representing scientific method, the scientific approach had become widely used within these fields, and 'hypothesis testing' was the methodology of choice. For the reasons discussed above, few people would defend scientific method today as the ideal approach to management research. Table 1.1 summarizes the issues involved.

Table 1.1   Comparison of issues in scientific method and management research

Scientific method	Management research
Must concentrate on a very narrow area of study	Usually involves a broad area of study
Provides an answer which relates to theory, but is often of little use on its own	Usually demands a definite answer, suitable for practical decision-making
All variables must be held constant except for one	Situations are usually so complex that not all variables can be controlled
Repeatable by any independent experimenter	May not be repeatable by another individual, in another situation or at another time
Results apply generally	Results are often not transferable between situations
Detachment of experimenter guarantees objectivity	Detachment of experimenter does not guarantee objectivity
Positivist view may be acceptable, particularly in studying inanimate materials	Positivist view is seldom likely to be acceptable, as human subjects are usually involved

PHENOMENOLOGICAL APPROACHES

Since management problems are generally the result of complex multifaceted interactions, a holistic approach to their study is preferable. Scientific method cannot provide this, because science is basically concerned with breaking situations down into elements which can be verified one by one. An alternative approach to that of scientific method is thus that of *phenomenology*, which aims to study a whole phenomenon in a concerted way. The *Oxford English Dictionary* defines a 'phenomenon' as 'a thing which appears, or is perceived or observed, applied chiefly to a fact or occurrence, the cause of which is in question'. In research terms it means a problem, structure or occurrence which has been identified for study. Strictly speaking, scientific experiments also deal with occurrences, but as discussed above, these are controlled 'phenomena', strictly limited in scope so that they can be studied.

Phenomenological approaches to research in management and the social sciences have developed alongside positivist methodology since the middle of the twentieth century. Early examples are the studies by William F. Whyte of social life in a US slum neighbourhood (1943) and of food service personnel at work (1948). Such situations are rich and complex in structure. Approaching their study from an experimental standpoint would not be a realistic proposition, because in the first place conditions and variables (including the presence of an observer) cannot be satisfactorily controlled. In addition, the results they yield are often so limited in scope or so hedged about by the experimenter's reservations that their usefulness is minimal. Thus it makes more sense to take a less structured approach to a wider field, but to consider carefully all the variables and contingencies which affect the study situation. Theory or hypothesis forms an essential part of the analysis, but phenomenology is not about hypothesis testing, because observations can never be sufficiently objective to make possible the rejection of one hypothesis in favour of another. Silverman (1993) suggests that the difference between scientific and phenomenological approaches is that in phenomenology hypotheses are generated, rather than tested. This is a helpful simplification in some ways, but falls short of the full picture, as has been discussed above.

Phenomenological studies may involve a wide range of data-gathering techniques, but in the social sciences they tend to concentrate upon 'qualitative' or 'illuminative' techniques. For example, the views or perceptions of subjects may be obtained through interviews, or a subjective observer may make structured observations of people or situations. There is increasing interest in techniques developed by other fields, notably the participant observation approach of anthropology. Since the objective is often to build as complete as possible a picture of a whole phenomenon, it is possible to use several different methodologies – for example, interview, observation, measurement and even experiment – in an integrated way. Critical comparison of the results provides a number of different perspectives and an opportunity to cross-check findings between methods. Thus phenomenological approaches tend to be rich and complex, unlike scientific studies, which may rely upon one methodology and one world view. Because of this complexity, it is less easy to generalize about holistic approaches in the same way as can be done with science.

Social researchers sometimes object to quantitative studies, equating them with positivism and scientific method. This may be a legitimate objection to the use of questionnaire methodologies in some branches of the social sciences. It is not a tenable position in management studies, since a whole range of quantitative measurements are an inherent part of the management process. Typical examples are weights, measures, processing parameters such as temperature or timing and numbers of personnel. Without these it may be impossible to understand the full complexity of a management phenomenon under study. Because cost and access are ever-important issues in management studies, it is often easy to justify questionnaire work (subject to suitable contingency considerations) as a quick, efficient and comparatively unobtrusive way to obtain social or psychological data. Quantitative data can contribute usefully to understanding a phenomenon and should not be neglected. As long as ethical questions have been satisfactorily answered, the argument for using questionnaires only breaks down if a scientific approach is followed uncritically. Two such typical situations are as follows.

- The circumstances and methodology are not adequately interpreted: for example, the researcher fails to consider all the possible variables, interactions and contingencies relevant to the situation under study.
- The actual (numerical) results are over-interpreted: for example, statistical techniques may add sophisticated interpretations which complicate the picture to an unjustifiable extent. Often it may be better to take the results on their face value.

The analysis of phenomenological data requires very careful consideration of methodological issues, i.e. the way in which the data have been gathered and all the factors and conditions involved. Due allowance must also be made for contingencies: aspects peculiar to the study situation which might not be transferable to other, similar situations. As with all research disciplines, phenomenological study demands very precise use of language. However, it frequently requires much greater richness of expression than scientific or experimental work, because of the complexity both of the perceptions being recorded and of the situations in which they occur.

Like all research methodologies, the phenomenological approach involves the proposition and examination of theories. Paradigms arise, just as in scientific studies, and they may be maintained or rejected according to their usefulness in explaining phenomena and their transferability between different situations. Perhaps the most persuasive paradigm in the management field is that of systems theory, which is discussed in detail in the next chapter.

AN INTEGRATED MODEL OF THE RESEARCH PROCESS

Earlier sections of the present chapter considered the inductive and hypothetico-deductive models as mutually exclusive approaches to understanding the research process. Yet neither is capable of adequately modelling the way actual research programmes develop. There are major objections to both of these simple models as explanations of scientific method. They are equally unsatisfactory models for phenomenological research, because the strength of such approaches is their heterogeneity. Phenomenological approaches, particularly those based upon case studies, offer the opportunity of exploring a range of methods, so that the results obtained from one viewpoint can be compared or tested against those from another. In addition, neither inductivism nor hypothetico-deductivism accounts for the observed tendency of research programmes to maintain themselves by continuously generating new questions (i.e. new anecdotal stages) for further studies.

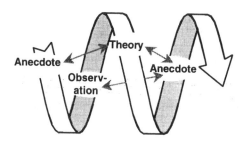

Figure 1.8 A generalized model of the research process

The proposed model shown in Figure 1.8 compensates for these deficiencies. It consists of a basically cyclic process, represented as a spiral, in which anecdote leads to observation, and thence hypothesis. The cycle spirals, rather than simply revolving, because the hypotheses generated at each turn give rise to new questions, which can form the anecdotal stage of a new cycle. This inductive process is perhaps the fundamental means by which human individuals set about understanding their environment. This is not only suggested by personal construct theory, but is also put forward by the protagonists of phenomenology as the 'natural' way to research the human environment. However, other interactions are not excluded. Anecdotes may suggest theories which require testing by observation (i.e. the hypothetico-deductive process). Observations may also lead directly to anecdote by suggesting new research questions. The spiral model thus has as its basis an overall inductive framework, but permits other processes wherever they are relevant.

This model thus contains elements of both inductive and hypothetico-deductive processes, and is relevant to all research approaches. It permits both the generation and the testing of hypotheses in any proportion, as demanded by the particular research situation, and thus blurs distinctions previously made between science and non-science. This is certainly the most appropriate model for research studies in management, where either the uncritical adoption or the uncritical rejection of hypothesis testing may seriously restrict the investigator.

TYPES OF RESEARCH

Academic research usually takes place for two primary reasons. It is a mental exercise designed to test students' ability to find, apply and examine knowledge. It can also generate new knowledge, which broadens academics' understanding of the field of study. This new knowledge is eventually incorporated into curricula to enrich student programmes. Thus academic research is destined for publication, teaching and wider dissemination. Questions of ownership, copyright or patent do not apply. The time scale of academic research may be fixed (for example, in the case of research for a higher degree) or it may be flexibly extended (for example, according to the amount of time available to an individual for private study). Either way, time scales tend to be fairly long – in excess of a year – and there is often no great urgency, except as a result of time limits on funding. Because academic research aims to contribute in a lasting way to the pool of knowledge, its methodology must be scrupulous. To ensure this, academic research papers are generally subjected to rigorous peer group review before they are accepted for publication. Such reports also tend to be written in a very precise way, which clearly defines the limitations of the findings.

Commercial research is usually undertaken for a specific purpose, such as to solve a particular problem, or to provide information for a specific strategic decision. It is always a professional concern, rather than a 'labour of love' by a motivated individual. Time scales tend to be short, i.e. weeks or months, and both the funding arrangements and the need for the information contribute to its urgency. Methodological precision is therefore often less important than speed. Some research may be carried out on an overtly 'quick and dirty' basis, in order to provide an approximation of the desired information within the all-important time frame. Cost–benefit considerations may exert a similar effect. Commercial research results are the property of the company which commissioned them, as are copyright and patent rights. They may therefore never be released to a general audience. Commercial research is usually reported in a simplified, easily readable format; often a verbal presentation is also made to the directors of the sponsoring company. Emphasis is upon the value of the results to the company rather than on details of method or accuracy.

There are obvious tensions between these two research outlooks, which tend to beset workers throughout the field. Researchers within industry tend to produce highly topical, strategically sensitive findings. These are generally restricted from publication by the companies within which they were conducted. Exceptions include material which provides good publicity or presents the company favourably in relation to its competitors. For instance, there are numerous accounts of successful quality management programmes in service companies. Despite these differences, academic and commercial research in vocational fields such as service industry management have much in common. In particular, they draw upon the same repertoire of research techniques and share the same background of published material.

The pragmatic nature of commercial research often obliges it to take a positivist frame of reference. Collection and processing of numerical data may be preferred to qualitative phenomenological approaches, which are frequently perceived as less 'objective' by boards of directors. Commercial research is also often used as a basis for taking risks, and is therefore required to be as representative as possible of the situation under study. As a result, quantitative techniques have tended to persist as a basis for measuring 'soft' data – attitudes, perceptions and intentions – for much longer in the management field than in other branches of the social sciences. A movement towards phenomenological methodologies is currently gathering momentum.

THE NATURE OF KNOWLEDGE

Knowledge, defined (OED) as 'theoretical or practical understanding of an art, science, language etc. ... the sum of what is known' is itself a very complex concept. For example, completely different intellectual skills are required to learn mathematics and French, and the two subjects are expressed in very different ways. Yet both are 'knowledge'. In order to make the sum of human knowledge more manageable, it is divided up into forms and fields. For example, mathematics and French are regarded as separate *forms* of knowledge, which require different skills and symbols to express them. Different branches within mathematics, such as algebra and trigonometry, are regarded as different *fields*. They use the standard techniques of mathematics (i.e. theorems and proofs) and they are expressed in similar mathematical symbols. Yet because of their different focus and approach, they are clearly different areas of knowledge. Forms and fields of knowledge are characterized by having their own symbolism, assumptions and values. Since the generation of knowledge necessitates research and enquiry, forms and to a lesser extent fields of knowledge have tended to evolve distinctive research methodologies. Paradigms arise and supplant one another in much the same way as they do in the sciences, though the criteria for acceptance may vary between different forms and fields.

The position of service industry management is interesting in this respect. The form of knowledge to which it belongs is social science. Within this broad area there is some discussion as to whether management in general, or branches of management, may be regarded as fields. For example, to judge by the subdivision of university management departments, marketing may be regarded as a separate field. Yet there is considerable support for the idea of a new field of 'services marketing' (e.g. Berry and Parasuraman, 1993; Fisk *et al.*, 1993). The growth of such separate fields depends partly upon the ability of the academic world to reach a consensus. It also depends upon the new field's capacity to establish its own specific assumptions (e.g. paradigms) and research methodology. This can only occur if practitioners possess a common consciousness of the evolving nature of methodology.

CONCLUSIONS

Research activities may be modelled in terms of four general, interlinked phases: preparation, planning, method/methodology and product. Formulation of a programme of research must begin with a research purpose and therefore with an understanding of the nature of investigative processes. These involve three basic stages – anecdote, observation and theory – and are thought to mirror the basic process by which all humans seek to understand their environment. This chapter has focused upon two principal models of the research process: induction and hypothetico-deduction. Inductive reasoning involves drawing hypotheses from observations by a process of analysis. Hypothetico-deductive methodology, on the other hand, involves proposing an initial theory (a rigorously defined hypothesis) which can then be confirmed or refuted by experiment. Experimental conditions are always strictly controlled, so that the hypothetico-deductive process always tackles a problem a small piece at a time; it is impossible to test all aspects at once.

Apart from these investigative models, the research process is concerned with building up a world view from a number of proven hypotheses. Such a 'meta-theory' is known as a paradigm, and is generally accepted by scholars until a new paradigm arises which explains the observed facts more convincingly. The examples presented in this chapter were mostly concerned with science, a particularly well documented research area, but paradigms, and hence 'thought revolutions', exist in all fields of knowledge. Although some philosophers claim that scientific knowledge is of a 'special' kind and more objectively based than that in other fields, this is by no means certain. In particular, it seems likely that consensus, rather than objectivity, is the key requirement for a paradigm to gain general acceptance in any field.

Two basic methodologies have been used in the fields of social science and management. A scientistic movement which persisted into the second half of the twentieth century was characterized by an uncritical application of 'scientific method' – primarily hypothesis-testing and experiment. The period since the Second World War has seen the rise of a phenomenological movement, which seeks to treat research situations in a holistic way. Phenomenological approaches may use a variety of different methods, but emphasize analysis and the induction of theories, rather than experiment, hypothesis-testing and deduction. However, close scrutiny of actual research progress identifies weaknesses in the two investigative models. A third, more comprehensive, model is therefore proposed, in which induction and hypothetico-deduction may coexist, the relative emphasis upon the two processes reflecting the overall ethos and the extent to which they allow meaningful hypotheses to be developed.

Knowledge may be classified into forms and fields. Forms of knowledge differ fundamentally in terms of symbols, structure and research methodology. Fields recognizably belong to a particular form, but many employ specific variations of symbols and research techniques. Service management represents a potential academic field, which is in the process of establishing itself and is to some extent in competition with other management subjects. In order to establish itself, it needs the freedom to develop an academic ethos, and particularly a research ethos, of its own. The generalized methodological model proposed in this chapter particularly suits a developing research area such as service management. It avoids over-dependence upon one single highly stylized model and allows the research process to approach more nearly the natural mechanism by which human individuals comprehend their environment.

REFERENCES

Berry, L. and Parasuraman, A. (1993) 'Building a new academic field – the case for services marketing', *Journal of Retailing*, 69(1), 13–60.

Bulmer, M. (1986) *Social Science and Social Policy*. Allen & Unwin, London.

Chalmers, A.F. (1982) *What Is This Thing Called Science?* Open University Press, Milton Keynes.

Conan Doyle, A. (1974) *A Study in Scarlet*. Pan Books, London.

Fisk, R.P., Brown, S.W. and Bitner, M.J. (1993) 'Tracking the evolution of the services marketing literature', *Journal of Retailing*, 69(1), 61–103.

Kelly, G.A. (1969) 'The role of classification in personality theory', in B. Maher (ed.), *Clinical Psychology and Personality: The Selected Papers of George Kelly*. Wiley, New York, p. 94.

Mayo, E. (1933) *The Human Problems of an Industrial Civilization*. Macmillan, New York.

Silverman, D. (1993) *Interpreting Qualitative Data*. Sage, London.

Whyte, W.F. (1943) *Street Corner Society: The Social Structure of an Italian Slum*. University of Chicago Press, Chicago.

Whyte, W.F. (1948) *Human Relations in the Restaurant Industry*. McGraw-Hill, New York.

2

Systems Theory and Research

INTRODUCTION

The systems concept is probably one of the most useful theoretical tools currently available for the management researcher. Broadly speaking, it assumes that the world is made up of identifiable systems – sets of components which work together, producing a total effect greater than the sum of the system's parts. This concept makes a stark contrast to the scientific view considered in the previous chapter, which basically assumes that everything may be broken down, and its component parts considered in isolation. Science takes this view largely because the experimental approach (which is the cornerstone of science) demands that only one aspect of anything is studied at any one time. The systems view is not opposed to the scientific view *per se*, it is just that a whole system cannot usually be considered in the context of an experiment, because the full richness of the system requires the simultaneous interaction of a large number of variables.

Systems thinking implies that observable phenomena consist of a large number of interacting parts. It is by no means a new idea. For example, the author and poet Jonathan Swift noted in the early eighteenth century that the world is made up of interlinked systems:

So, naturalists observe, a flea
Hath smaller fleas that on him prey
And these have smaller fleas to bite 'em
And so proceed ad infinitum.
(*A Pastoral Dialogue between Richmond Lodge and Marble Hill*)

The converse observation, that objects seem to be clumped into ever larger systems, was made at about the same time by Alexander Pope:

Observe how system into system runs
How other planets circle other suns.
(*Imitations of Horace, To Mr Fortescue*)

This was the period of early scientific successes, by Newton and others. The solar system had just been discovered (observing stars through the telescope would eventually lead to the discovery of galaxies and other astronomical supersystems in which the stars took part). At about the same time, the microscope was making it possible to see ever smaller systems of living things.

However, the development of experimental methods in science shifted the emphasis of enquiry from interrelationships and groups to a closer study of the component parts of things. This approach spread until it permeated all research areas, including management and the social sciences. Experiment and hypothesis-testing became the principal approach to studies in these fields until the 1950s. Probably the earliest paper to propose an alternative view was that of Boulding (1956), who introduced general systems theory as an appropriate way to interpret research into management phenomena. Even then, the new approach had to be given a 'scientific flavour', and Boulding's paper was subtitled 'The skeleton of science'. Since Boulding's time, many writers have taken up the systems cause, perhaps the best known being Kast and Rosenzweig (1968, 1985) and Bertalanffi (1968). The general systems view identified by these authors makes it possible to divide up the world into interactive 'bundles' of components and to identify the structural relationships between the components themselves and between discernible bundles of components. It also makes it possible to seek out new properties, different from the individual properties of the original components, and caused by the interrelationships between them. General systems theory provides a useful analytical tool for understanding complexity in typical management situations, such as groups of people or organizations. It also provides the basis for two analytical techniques, both of which may be used in management research situations. These are systems engineering and soft systems methodology, both of which are discussed in the present chapter.

Systems theory and systems methodologies have certain inherent disadvantages. The most important of these is that every system is unique. The findings from a systems study are often only applicable to the subject of that study and it is impossible to transfer them unmodified to any other situation. They may also only be relevant to the particular time the study was undertaken, becoming progressively less applicable as time passes. Changing from an experimental research approach to a systems approach may thus mean abandoning all pretence to 'universal applicability' of the results. However, it is doubtful whether the results of any 'experimental' management study were ever truly universally applicable, because it is never possible to control all the variables completely. The essential problem in any management research is to understand the full complexity of the situation. General systems theory provides a framework for doing this, and is thus the most compelling paradigm in current management thinking and research.

GENERAL SYSTEMS THEORY

The basic premiss of general systems theory is that the world is made up of identifiable systems. The *Oxford English Dictionary* defines a system as 'A set, or assemblage of things connected, associated or interdependent, so as to form a complex unity'. From this it follows that a system has the following properties.

- It is *identifiable*, i.e. it must be possible for an observer to discern it and to show (or at least to make plausible case) that the system exists.

- It possesses *emergent properties*, i.e. properties which are not possessed by its individual components, so that the system can behave in some way that the individual components cannot. An interesting feature of emergent properties is that they must appear independently at all systems levels. For example, each of the components of a system is a system in its own right and has emergent properties not possessed by *its* subsystems. Similarly, the emergent properties of a system are lost within the new emergent properties of the supersystem of which it is a part.

If the world is to be expressed in terms of systems, where does one start? There are three logical places. It might be possible to begin with the smallest possible thing and build up into subsystems and a higher system. It is also theoretically possible to identify the largest possible thing (the universe, for example), and break it down into ever smaller subsystems. Neither of these options is helpful for researching services management, where it is easiest to start from human individuals or groups. However, this serves to introduce another feature of systems, that of hierarchy. Every system is made up of *subsystems*, each of which is a system in its own right, made up of increasingly smaller subsystems. At the same time, every system must be combined with other systems at the same level of the hierarchy into a larger structure, or *supersystem*. These must in turn be combined into still higher structures, and so on. The hierarchical relationship of systems is shown in Figure 2.1. Each system has three interactional dimensions. At the 'lower' level, its properties are influenced by the subsystems within it. At the intermediate level, the system can be considered as interacting with other, parallel systems. These in turn interact to produce a higher level still, a supersystem. One task faced by the researcher is to decide the level at which to stop, because as in the quotes by Swift and Pope at the beginning of this chapter, the continuous hierarchy of systems can go upward or downward *ad infinitum*.

In order to be identifiable within its hierarchy, a system must possess a *boundary*, *sub-units* (subsystems) capable of interacting together and an *environment* located outside the system boundary. Although a system must be distinguishable from its environment (otherwise one could not specify its existence), almost all systems interact with their environments in some way. This interaction involves another important defining feature of a system: the inputs and outputs. Systems can also be characterized according to the degree of control they exert over their inputs and outputs. A system which has a great many inputs and outputs, over which it exerts comparatively little control, is said to be a permeable system. An impermeable system is much more selective about the materials, information, personnel etc. which it allows to enter or leave.

SYSTEMS CLASSIFICATIONS

The value of general systems theory is that it provides the researcher with a flexible basis upon which to build analytical structures. It might be still more helpful if there were a recognized general approach to classifying systems as a whole. No universally accepted classification exists, although several have been suggested. Two useful guidelines for the researcher are those of Boulding and Jordan, discussed below.

Boulding's (1956) classification of systems is intuitive, informal and based upon the variety of ways in which the system can move or act, and hence upon the complexity

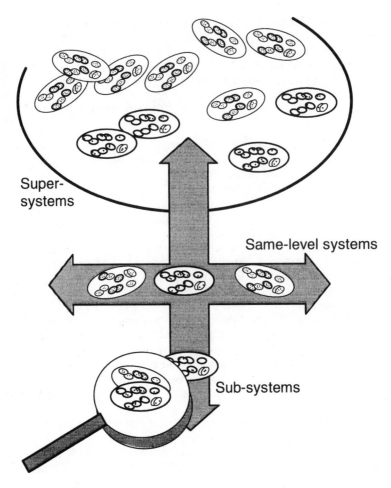

Figure 2.1   Hierarchy of systems

of its interaction with its environment. For example, he differentiates structural systems, where the components have no movement, simple or intermediate systems, where movements or activities are more or less predetermined, and complex ones, in which the component parts have increasing levels of self-determination. Boulding's classification is shown in Table 2.1. It makes it possible to identify management research as occupying a higher systems level, i.e. level 8: socio-cultural. It also suggests that there may be further levels or sub-levels, located between level 7 and level 8 or between levels 8 and 9. Boulding's classification explains why Mayo's Hawthorne study, discussed in the previous chapter, did not give the results expected. It was evidently based upon an inappropriate systems view of the working environment. It assumed that people at work make up a 'level 2 system' in which the structure is well defined and the activities are predetermined. What the researchers actually discovered was that the workplace is a much more intricate system, in which workers, management, researchers and conditions interact in complex, self-conscious ways.

Table 2.1 Intuitive hierarchy of systems (adapted from Boulding, 1956)

Level	Characteristics defining each system level from the previous one	Examples	Relevant disciplines
1. Structures and frameworks	Static	Crystal structures, buildings	Description, verbal, pictorial, chemistry, architecture, etc.
2. Simple machines	Predetermined motion or equilibrium	Clocks, machines, the solar system	Physics, classical mechanics
3. Control mechanisms	Feedback loop control	Thermostats, homeostasis mechanisms in organisms	Control theory, cybernetics, basic physiology
4. Open systems	Structurally self-maintaining within narrow environmental limits	Flames, biological cells	Cell biology, biochemistry, chain reaction chemistry
5. Lower organisms	Functionally organized for survival within fairly wide environmental fluctuations	Plants, bacteria, simple animals	Botany, invertebrate biology
6. Animals	Ability to learn and thus to cope with more extreme environmental variation	Birds and animals	General biology
7. Man	Self-consciousness, knowledge of knowledge	Human beings	Biology, psychology
8. Socio-cultural systems	Roles, communication, shared values	Families, organizations, nations	Social sciences, history, anthropology
9. Transcendental systems	Inescapable unknowables	God, the human soul, nirvana	Philosophy, religion?

Jordan (1968) proposes a quite different style of classification, based upon the interaction between three pairs of dimensions. These are defined as follows:

- rate of change, which may be *structural* (static) or *functional* (dynamic);
- existence of purpose, i.e. a system may have a purpose (*purposive*) or it may not (*non-purposive*);
- connectivity, i.e. a system may be interconnected in a predetermined (*mechanistic*) or a self-determining (*organismic*) way.

These six bipolar dimensions give rise to eight possible combinations, which can be used to classify systems as shown in Table 2.2.

Table 2.2 Classification of systems (adapted from Jordan, 1968)

Classification	Example
1. Structural purposive mechanical	Road network
2. Structural purposive organismic	Suspension bridge
3. Structural non-purposive mechanical	Mountain range
4. Structural non-purposive organismic	Any physical system in equilibrium (a soap bubble, for example)
5. Functional purposive mechanical	A production line (assuming that a breakdown of one machine does not affect other machines)
6. Functional purposive organismic	Living organisms
7. Functional non-purposive mechanical	Motion of waves on the seashore, shadow patterns thrown by a tree in the sunshine
8. Functional non-purposive organismic	The space–time continuum

Jordan's classification makes it possible to conceptualize virtually all management research situations. The Hawthorne situation, for example, was originally conceptualized as 'type 5', but it became necessary to recharacterize it as 'type 6' in order to understand the observations that were actually made. Management research always deals with purposive systems, and it is usually beneficial to define a system under study in terms of its purpose. Management researchers may, however, seek to identify non-purposive behaviour in an attempt to focus or eliminate it.

Jordan's classification also exemplifies another important principle of general systems theory. This is that all systems features – boundaries, emergent properties, super- and subsystems, outputs and inputs – are arbitrary devices which permit a real situation to be analysed. Thus the specification of a system is entirely under the control of the observer, and has no objective 'reality'. It is usually necessary for the researcher to justify choices; it is never necessary to 'prove' objectively that they exist. General systems theory is interested in relationships, structures and interdependences *as the observer sees them*. It is thus a phenomenological viewpoint. There are no 'fixed' points in systems thinking.

This flexibility is demonstrated by Table 2.3, which shows how 'areas' of management responsibility can be subdivided. 'Areas' may mean geographical regions,

Table 2.3 Areas into which 'management responsibility' can be subdivided

'Areas' 1	'Areas' 2	'Areas' 3	'Areas' 4
1. marketing	customer segment A	travel	north
2. personnel	customer segment B	accommodation	north-west
3. operations	customer segment C	catering	south
4. finance	customer segment D	entertainment	south-east
5. development	customer segment E	liaison	east
6. research	customer segment F	customer care	west

organizational or practical functions or customer responsibilities. The four areas shown in the table represent only a few of the ways in which the original field 'management responsibilities' can be divided up. The actual areas chosen may depend upon the personality and interests of the researcher, upon the *status quo* of the organization under investigation or even upon educational or management 'fashion'.

All these areas are 'right' in the sense that they are valid subsystems. All have identifiable boundaries, subsystems, supersystems, inputs and outputs. The differences between the columns 'Areas 1' to 'Areas 4' are those of structure, interrelationship and interaction. The choice of which subsystems ('areas' in the table example) to use in an analysis depends on the needs and objectives of the research.

To summarize, the main point of general systems theory is that a system must be identifiable, i.e. it must have

- subcomponents which interact with one another;
- an identifiable boundary;
- an environment, from which it is distinct;
- inputs and outputs;
- a purpose (for most systems in management research).

A system must also demonstrate *emergent properties*, demonstrated by all the components working together, but not by individual components in isolation. Systems theory is about relative aspects, such as structure and relationships, as seen through the eyes of an observer. It therefore deals with phenomenological issues, rather than with experiment, objectivity or positivism.

'HARD' SYSTEMS METHODOLOGY

One practical use of the principles of general systems theory is the analytical process known as systems engineering. This approach grew from Second World War weapons programmes, which required the precise control of interacting components, not only within the weapons themselves, but also in the organizations and structures which were set up to develop them. Systems engineering aims to deal with a known problem, which has been clearly defined. The system which is set up to solve or overcome the problem is also assumed to be clearly definable. Often its objectives and characteristics can be expressed and modelled in mathematical terms.

The solution of a typical systems engineering problem involves specifying the system boundaries, subsystems and emergent properties. Relationships between all of the subsystems are modelled, usually with the aid of a flowcharting procedure. The assumption is that inputs, outputs, interactions and feedback loops can be specified exactly. When they are identical to the specification, the system will be operating in the most efficient way. A simple analogy is that of a clock, which contains a number of individual components and sub-units, intermeshed in such a way that a new emergent property not possessed by the components (i.e. that of telling the time) is achieved. The initial systems engineering problem (now obscured by the mists of time) was to mark the times of day when services should be held in monasteries. Because it relies upon detailed specification and precise control, systems engineering has been called a 'hard systems' approach to problem-solving (Kirk, 1995). Systems engineering procedure consists of seven stages, as shown in Table 2.4.

Thus the systems engineering approach is a technique for understanding the

Table 2.4   Systems engineering procedure

Step	Description
1. Problem identification	Often this process involves clearly specifying a physical need
2. Choice of objectives	The physical needs are defined and placed in the context of the value system within which they must be met, i.e. the trade-off against cost, time-frame and resources
3. Systems synthesis	Various alternative systems are suggested which may be able to satisfy the need (or solve the problem) and meet the objectives
4. Systems analysis	The various alternative systems are examined carefully to identify which will best meet the objectives
5. System selection	All the criteria are weighed up and the most promising of the alternative systems is selected
6. System development	The chosen system is optimized and scaled up for use in the real world
7. System engineering	Once adopted, the system is continuously monitored, developed and updated to match changing conditions in the workplace

practical detail of systems. It brings with it a wealth of analytical techniques, such as flowcharting, which can be used to understand the interrelationships between many different types of systems components. However, it is most suitable for developing systems which deal with machines and materials. Its weakness is that the level of control required can only be exercised with systems components which have little or no scope for independence, those at level 2, or at most 3, of Boulding's classification. Thus, systems engineering is unsuitable for systems composed (for example) of groups of people.

This might seem to make systems engineering unsuitable for any application in management problem-solving or research, since, as argued above, most systems in the management field involve interactions with personnel. However, networking and critical path analysis are examples of 'hard' systems techniques which can readily be used in services management. The management fields of operations research and process engineering depend heavily upon systems engineering, which can be used to understand many different types of material- and information-processing. It is true that traditional operations research, which was largely concerned with the flow of paperwork administration systems, has now been largely superseded by computer technology. However, computer programs are themselves examples of systems engineering, and a knowledge of this field is essential to modelling the technical aspects of modern information systems: global reservations systems, retail stock control systems, hotel premises management systems, financial transfer systems and so on.

Process engineering may also be relevant to service industries. For example, it can play a part in the design of food processing systems for catering. Just-in-time (JIT) and stock control systems are further examples of engineerable systems which play an important part in certain service industries. Harris (1989) identifies a number of ways in which this may be done within different types of service context.

Example 2.1   General Systems Theory and Process Engineering in Catering

An example of systems engineering in action is the hazard analysis and critical control point (HACCP) system. This was originally developed by NASA to produce food of exceptionally high microbiological safety for use in spacecraft. It was developed by regarding the food production process as a system, the components of which are the production stages. Thus, harmful bacteria can only get into the food from a contaminated input to the system, or from a faulty process. The HACCP system has proved itself so effective that the World Health Organization recommends it for use in all food production processes. The HACCP procedure involves defining the food production process as a system, and identifying all inputs and outputs. These are then catalogued, and individually assessed for inherent hazards and risks. The process is then flowcharted and all the process stages are assessed according to their level of risk. After this, standards can be set for each critical process stage, and monitoring and documentation procedures set up to control unavoidable risks.

HACCP is easiest to apply to inflexible food production processes with a limited number of outputs. Real kitchens are usually more complex systems, dealing with a wide range of products and a volatile demand. Thus, the real world often requires 'softened' versions of the HACCP procedure, in which standards and procedures may be blurred, but a level (perhaps less rigorous) of hygiene is nevertheless achieved. Thus systems engineering approaches can be more or less rigorous, as circumstances require, and it is possible to use elements such as flowcharting flexibly in service situations.

Thus, 'hard' systems analysis may be generally useful for modelling the way in which the components (or subsystems) of a system interact. Several such models are usually possible, and the hard systems procedure involves evaluating them and selecting one for use. This underlines the fact that a systems model of any kind is an arbitrary device, and only ever an approximation to the 'real world'. Simpler systems, made up of mechanical, 'level 2' components, are more susceptible to hard systems modelling. In such cases, modelling is more likely to be rigorous and the output and behaviour of the model are more likely to correspond to the way the 'real world' system actually works.

Researchers may become so attracted by the rigour and simplicity of hard systems that they ignore their inappropriateness (and hence inaccuracy) in complex management situations. Hard systems deal essentially with simple, mechanical components. They therefore cannot take into account the full complexity of the business environment. A new systems model would have to be identified for each supersystem, and even if it could be found, it would probably not be able to account for the complexity and unpredictability inherent at the supersystem level. Hard systems are also inherently unsuitable for modelling interpersonal interactions, such as the flexible and unpredictable 'service encounter', which is at the heart of all service operations. Such problem areas are best modelled by a more comprehensive procedure known as 'soft' systems analysis.

'SOFT' SYSTEMS

Systems engineering and the 'hard' analytical approach discussed in the previous section take a tactical approach to problem-solving. They assume that the problem can and has been clearly identified. Systems engineering then sets about solving this identified problem in the most practicable way possible. It works by mechanical algorithms, meshing together the components of an identified system in a precise way. By contrast, 'soft' systems thinking is strategic in nature. It seeks to define and redefine the problem, looking at it from different standpoints, in order to include the full richness of the picture. For example, all aspects of the environment must be taken into account, together with the perceptions of the 'problem owner', who may also be influencing the problem. While 'hard' systems methodology aims to solve problems, 'soft' systems methodology seeks to identify them, clarify them, place them into context and rationalize them.

Example 2.2   Hard versus Soft Systems Problems

A problem is identified with unsatisfied customers (and loss of business) in a chain of travel agents. At first sight it appears to be a difficulty of communication. The problem is therefore articulated as: 'How can we speed up communication, particularly ticketing, bookings and reservations in our outlets?' The answer is to redesign the software systems used for these transactions. Engineers are called in, who modify the systems, enabling instant, worldwide communications, with much shorter delays than were previously experienced. However, the problem continues. A new analysis is made of the situation, which takes into account a number of factors which were not included in the original assessment of the problem:

- the attitudes of customers and staff;
- changes in the market segments being served by the chain;
- high street competition;
- the way information, tickets, etc. are forwarded to customers;
- the way complaints are dealt with.

From this it can be recognized that the problem is not as simple as previously supposed. A new plan of priorities for action is drawn up. New staff activities and training programmes are developed. More competitive service packages are designed. New procedures are instituted for forwarding information, delivering tickets and answering telephones. Customer satisfaction is seen to improve.

This example is not intended to suggest that the new communications software was not effective. It probably contributed substantially to the solution, as soon as the other factors were taken into account. The real problem, however, was that the full context of the problem had not been appreciated. It had therefore not been realized that a number of strategic measures were required, rather than the simple, 'obvious' tactic of speeding up communications.

Soft systems methodology is just as much a legitimate product of general systems theory as is systems engineering, but its emphasis differs considerably. Systems engineering looks *down* the hierarchy to the subsystems in order to understand and manipulate system function. Soft systems methodology looks *up* the hierarchy towards the supersystem, and seeks to understand the broad context and complexity of the situation. The soft systems approach stresses two main aspects of problem-solving. The first of these is the breadth of the analysis. Systems engineering virtually defines its systems as closed, so that it can analyse and control the subsystems. By contrast, soft systems methodology deliberately looks for interactions between the system and its environment, drawing and redrawing the system boundary to include as many aspects of the problem as possible. In Example 2.2, the system chosen for the second analysis could have included wider political, economic and social factors, as well as the ones identified. The fact that it did not do so was a matter of choice on the part of the researchers, who did not feel justified in extending the system boundary so widely.

Soft systems analysis places great importance upon the point of view of the problem owner. Problems are frequently influenced by what is termed the *Weltanschauung* – the unquestioned image or model of the world held by key people within the system. To an outsider the viewpoint (*Weltanschauung*) of the main players may appear to cause the problem, or to prevent the implementation of an apparently obvious solution. Thus it must always be taken into account during the problem-solving process.

SOFT SYSTEMS METHODOLOGY

Soft systems methodology can be summed up in the seven-step model shown in Figure 2.2, which is derived from Patching (1990). The numbered sequence of stages is

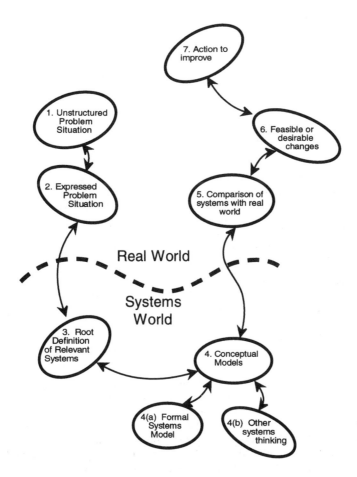

Figure 2.2　Soft systems methodology model, after Patching (1990)

only presented as a learning aid. In practice, the stages need not necessarily follow one another in the order shown. (In the figure, this is expressed by double-ended arrows between the stages.) Soft systems analysis often also involves much iteration, as different likely seeming models are successively refined and tested. The following text explains the seven stages of soft systems methodology in outline. Readers may find further details and examples in David Patching's excellent book on the subject (Patching, 1990).

1. *Unstructured problem situation.* An unstructured problem is any situation where a mismatch can be perceived between the real world and what might or should be. The existence and nature of the problem are a matter of perception by one or more individuals. A problem therefore never exists in isolation. There is always a problem owner, defined as the person(s) who stands to gain most from an improvement in the problem situation. The problem owner is also responsible for making the changes necessary to alleviate the problem. Put in this light, it becomes clear why quality circles and employee empowerment are so effective (see Teare *et al.*, 1994). Both approaches sensitize employees to problem situations, giving them ownership and the power to do something about the problem.

2. *Expressed problem situation.* Expressing the problem situation involves collecting a great deal of information about the organization, department, situation and scenario in which the problem takes place. Whereas the 'problem situation unstructured' stage asks 'what?' (or even 'approximately what?'), a good way to approach problem expression is to proceed through a standard format of questions, such as who; when; how; where? A procedure of this kind is outlined as the basis for refining a research idea in Chapter 3 of this book. The outcome of stage 2 (the problem expressed) is a diagrammatical 'rich picture' which shows as many details as possible about the problem scenario, in the most accessible form. This is not a search for systems. The rich picture provides information from which potential systems features such as boundaries, environment, inputs and outputs may later be identified. Another way to approach the expression of a problem is to look for elements of structure and process and examine relationships between the two. For example, this may be done by asking questions about the way activities are resourced and controlled. Problem themes may also be used to focus attention upon particular elements of the problem. As Figure 2.2 shows, the soft systems procedure then leaves the real world behind and plunges into an idealized 'systems world', where models can be developed unhindered by the constraints of the real world.

3. *Root definitions of relevant systems.* A root definition describes in detail the nature and purpose of the system. Although systems boundaries, inputs and outputs are the starting point for the root definition, the real focus is upon the human players in the problem situation (i.e. all those who perceive the problem, could influence it or are affected by it). The mnemonic CATWOE provides a checklist to help the definition process. The letters have the following meanings:

C   *Clients* of the system, i.e. customers or others who benefit from the system outputs.

A   *Actors*, i.e. everyone who carries out any activity within the system.

T   *Transformations*, i.e. changes which take place within the system or are caused by it, such as the conversion of inputs to outputs.

W   *Weltanschauung* or *world view*, i.e. the assumptions which are made about the system and its environment by owners, actors, customers, etc.

O   *Owner(s)* of the system, i.e. the person(s) to whom the system is answerable and who has responsibility for it. One definition of the system owner is 'the person who could make the system cease to exist'.

E   *Environment*, i.e. the other systems, supersystem, etc. which surround the system and interact with it.

Several different root definitions and system models are possible for any given situation. Boundaries, inputs and outputs may be drawn in different ways, describing different systems, with different *CATWOE* features. A common type of iteration in soft systems methodology is between the rich picture and the root definition stage, as successive plausible systems are defined.

4. *Conceptual models.* A conceptual model should show the minimum number of activities necessary to achieve the *transformation* as stated in the root definition. These activities are represented by verb-dominated phrases such as 'take customer's order', 'enter order at stock control workstation', 'collect goods' and so on. A conceptual model should have the eight characteristics of *formal systems models* shown below:

(a)   It must have an identified *ongoing purpose*, i.e. it must exist for a given reason and achieve an identifiable change or transformation.

(b)   Its performance must be *measurable* in terms of its effectiveness (i.e. the extent to which it achieves its goals) and its efficiency (i.e. the way it utilizes its inputs to produce its outputs).

(c)   There must be identifiable decision-making processes and mechanisms for regulation and control.

(d)   It must possess *components* that are themselves identifiable systems and interact to produce the transformation.

(e)   It must exist as part of a wider *supersystem* or 'system of systems' and interact with its environment.

(f)   It must have a *boundary* which encloses its component systems, activities and control mechanisms.

(g)   It must have identifiable *inputs* and *outputs*.

(h)   It must have a finite existence and stability despite fluctuations or disturbance in its environment.

The analyst's job is to identify these features within the conceptual model and match them up to the rich picture and the root definition. This requires considerable movement back and forth between stages 4, 3 and 2 of the soft systems methodology model (Figure 2.2). The procedure is very flexible, and though it is desirable to use the formal systems model as shown in stage 4(a), other systems thinking may be used. This is implied by stage 4(b). Stages 2 to 4 may aim to develop several possible systems models – at a later stage these are evaluated and the most promising candidate is chosen. It is also frequently necessary to backtrack from later stages, as models are found wanting when compared to the real world situation.

5. *Comparison with the real world.* The sequence of stages now emerges into the real world again. The model is scrutinized to see whether the components, structures and activities it represents actually exist in reality. One recommended way of doing this is by orchestrating a debate between researchers and problem owners. The former usually support the idealized systems view, while the problem owners may object on the basis of their practical experience. Systems models also make assumptions about the way the real world works, making it possible to consider such issues as effectiveness, efficiency and productivity. Comparing the model with the real world

may suggest changes that could be made in the real world situation to overcome the original problem.

6. *Feasible or desirable changes.* Changes identified from the comparison exercise should be carefully examined in order to identify inherent advantages and problem areas. Although it is generally possible to identify a number of possible problem-minimizing changes at stage 5, some of these may involve trade-offs with other goals or values of the organization and may therefore not be desirable. Some models may require unreasonable inputs of resources or unwarrantable changes, and may therefore be unfeasible. However, some changes may be both feasible and desirable.

7. *Action to improve.* When a model and a set of acceptable changes have been identified, it is necessary to consider how they can best be implemented in the real world situation. A development strategy should be drawn up, detailing the structural and procedural changes which must be made and the agencies, structures or individuals responsible for them. It is also necessary to consider tactical issues, such as the timetabling of events, resourcing, training and staffing at this stage.

Soft systems methodology provides a series of frameworks for research, rather than just one. It gives a clear view of the problem context and can formalize and focus thought processes, providing a basis for choosing 'what to do next', and because it consists of an essentially reversible series of stages, it can provide a useful kit of tools for identifying, processing and developing ideas. However, it has a number of drawbacks. Although in skilled hands it can be a rigorous and disciplined approach, it tends to be very intuitive, differing qualitatively between different individual analysts. Literature on the subject therefore tends to be rather vague. Authors such as Patching (1990) have tended to demystify soft systems methodology by giving clear-cut practical examples. These may, however, give the impression that this methodology is only for analysing problems in organizations, that the whole procedure should be followed through and that a practical outcome of some kind should result. It is also implied that as a general rule projects should start with soft systems methodology and become progressively 'harder' and more systems-oriented as they progress towards completion (stage 7, as described above, is a case in point).

Although soft systems methodology can be and is used in this way, none of these assumptions is necessarily correct. Techniques of both 'hard' and 'soft' systems thinking are available to the researcher, but the nature of research makes it desirable to take a very flexible approach in their use. It is often helpful to a regard a problem as unstructured from the outset and to approach it through a rich picture. It is also helpful to implement a structured system (such as a detailed programme of research activities, or a specific identified solution to a problem) through flowcharts, time-tables, critical path analysis or other manifestations of systems engineering. In between it is frequently necessary to draw diagrams and to make models of varying flexibility to express and analyse real world situations. That is all that can usefully be said, except that above all the researcher should keep an open mind about the techniques and approaches available.

Example 2.3   A Research Question and *Weltanschauungen* in Tourism

People's use of leisure time seems to be a fruitful area for research. Yet the actual research *question* is far from clear. What exactly is it that we wish to know, and for what purpose? Should we target tourists from countries other than our own, or should we target only those in our own country – or only those in Western countries?

Clearly, this research question requires clarification, and one way to do it is to draw up a rich picture. Since the chosen topic area is so wide this requires decisions about what should or should not be included. A world view (*Weltanschauung*, plural *Weltanschauungen*) will emerge. For example, the researcher may decide to tackle the problem from the point of view of international tour operators; i.e. as a typical piece of commercial consumer research. Here the focus might be upon identifying customer segments with particular lifestyles and interests. However, it would be equally legitimate to approach the research from another *Weltanschauung*, such as the consumer's point of view (groups such as the Consumer's Association do this all the time). The emphasis might then change, to focus upon the availability of services for particular interest groups, or upon value for money, or specific perceived problems such as the attractiveness and sustainability of resorts.

THE RESEARCH PROCESS AS A SYSTEM

Systems thinking can help in a number of ways with the design and structuring of research programmes. Not only can research topics and subjects be modelled as systems, but the research procedure itself can be regarded in this light. For example, a 'typical' research process can be represented as a systems model, as shown in Figure 2.3. According to this model the process has four stages, which may be thought of as progressively 'harder' systems as the research progresses. Early stages of the research process are seen as very iterative, i.e. they involve a great deal of examination and re-examination of the aims and basis of the research, its hypotheses/relationships and methodology. As the project takes shape, these original assumptions become more and more accepted, and less iteration is needed.

Preparation

The 'preparation' stage of research often consists of idea generation. This is particularly true in academic situations, where a student may be asked to identify a topic of interest. This is a particularly difficult task, and often undergraduate (and sometimes even postgraduate) projects are chosen by tutors. Unfortunately, the skill of choosing what to tackle next is perhaps one of the most useful 'life skills' that a university may hope to teach. We would like to encourage more students and institutions to work in this way, and soft systems thinking is therefore offered as a basis for topic selection and development, discussed in this and the next chapter. The tasks of the preparation stage are to identify a number of broad topic areas and appropriate methodologies. Topic areas can then be screened according to a list of criteria, and either rejected or selected for further development. Almost all the major decisions are usually made at the preparation stage, which may be therefore be critical to the success of the project. The iteration processes shown in Figure 2.3 apply not only between the preparation and planning stages, but also amongst the 'planning' subsystems: idea generation, literature searching, methodology choices, etc. It is important that this stage of the process is flexible and dynamic, even after an apparently suitable topic has been chosen.

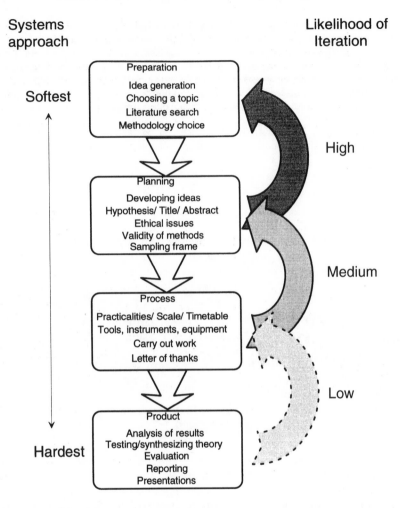

Figure 2.3   A systems view of the research process

Planning

The development of research ideas (unlike their generation) can be comparatively
structured. Many, even most, can be reduced to a simple statement of the type 'X is
related to Y in some way'. Idea development then consists of clarifying the nature of
X and Y and of the relationship between them. This relationship may boil down to a
research hypothesis/null hypothesis, which can be tested by gathering and analysing
quantitative data. Alternatively, it may be a loose configuration for which more
specific hypotheses may be induced from qualitative research results. Identifying and
clarifying the relationship (and even precisely defining X and Y) are still difficult, but
at least there are clear criteria for making decisions, which may not be the case at the
idea generation stage. The planning stage also involves a more detailed consideration
of the research methodology to be used. Methodological choice affects not only the
nature of results, but also the actual question that is asked, and therefore it tends to

colour the whole project. The choice of sample, for example, affects the size and scope of the work, its cost and time scale, as well as the representativeness of the results. The chosen methodology may also introduce ethical questions of a more practical nature than those discussed in the previous chapter. For example, there may be questions of the ownership of the data, the privacy or anonymity of both individual respondents and the organization being studied. If the intention is to publish the results, this must be clear to everyone at the start. Safeguards should be put in place to ensure that the problem owner(s) have plenty of opportunity to read and if necessary veto what is going to be published.

Process

Research is by nature a flexible and even formless activity. It is therefore difficult to generalize about its practical implications. However, practical issues such as the collection of data usually need to be coordinated. This involves clearly identifying, scheduling and timetabling the work that needs to be done. It may also be worthwhile to prepare a flowchart and a critical path analysis of the project. All programmes benefit from some kind of practical planning, which provides a structure and time scale for the work. (It may also impress business organizations that the research is being taken seriously and is not 'merely academic'.) However, some flexibility must also be retained. For example, the success of organizational research may depend upon interviewing a particular individual. If that person can spare ten minutes immediately, but is then abroad on business for a month, it makes sense to conduct the interview immediately, whatever the schedule might say. It is usually also necessary to organize letters of introduction and thanks.

Product

Analysis of results usually occurs throughout the practical stages of a research project. Researchers are usually agog to see what their work has produced. Techniques and instruments (questionnaires, for example) must be tested for accuracy and validity. It is also necessary to keep a check on the progress of the project, as otherwise it may lead up blind alleys or depart from its objectives. In the authors' experience this requires the production and examination of a large amount of data, not all of which contributes to the research project as a whole. Analysing results at the 'product' stage is often a heartbreaking exercise of teasing out the wheat from the chaff. A PhD study should of course keep as many of these extraneous data as is necessary to demonstrate that the candidate has identified blind alleys, kept to objectives and justified every course of action taken. In research reports for clients, however, or papers for academic journals, results must be pared down until they present a coherent argument. Anything more detracts from the work. The 'product' stage should be seen as presenting the argument and the supporting data in the clearest, most accessible way.

Thus the sequence preparation, planning, practice, product models the research process as a system. The early stages are best viewed as 'soft' systems, and the model becomes progressively 'harder' as more and more practical aspects of the research process are considered. This systems model provides a helpful overview and sense of logical flow. On the other hand, it is extremely general, and this severely limits its usefulness. The rest of this chapter and all of the next aims to put flesh upon the bones provided by this model.

PROCESSES OF THOUGHT

Thought processes can be subdivided into two types: creative and algorithmic. Creative (also known as intuitive) thinking is spontaneous, usually involving some kind of mental 'leap'. Often, the greater the 'leap' that must be made, the more valuable is the thinking. If a deep-sea fish were to 'discover' salt water this might constitute a very significant thought in the fish world. Its originality, 'difficulty' and significance come from its context. Deep-sea fish presumably take their environment for granted because they are so closely involved with it. To make the mental leap that could consider alternatives to being immersed in sea water, or place sea water in a relative environmental context, is extremely creative because it comes from an intuitive process that is impossible to describe. The 'cleverness' of a creative thought lies in its originality.

Algorithmic thinking, on the other hand, operates in terms of rules and frameworks. An *algorithm* is defined as 'a logical or computational procedure that if correctly applied ensures the solution of a problem' (*Collins Concise Dictionary*). Thus, an algorithmic thought is one which has been arrived at by the rigorous use of a logical procedure. A rocket scientist who uses Newton's laws of motion and gravity to send people to the moon is applying an algorithm (the laws of motion, etc.) to solve a problem in this way. The 'cleverness' of algorithmic thinking lies in its rigour and in its ability to follow a complex chain of thoughts, arguments and events to its accurate conclusion. Versatility is also important, since an analyst with a large range of tools is often more effective than one who is only skilled with a few. 'Hard' systems methodology and systems engineering would seem to be primarily concerned with algorithmic thinking, since they aim to set up rigorous systems for modelling the world. This is of course an over-simplification. Stages 3 to 5 of systems engineering procedure – 'systems synthesis', 'systems analysis' and 'system selection' – clearly demand some creative thought. In addition, the initial stage, 'problem identification', is usually intuitive, because it does not question the environmental scenario from which the problem arises. By the same token, it is erroneous to regard soft systems methodology as primarily concerned with creative thinking. The soft systems procedure is itself a kind of algorithm, although it is sufficiently flexible to allow considerable creative thought.

Throughout the twentieth century, Western cultures have been increasingly pre-occupied with individualism. One consequence of this may be that students beginning research regard creative thinking as more productive and interesting than algorithmic thinking. There is a tendency to rush off and work in isolation, rather than seeking advice from tutors, classmates or the literature. There is also a tendency to regard work with quantitative data and existing techniques as less rewarding than comparatively unstructured qualitative work. In fact, all research processes require both creative and algorithmic thought. Creative thought can suggest a new fruitful area for study, or a new technique or theory. Algorithmic thinking is necessary for carrying out every kind of investigation and for analysing the results. It is always important to find out what is already known and to consult the work of others, and this in turn always has an algorithmic dimension. Neither creative nor algorithmic thought can be used without the other – at least not in effective research.

The first two stages of the research process shown in Figure 2.3 are used in the sections below to demonstrate how soft systems methodology can be used to firm up potential research topics and to identify suitable activities and techniques for the research process.

IDEA GENERATION

Idea generation is the first and arguably the most important creative activity in a research process. It aims to provide the raw material from which the research topic will be identified. It is possible to structure the process. For instance, brainstorming is a useful management technique, and can be used to generate a large number of ideas. Effective brainstorming requires a group of between five and twelve individuals. All should enjoy equal status within the group and there must be no criticism of the ideas or comment on them as they are generated. The group elects a leader who leads the session, writes down the ideas as they are generated and encourages quiet individuals to participate, so that everyone puts in ideas. The leader also acts as umpire if anyone feels that the rules have been broken. Although brainstorming may be used in a very general way, it often works best if the field is first narrowed by specifying a particular problem or area. The aim is to identify as many ideas (of whatever quality) as possible. These are written down on a flip chart or overhead projector so that everyone can see the list grow.

Brainstormed ideas may be analysed by several techniques. One of these is mind mapping, which models the association between loose ideas and a particular theme. It can be used by a group or an individual to clarify thinking, capture ideas or determine the scale of a situation or opportunity. The issue most central to the problem is written on the centre of a large sheet of paper (or flip chart). Subthemes and issues relating to this central theme can then be identified from the brainstormed list of ideas, or they may arise spontaneously during group discussion. Key words describing each of these issues are written down and joined to the central theme by lines, to build up a spider's web of relationships which branch and sub-branch outwards from the centre. Finally, the mind map is reviewed. It is best to select at least three subthemes for further development.

Although techniques such as brainstorming and mind mapping are useful for identifying and analysing potential topics, they do not address the most central problem in topic selection. This is that a research topic often has to be chosen in a way which suits a number of different (and not always visible) stakeholders. The most suitable way to address this area of the problem is through the early stages of soft systems methodology. Rich picture generation and root definition (using the CATWOE mnemonic) are particularly useful in this respect.

THE RESEARCH TOPIC IN CONTEXT

Factors influencing the choice of a research topic differ according to the nature and purpose of the research, but in general terms they can be identified and contextualized using a rich picture diagram. Such a diagram is shown in Figure 2.4. It is of course impossible to generalize about any specific research situation, and the diagram

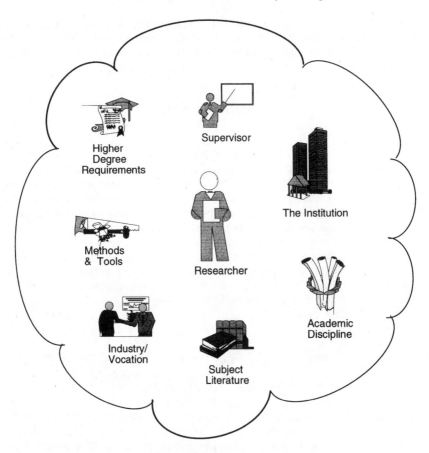

Figure 2.4 Rich picture of research topic choice

is drawn for a hypothetical service industries management researcher, based in the academic sector. However, many of the issues it raises will be relevant to all research scenarios. The diagram's value in this case is that it puts the problem of topic identification into a manageable context. This approach may be more or less valuable according to the situation, but it serves here to illustrate both the problem and the way soft systems thinking can be employed in research. The diagram shows, in unstructured form, all the factors which may affect topic choice, and these are individually discussed below.

The Researcher

All researchers bring preferences, attitudes and values to their work, which are (or should be) reflected in the choice of topic. The 'researcher' shown in Figure 2.4 is a student, perhaps a graduate or undergraduate. Such a researcher is often central to an academic research project, generally becoming very involved with it, lavishing creative energy on it and putting many hours of work into it. This is necessary in order for learning (often the most valuable and formative learning in an individual's career) to take place. Therefore, it is crucial that a project is perceived by a student researcher as interesting and valuable. This is less likely to be a key issue in industrial research, where topics reflect company objectives, but even in this situation it is valuable for researchers to know their own feelings and interests and to act accordingly as far as possible.

It is frequently difficult to identify a topic of personal interest. An individual may find it a problem to differentiate between fine shades of interest or value, or may just not feel any 'ownership' of topics in the particular subject. It is often necessary to go back to first principles and ask 'Who am I?' One way to do this is to think back to some time in childhood and try to identify the things that were interesting then. Aptitudes change between childhood and adulthood, but values and real interests – the things which really make people tick – often stay unchanged in the back of the mind. Such soul-searching is unlikely to define a topic precisely, but it can provide useful pointers. For example, a childhood interest in transport might be expressed in a PhD study of airports as an aspect of international tourism.

Methods and Tools

It is equally important that the topic choice involves methods and techniques which take into account the researcher's skills and aptitudes. For example, someone with a limited background in mathematics might be well advised not to undertake a project involving extensive quantitative analysis, survey work or statistical psychology. On the other hand, if the researcher's mind is made up, mathematical skills are 'algorithmic' and should be comparatively easy to learn in the context of the study. A more difficult (and more common) situation is one where the work requires social skills for handling unfamiliar categories of people. This may be the case, for example, if the research involves gathering sensitive material inside an organization. Skills of this kind are largely intuitive and if the would-be researcher does not already have them they may be much harder to learn. Personality is also very important; as discussed in Chapter 1, predispositions may extend beyond the actual topic to the methodology chosen to carry it out. Choice of methods may also include other personal issues of ethics and morality.

Academic Discipline

Figure 2.4 shows the academic discipline exerting an influence on the choice of topic. The academic discipline is in effect the framework within which the topic takes form. It also restricts the topic. For example, a study of the skills demonstrated by the branch managers of a bank would be an acceptable choice of topic in the field of service industry management; the skills of production managers in manufacturing industry are clearly not relevant. But what about bank services marketing: is that a service management topic, or merely a peripheral one related to the field? The problem seems innocuous expressed in this way, but in fact there are a great many grey areas. A good rule is 'if in doubt, always choose the topic which is least ambiguous'. Another way to deal with the decision is to identify the 'customer' of the research: industry, other academics, the general public, etc. It is also possible to reassess topic relevance at the CATWOE stage, the 'C' standing for 'customers'.

Degree Requirements

Research is widely used in academic establishments as a means of teaching and assessing students. At undergraduate level, a research dissertation can demonstrate students' ability to direct their own learning within the confines of an academic subject. A master's thesis has a similar goal, but the candidate must usually also conduct some primary research (i.e. data gathering). The emphasis of a master's degree (particularly a research-based one such as an MPhil) is generally upon research techniques. By contrast, a doctoral candidate (i.e. for a PhD award) must break new ground by investigating a brand new topic, or perhaps developing a new technique. The main criterion is that the research adds new knowledge to the subject base.

The requirements of academic awards may have considerable influence upon topic choice, and this often means that the scope of a study must be chosen carefully. If it is too wide it may not be completed in time, but if it is too narrow it may not match the academic criteria. Doctoral studies often begin as MPhil programmes, with an option to extend the work to PhD. Thus they have to have an approximate plan of development, indicating which part of the research corresponds to the MPhil and which to the PhD.

Subject Literature

Academic research must demonstrate that it builds upon existing knowledge. This is usually achieved by surveying the literature to find out what others have done in the field. In order to meet the criterion of adding new knowledge to the subject base, a PhD study must also demonstrate that the same work has not been done before by someone else. Activities of literature-searching, reviewing and referencing are thus essential to the academic research process. They are also an important (but sometimes overlooked) component of commercial research. For example, much time and effort may be saved in market research by surveying national statistics, industrial digests and other sources which supply invaluable information about market segments and competitors.

Researchers learn to read subject literature to some extent on undergraduate degree programmes. However, research literature must generally be read with extreme care and analysis, and usually it takes time to become familiar with the literature. This learning process is best begun at the outset of a project, while the topic is being chosen. It will continue throughout the programme, and is in many ways as important as the primary research activities themselves.

Industry

There may be a temptation almost to forget the needs and interests of industry in the face of the stringent requirements of the academic world. Vocational subjects such as service industries management cannot afford to do this. Research topics should reflect current issues and trends in the appropriate industries, and ideally they should provide outcomes which practitioners are likely to perceive as useful. All researchers should question the significance of the research and ask themselves who is going to benefit from it. To some extent this can be achieved by going through the CATWOE procedure, but the question of significance is so important, and so difficult to gauge, that it should be constantly addressed. For example, it is worth scanning the trade literature for the latest developments and asking industrialists for their opinion.

The Institution

Research carried out within industrial companies must generally meet clear cost–benefit criteria, and companies therefore need to direct and control their research efforts closely. Academic research has different aims and criteria, but certain factors, notably cost, are nowadays as tightly controlled as in industry. Academic topics are intended to be vehicles for learning, and institutions often allow candidates considerable flexibility of choice. However, some consider that the learning process is best served by restricting student choice to a prescribed list of topics. In fact, few institutions have an unlimited range of expertise and most are forced to restrict the range of topics offered to those they feel competent to supervise. Academic institutions also usually have identifiable areas of strength, and it is to a candidate's advantage to work within these or to move elsewhere. Supervisory support will be more effective in an institution's area of strength, and so will library and technical facilities. It is encouraging to work alongside others on parallel projects in a vibrant research group.

Supervisor

Academic research departments strongly reflect the personalities of individuals within them. Therefore, many of the issues discussed above under the heading 'the institution' also relate to the available supervisors. In addition, an allocated supervisor is familiar with the academic subject and the topics which are most likely to be worthy of study. However, the supervisor ought to play a key role in a research project, forming a close relationship with the candidate. German researchers use the term *Doktor Vater* (doctor-father) to emphasize the close bond which normally develops between the supervisor and candidate. If personality clashes seem likely to occur between the two, it is best to re-evaluate the choice of supervisor, and this may in turn affect the choice of topic and the way the research is conducted.

ROOT DEFINITIONS OF THE 'RESEARCH SYSTEM'

The rich picture described above places the choice of a research topic in context. It also makes it possible to identify potential systems within this context. Figure 2.4 was drawn up solely to illustrate the factors involved in *choosing* a research topic. Although this may be helpful, the issue of real interest is the *development* of the topic and its subsequent realization as a piece of research work. Topic choice is in effect only one part (the first of the four stages) of the larger system outlined in Figure 2.3. It is probably most productive at this point to structure more of the stages. This can be done by carrying out the CATWOE analysis, as follows.

Clients

Clients of the research project must be identified. There may be several of them, and some may have to be eliminated as not being relevant to the particular *Weltanschauung* which characterizes the research. Typical clients may be a funding agency (which obtains useful information or data for its money), an examining panel or a university research degrees committee (who will receive the completed thesis). The researcher (who gains learning) may also be regarded as a 'client', but other possible clients are the company in which the work is carried out or the organization which originally commissioned the research.

Actors

All the agencies mentioned above may be regarded as actors who participate in the system, but the 'actors' category also includes the researcher and the individual respondents whose information will make up the research data. The list of actors should seek to exclude those whose role is tenuous or minimal.

Transformations

In order to define a transformation it is necessary to define the system inputs and outputs. This again depends upon the viewpoint within which the research project is defined. Research extracts data from the environment, but it also analyses and extracts knowledge from data. Research projects usually obtain knowledge from the work of others, through the subject literature. In an academic environment, research may be regarded as a means of transforming an unqualified individual into one who possesses a qualification.

Weltanschauung

In a sense, the concept of *Weltanschauung* summarizes the CATWOE process. This stage of systems analysis is about deciding the context in which the system is to be modelled. The context depends upon the system environment, boundary, inputs and outputs. It also defines the roles of people, groups and influences which differ depending upon the context and situation, as described above. A *Weltanschauung* is generally the particular point of view of an individual or group. Typical examples might be:

- the viewpoint of the researcher;
- the viewpoint of one or more of the people, groups or organizations who take part in the research (e.g. as respondents);
- the viewpoint of the funding body;
- the viewpoint of the sponsoring institution;
- and so on.

Each different 'world view' generally carries with it different possible customers, actors, inputs and outputs.

Owner

Soft systems analysis was originally developed for solving clients' problems in consultancy situations. In such contexts it is important to identify a problem owner, because the problem itself may be a matter of perception. This aspect may not be as significant where a research system is to be defined. In academic research, the 'problem owner' is often the researcher, while in industry-sponsored projects it is usually the sponsoring department.

Environment

Aspects of the research environment were discussed above under the heading 'The research topic in context' and are shown as a rich picture in Figure 2.4. However, there is more to 'context' than this, and it is vital to be able to place a project in its wider environment. For example, it is important to study the subject literature, so that the project does not repeat the work of others, and equally to make oneself aware of current trends related to the subject. This is particularly true of long-term projects, which may be rendered irrelevant by the passage of time. In extreme cases, others may undertake and publish the same work, preventing its submission as a PhD study. It is wise to choose topics which will produce interesting results whichever way they turn out. Such topics are said to have *symmetrical outcomes*. For example, a study of retail service might be of little interest if it showed that customer satisfaction was greater if service quality was improved (because most retail managers would feel they know this anyway). A study which showed that service quality had no effect upon customer satisfaction would be much more contentious and therefore interesting. However, the problem of asymmetry can often be overcome by changing the focus or style of the study. For example, research which could offer a mathematical relationship between service quality and customer satisfaction (or measure either of these 'quantities' in a convincing manner) would probably be of interest, whatever actual relationship it discovered. This is because the measurement itself is difficult, and, if achieved successfully, would be of great use to retail managers.

CONCLUSIONS

Systems thinking pervades management education (and consequently management research) in ways which are not always recognized. Systems methodologies provide a convenient way to tackle far-reaching and intractable management problems. Two types of methodology have been examined here. Systems engineering assumes that the problem to be studied is well understood and the system is clearly identifiable. It provides a useful kit of tools – flowcharting, timetabling, critical path analysis and so on – which can be used to break a problem down into its component parts. These may then be rearranged into a more coherent and functional whole. By contrast, soft systems analysis aims at structuring a characteristically vague problem. This is done by identifying all environmental factors which may possibly be relevant and then establishing an appropriate *Weltanschauung* or perspective, from which a workable systems model may be defined and modelled. Although many soft systems situations are of a high order of complexity, some systems or parts of systems may be sufficiently simple for a systems engineering approach to be employed. Systems methodologies are therefore valuable research tools, which are particularly suited to studying phenomena in organizations and to analysing processes.

The present chapter has illustrated how soft systems methodology may be used to tackle the problem of choosing a research topic: an unstructured problem which frequently besets inexperienced academic researchers. Only certain stages of the methodology have been employed and the application has been both cursory and general. Rich pictures and systems diagrams may well help in identifying a practical problem and deciding upon a suitable way to tackle it. The student is not recommended to waste much valuable time drawing and redrawing diagrams of the process of topic choice, as has been done in this chapter. On the other hand, certain elements of systems thinking are highly appropriate for understanding the research process and placing it in context. The systems theme continues into the next chapter, which explores the process of refining and developing a research idea into a proposal.

REFERENCES

Bertalanffi, L. von (1968) *General Systems Theory*. Braziller, New York.

Boulding, K.E. (1956) 'General systems theory; the skeleton of science', *Management Science*, 2(3), 56–68.

Harris, N. (1989) *Service Operations Management*. Cassell, London.

Jordan, S. (1968) *Themes in Speculative Psychology*. Tavistock, London.

Kast, F.E. and Rosenzweig, J.E. (1968) 'General systems theory: applications for organization and management', *Academy of Management Journal*, December, 447–68.

Kast, F.E. and Rosenzweig, J.E. (1985) *Organization and Management: A Systems and Contingency Approach*. McGraw-Hill, New York.

Kirk, D. (1995) 'Hard and soft systems: a common paradigm for operations management', *International Journal of Contemporary Hospitality Management*, 7(4), 13–16.

Patching, D. (1990) *Practical Soft Systems Analysis*. Pitman, London.

Teare, R., Atkinson, C. and Westwood, C. (eds) (1994) *Achieving Quality Performance*. Cassell, London.

3

Planning Research

INTRODUCTION

The planning of research usually begins with the identification and clarification of the problems to be researched, and then with suggestions for suitable methods and techniques. For example, soft systems methodology can be employed at this stage, as discussed in Chapter 2. However, many research projects then follow a more structured approach. In academic research, the preferences and aptitudes of the researcher often predetermine the choice of topic and of methodology. Many research problems begin life in rather a vague form and require clearer definition before they can be tackled. After this stage, however, research planning may take a more linear and systematic course. This is likely to be less iterative than the process of topic selection, and usually involves aspects such as timetabling and scheduling, often requiring a 'harder', more pragmatic view of the work. Figure 3.1 shows this part of the process in context. The first of the four boxes (shown in grey) has already been discussed in the previous chapter. The present chapter deals with the remaining three. It discusses the elements of planning which underlie the implementation, analysis and reporting of research, and also traces the final stages of the topic development process.

PLANNING THE SCOPE: DEVELOPING A RESEARCH IDEA

Soft systems methodology can make it possible to identify suitable, practicable areas of interest and appropriate ways to tackle them. However, research ideas identified in this way usually still require considerable development. They are generally broad areas, rather than specific topics, and may need to be cut down to a manageable size. This may be achieved by:

- identifying and adding new terms to qualify and hence restrict the area of interest;
- narrowing the area of interest vertically, i.e. reducing the organizational/social scope;

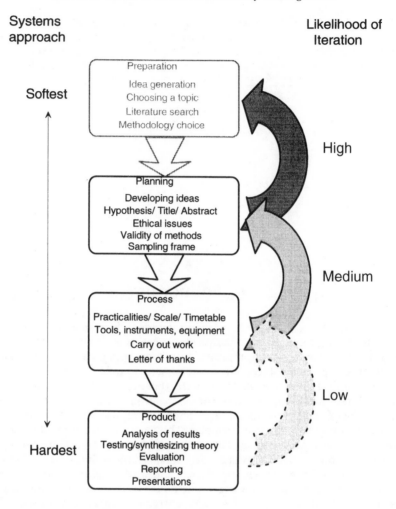

Figure 3.1 A systems view of the research process

- narrowing the area of interest horizontally, i.e. reducing the geographical, topical or numerical scope;
- intensifying the methodological focus.

These approaches are discussed in more detail below. Any or all of them may be used, depending upon the nature of the topic and its original depth and breadth. The four approaches overlap in many ways, and are to some extent dependent upon one another. However, it is generally worthwhile considering all of them, in order to achieve the best focus possible.

Identifying New Terms

An initial research idea frequently takes the form: 'I want to do some work on X using Y technique(s)'. For example, a researcher may identify service quality as an interesting field for study, and may feel that a case study approach might be the most appropriate or interesting. A quick literature scan may reveal that a large number of authors have already completed studies in this area, many using a similar approach. An effective way to cope with the problem is to introduce a new term into the research idea. For example, the study of service quality may be restricted to one particular type of service industry, such as restaurants or banks. Other terms which can be used to restrict the scope of a topic are:

- geographical locations (for instance, cities, regions or countries);
- departments of a particular type of business organization;
- customer groups (for example, market segments based upon socio-economic or lifestyle criteria);
- worker groups (for instance, the way front-line workers affect quality, or back-of-house and service workers interact);
- areas of environmental focus, such as technological, economic, social, political or legal;
- areas of management focus, such as decision-making;
- management functions, such as marketing.

It is possible to reduce the scope of a research topic still further by introducing several terms together. Terms may also be suggested by the chosen methodology. For example, it is often most convenient to carry out a case study on a comparatively limited basis: in one organization or department, with a few selected individuals from one customer segment, or some such defined scenario. On the other hand, survey work usually demands a wide geographical location, many individual respondents, a number of organizations or even different countries.

Sometimes it is productive to investigate potential cause–effect situations. For example, the researcher may choose service quality as the first term and organizational downsizing (i.e. the flattening of the organizational structure) as the second. The two-term research idea then looks like this: 'Service quality and organizational downsizing'. This implies an unspecified relationship between the two. But it is also possible to propose a more formal, causative relationship between them, if the researcher suspects that one term causes the other, or is influenced by the other in a clear-cut way. For example, a plausible causative relationship is summed up in the research idea: 'Effects of organizational downsizing upon service quality'. This may be further qualified by adding more terms, e.g. 'Effects of organizational downsizing upon service quality, as measured by customer satisfaction', or 'Effects of organizational downsizing upon service quality in four star hotels'. Such an idea may be stated as a formal hypothesis and then tested, to establish that the null hypothesis is incorrect. Alternatively, it may be treated in a more phenomenological way, by gathering and evaluating data which support, contradict or qualify the original idea.

Narrowing the Area of Interest Vertically

Another way to structure and define a research topic is through the level of analysis. This may also be called the vertical perspective, because the different levels are considered to be arranged one above the other in a vertical hierarchy. The following levels make a useful starting point for narrowing a research topic down:

- *international level*, i.e. comparison between the practices, attitudes, etc. in different countries;

- *societal/national level*, i.e. comparison between different strata of society (e.g. different socio-economic groups, nationwide);
- *industrial level*, i.e. comparison between different industries (e.g. banking and retail) or between different industrial sectors (e.g. the manufacturing and service sectors);
- *organizational level*, i.e. comparison between two different organizations in the same sector;
- *group level*, i.e. comparison between groups within the organization (e.g. different departments or occupational grades);
- *individual level*, i.e. in certain circumstances it may be worthwhile making comparisons between individuals (e.g. the experiences of the individual customers of a service).

Other levels may be identified, depending upon the needs of the situation. It is also possible to conduct projects at more than one level simultaneously. These are complex, time-consuming and beyond the scope of the individual researcher, but may be undertaken by research teams, or by consortia of teams from different institutions.

Narrowing the Area of Interest Horizontally

The 'horizontal focus' of a project refers to the sample or subject size upon which the research is conducted. Typical 'horizontal' groupings are as follows:

- *geographical*, i.e. one particular country, group of countries, region of a country, one particular town or city;
- *market segment groupings*, e.g. socio-economic groups, groups based upon age, religious affiliation, lifestyle, etc.;
- *specific subject*, such as one particular organization.

These groupings appear similar to those in the vertical levels, discussed above, but they are not by any means identical with them. For example, it is possible to narrow the scope of an international project by restricting it to a few specified countries. In the same way, a case study conducted on a 'national' basis may restrict itself to one or two particular organizations. In such circumstances it is usually necessary to argue convincingly that the particular organizations chosen are typical of the industry as a whole.

Intensifying the Methodological Focus

The level and sample size used in a study are to some extent dictated by the chosen research methodology. For example, surveys tend to require large samples in order to achieve statistically significant results. Interviews, on the other hand, may take up so much time, and produce such rich results, that it is only feasible to study a small sample, a single organization or an identified group of individuals. The higher levels (national and international, for instance) offer good scope for survey work, but interview and other techniques can also be used, depending upon the nature of the problem. Small samples may be perfectly appropriate.

Intense methodologies are those which produce a large amount of potentially complex data from a relatively small sample. It may be possible to narrow a research project down by moving from a comparatively 'diffuse' methodology such as a questionnaire survey to a more intense one (e.g. an interview or ethnographic study). However, it is also necessary to justify the chosen methodology, particularly where it restricts the sample size and may as a result be studying an atypical area. On the other hand, it may be possible to use both types of methodology in such a way that the results from one technique support those from another. Two approaches are available for this. Triangulation generally involves different techniques at more or less the same hierarchical level of study. Case study methodology, on the other hand, uses increasingly intense methodologies, focusing on smaller and smaller subgroups within the sample. In this way it is possible to provide a view of the study subject which possesses both breadth and richness.

The most important thing about defining and narrowing a research topic is to justify the way in which it is done. This depends partly upon the research objectives. If the aim is to discover something from a limited survey sample that applies generally to a whole population, then it is important to show that the chosen sample is typical of the whole. This may dictate both the sample size and the methodology employed. However, it is often impossible to be sure that research results are generally applicable, and it is therefore reasonable to use small (and not necessarily representative) samples, particularly when the technique used produces rich data. It is also possible to justify a project in terms of access. For example, the researcher may have access to one company rather than another, owing to geographical location or to personal circumstances. This is a perfectly legitimate justification of a choice. It is harder to justify opportunistic research, undertaken just because a particular subject happens to present itself at a particular time. It may be necessary to find other factors which appear to support the choice. However, such impromptu research opportunities should always be grasped, as they may provide valuable insights and stimulate other research in the area.

Example 3.1   Refining a Research Idea

As discussed in Chapter 2, research topics may be developed from the output of a brainstorming session. For example, the session might produce a series of ideas: hospitality industry, employee attitudes, technology, career progression, food and beverage service and so on. One way to develop this list into a research topic is to arrange the ideas in order of relevance around one central subject or theme, such as human resource management. A good way to achieve this is to use the technique known as mind mapping, discussed in Chapter 2, which enables the ideas to be fitted together (for example) as follows.

> A study of the effects of introducing food technology upon the perceived career paths of food service staff.

Each of the terms in this statement (introducing, perceived, career and food service) serves to narrow the scope of the project: it is not merely about human resource management or food technology in the hospitality industry, nor about attitudes to technology. It could be converted into a rigorous hypothesis/null hypothesis, i.e. that the introduction of new technology does, or does not, influence employees' perceptions of career progression. This could be tested and supported or falsified by a suitably designed process of enquiry. The topic could also be narrowed still further by choosing a particular aspect of food technology: a new type of cooker or a new type of pre-prepared food.

This topic may be narrowed still further by narrowing the particular vertical 'slice'. For example, if sufficient resources were available, it might be desirable to compare perceptions of careers and technology in two or more different countries. A less ambitious project may have to be content with a single case study of a single company. Further narrowing could be achieved by taking a particular horizontal 'slice'. For example, an international study might choose to compare findings in two particular countries (perhaps for reasons of convenience, contacts or access). If the project could not conduct a widespread survey of establishments in the two chosen countries, it might nevertheless choose two representative sets of restaurants and examine each of them on a case study basis. Alternatively, paired case studies could be conducted at single establishments. Another way to tackle the study might be to conduct a fairly widespread, but cursory, survey, followed first by more detailed questionnaires and then by interviews, focusing in on ever-smaller subsamples, but providing data of increasing depth and richness.

PLANNING THE CONTEXT: SEARCHING THE LITERATURE

Literature searching is an important part of developing and justifying a research topic. It is equally important during the implementation and reporting phases of research work. Literature fulfils the following functions.

- It places the research work in *context*; for instance, a project in service industry management may need to draw upon literature from several other disciplines – psychology, sociology, marketing, accountancy, etc. – to provide the techniques and rationale upon which it is based.
- It provides a *background*, i.e. previous work by other authors, upon which the project builds.
- It makes it possible to *build upon existing knowledge*, and also to prove that *new knowledge* is being generated.
- It enables the researcher to prove that *plagiarism* has been avoided.
- It saves time and money, *avoiding duplication* of effort between different researchers and institutions.

Reading, reviewing, referencing and writing are an essential part of being a researcher, and they are complex skills which take time to learn and apply. The earlier one can begin learning these skills, the better. At the planning stage it is most important to learn to access literature sources and to read.

Accessing the Literature

Broadly speaking, there are three types of literature source, which may be identified as primary, secondary or tertiary. These have the following characteristics.

Primary sources are those which contain the actual results and original thoughts or opinions of other authors and researchers. For academic studies these are journal articles, edited volumes (i.e. books of articles) in which the chapters are often rather longer and more substantial than those in journals, books and conference proceedings. The last may appear in several forms. Sometimes they are informally bound and made available only to conference delegates. However, they are an important source of information and there is a growing tendency for them to be published as edited collections of articles, either in book form or in a dedicated issue of a journal.

Academic articles may be of several types. For example, research articles present the results of a particular project, while discussion papers may put forward new ideas for scrutiny and discussion by other academics. Review papers summarize the work of a number of authors on a single topic area, usually adding the commentary of the review author. Some journals also feature 'research notes' or 'research communications' – brief interim accounts of work in progress which has produced early results. Examples of relevant journals are the *Service Industries Journal*, the *International Journal of Service Industries Management*, the *Journal of Retailing* and the *International Journal of Contemporary Hospitality Management*, but there are numerous others.

Secondary sources contain summaries of articles, called *abstracts*, or sometimes *bibliographies*. They provide a way to absorb the contents of articles quickly and to negotiate a way through a vast amount of literature. Examples are *ANBAR Abstracts*, the *HCIMA Bibliography* and *Abstracts in Hospitality and Tourism*. These are published regularly in book form, and may be available in libraries, where they can be searched using the index in each volume. However, it is increasingly possible to find abstracts on public databases or on CD-ROM. An example of the former is *ABI Inform*, a business abstracting service. This is available (along with numerous other abstracts) through DIALOG, an international subscription, on-line database service. Readers may gain an idea of how to access a database of this kind through Chris Parker's (1991) article on the subject, but technology is constantly changing and it would not be appropriate to give detailed operating instructions here. An example of an abstracting volume on CD-ROM is *World Hospitality and Tourism Texts* (WHATT) published jointly by the University of Surrey and the Hotel, Catering and Institutional Management Association. It is held by many libraries on subscription and is regularly updated.

Tertiary sources allow access to an even greater amount of primary literature, but provide less detail about each item – usually only the title, author and publication details. Tertiary sources are of two main types. *Indexes* are bound volumes (i.e. books) which can be searched alphabetically, e.g. the *British Humanities Index*. The other important type of tertiary source is *Books in Print*, available for several countries and in several languages. An example is *British Books in Print*. As the title suggests, this volume provides brief, but regularly updated, details (title, author and publication details) of all books in print in the United Kingdom, both fiction and non-fiction. *Books in Print* is now available on microfiche and as an electronic database rather than in book form. In fact, the use of tertiary sources has declined slightly since the 1980s. This is probably because CD-ROMs and on-line databases have made it possible to conduct exhaustive searches on abstracts and whole articles, rather than merely on titles, as hitherto. Enormous numbers of literature sources are currently available for searching in this way, and the number continues to grow constantly. However, at the time of writing, downloading of full-text articles is slow and inconvenient, and the ASCII format of the databases makes it impossible to download graphics (illustrations and figures).

This discussion has concentrated upon academic literature, but in a vocational subject, such as service industries management, many other types of source are relevant. These include:

- *government sources*, such as statutes and parliamentary proceedings;
- *trade literature*, such as the periodicals of professional associations or specialist literature for financial services, hoteliers or retailers;
- *general sources*, such as newspapers and magazines for the general public.

To these should be added non-literature reference sources: films, videos, television and radio programmes, publicity materials and so on. All may provide the researcher with important information in an accessible and quotable form.

Where to Search

The most important sources of primary, secondary and tertiary literature are libraries, professional bodies and the Internet.

Libraries hold a variety of indexes, abstracts, journals, edited collections and textbooks. Actual holdings depend upon the type and purpose of the library. Public libraries tend to hold many items of general interest, but are usually quite restricted in terms of specific subjects (such as management in the service industries). Educational establishments usually have good holdings of academic books and journals (particularly if they have a faculty of service industries). However, their holdings of trade journals may be limited. However, trade journals are often to be found in the libraries of specific trade associations, although these may only be available to association members. Most libraries can also obtain any kind of article through interlibrary loans if they do not have it themselves. Libraries often hold reference volumes such as *Books in Print* on microfiche or on CD-ROM. Increasingly they also hold subscriptions to public on-line databases such as DIALOG, although they usually prefer to have a librarian conduct the search rather than teaching staff, students or the general public.

Professional bodies may open their library facilities to their members, or provide a postal service on request. They tend to specialize in trade literature, but may also hold academic journals in vocational fields. Often they have the latest information on legal matters affecting their particular industry, and can provide copies of government consultative documents, white and green papers, notices, European Union directives and so on. Professional bodies usually also hold a variety of statistical information and marketing data relevant to their particular industry.

Most academic institutions are able to offer *Internet* access to their staff and students through the Joint Academic Network (SuperJANET). This may or may not include on-line literature searching facilities. However, private Internet access is increasingly becoming available to the general public. All it requires is a computer, a modem and a subscription to an Internet server. There is a growing number of commercial access providers, such as *Compuserve* and *Microsoft*, who offer e-mail services plus access to the World Wide Web and various public database systems, including DIALOG. Customers can thus tap into a vast array of information, including details of businesses, companies and the stock market, as well as most of the types of literature described above.

How to Use Literature

Since literature will be an important feature of all aspects of a researcher's life, it is best to attempt to tackle it systematically from the start. This can be done by entering bibliography details upon file cards, in an electronic database or in a specialized system such as Microsoft *Reference Manager*. References should contain full details of the author and title, as well as publication details (date, publisher and place of publication for a book; date, volume, issue and page numbers for a periodical). If cards are used they should be large enough to take notes about the content of the article, the reader's opinions of it, etc. File cards should be organized in alphabetical author order. It may be possible to search electronic filing systems by key words as well as by authors. Whatever system is chosen should be continually updated (electronic systems should also be carefully backed up), and nothing should ever be thrown out.

Reading is another important aspect of literature use. Many specialist works on study skills provide advice on how to read: for example, *Improving Study Skills* (Lashley, 1995). It is possible to make detailed prescriptions and to break the process down into a number of set stages. However, for the purposes of this book, a simple approach is presented, summed up as *skim*, *mark* and *make notes*. These are described below.

Skimming a work consists of getting through it as quickly as possible, to get an overview of what the writer is attempting to express. This can be done in several ways. It is possible to dip randomly into a work, stopping here and there at particularly interesting passages. Sometimes it is possible to make this process more systematic, by looking first at a table of contents. Alternatively, there may be subheadings to guide the reader through the work. Some journals require authors to insert subheadings at regular intervals, and this can help a reader considerably. It is possible to 'tune in' the eye to pick out certain key words, and this is another helpful way to negotiate an article. Research articles are frequently difficult to read. The linguistics scholar Stephen Pinker (1994) cites them as one of the most notorious sources of incomprehensible English. This is partly because of the complexity or novelty of the ideas expressed. In any case, it is very important for researchers to learn how to read, study and exploit such literature, which is an essential source of new ideas and techniques.

Marking passages is another important part of reading. Research articles are usually densely packed with ideas and information. It is important to remember where things are, as many of them will be built into research proposals, research articles or reviews. A good way to mark passages is with bookmarks of clean paper that can be annotated as reading progresses. The bookmarks may also be removed later, and provide a useful guide to what information is available and where it is located in the text. In any case, it is useful to have a means of recording which articles (and which parts of articles) are most useful and why. Such notes can often be added to actual, or electronic, filecards.

Making notes (annotation) is the most important part of reading research articles. It provides a way to get the ideas expressed in the text into the reader's own words *during* the reading process. Everything of interest in the text should be annotated, and so should any ideas or questions which come to mind during reading. Notes should always attempt to put the ideas in a different way from that expressed in the text. They should aim to simplify the text and to enhance it. If possible, they should synthesize the reader's ideas with those of the writer, because this is the nature and purpose of reading. Notes should never repeat what is in the text. If the writer's words are so appropriate that it is important to save them for quoting later, they can be marked with an editing highlighter pen. Such pens can be used to give the impression that a document has been read – busy people frequently highlight the minutes of committees for this purpose. If real reading and real understanding are required, highlighting in this way is a dangerous practice. It is possible to fool oneself that a piece of heavily highlighted text has been read, when it has *only* been highlighted. Few research articles contain many quotable extracts, so annotation, rather than highlighting, is the most reliable way to tell whether an article has been carefully read.

Postmodernist literature critics (for example Roland Barthes) say that 'the reader kills the writer'. This implies that to gain ownership of (to truly understand) the written word, readers must put the expressed ideas into their own words. The essential thing about reading is as far as possible to get inside the written word and make the ideas it contains one's own. Thus, a good review should say something new about the original written text (and so should notes written in the margin of a text). The fewer of the original writer's words that remain, the more learning will have taken place.

PLANNING IMPLEMENTATION

During idea development an appropriate research methodology will often suggest itself, providing a starting point for planning the study. Implementation also requires careful planning of the actual design of the work, the timing and the personnel required to undertake the project.

Study Design

Four main types of study may be appropriate for research into service industry management: case studies, surveys, archival studies and experiments. These can be broadly outlined as follows.

- *Case studies* generally focus on the questions how and why, typically using a variety of techniques or subsamples and focusing from a comparatively broad outlook to a progressively narrower subject area. They are an effective way to make a detailed study of an area in which the researcher has no control over influencing variables.
- *Surveys* generally ask who, what, how many or where. They tend to include relatively large samples and wide fields of study, often using questionnaires or standardized interviews. Surveys provide a good way to summarize the status of a large group of individuals, companies, etc.
- *Archival studies* typically ask how much, how many, who, when or where. As the name suggests, they rely upon a detailed analysis of statistical or archival sources, rather than upon primary research methodologies. Archival studies are an effective way to increase knowledge in an area where considerable information exists, but there are few theories.
- *Experiments* ask how or why, and usually seek to falsify or confirm a careful formulated hypothesis. Generally, they aim to compare a 'treatment' sample (for which one single defined variable has been changed) with a 'control' sample (for which this variable remains unchanged). The experimental approach assumes that the researcher has control over all relevant variables, and that all but one (the test variable) can be held constant.

These four types of technique can be used in various ways. For example, case studies and surveys may deal with single situations, or with multiple ones. A single situation ('one off') study examines one single situation at one particular time. It has the advantage of concentrating its focus, but may not be able to set its findings in context, because there is no basis to make a comparison. Case studies and surveys may be made on a comparative basis in two ways. Horizontal studies compare different samples. For example, it is possible to compare two different market segments or nationalities by means of a survey. A case study might compare two different organizations, or two departments within an organization. An alternative type of comparison is the longitudinal study, which examines one subject over a period of time. For example, a case study could draw inferences about the before/after effects of a particular change within an organization. A longitudinal survey might follow the same group of managers at parallel points in their careers.

The design of experiments is complex, because of the need to control all the variables rigorously. Numerous formats have been devised for doing this. For example, biologists and medical researchers use the following standardized experimental designs:

- randomized experiments (in which the 'treatment' and 'control' individuals are randomly allocated within the population as a whole);
- randomized block experiments ('treatment' and 'control' individuals are randomly allocated within different groups called 'blocks');
- Latin square experiments ('treatment' and 'control' individuals are systematically allocated in a way which cancels out differences between blocks and treatments).

Each of these designs calls for a different kind of statistical analysis, all of which are discussed in more detail by Ott (1984). Ryan (1995, p. 33) mentions an experimental design known as the Solomon four-group comparison, which may be used in before/after survey studies. Here the sample is divided into four groups, as follows:

- group 1 undergoes the change, and is interviewed/surveyed both before and after it;
- group 2 does not undergo the change, but is interviewed/surveyed in parallel with group 1;
- group 3 undergoes the change, but is only interviewed/surveyed afterwards;
- group 4 does not undergo the change, and is interviewed/surveyed in parallel with group 3.

In this way, the design seeks to control for any changes which are unrelated to the change being investigated. It also makes allowance for the possibility that the first questioning may affect respondents' answers at the second stage of the survey. Research designs of this kind aim to give the researcher maximum control of the data and of the circumstances under which they are obtained.

Study Criteria

Quantitative studies are essentially about taking measurements, so a few words about measurement theory are appropriate here. In order to be useful, any measurement must have two criteria. It must be accurate and it must be precise. Accuracy refers to the measurement's ability to reflect the 'real world'. For example, a tape measure should read one metre if the dimension of the object it measures is one metre. A clock should show one o'clock at exactly one o'clock. Precision, on the other hand, refers to the readiness with which a measurement can be duplicated. For example, if the tape measure measures one metre the first time, it should do so on all subsequent occasions, no matter who is using it. Accuracy and precision may be virtually independent. For example, a crude measuring device may give widely spaced readings, with an average very close to the real value. On the other hand, a very precise measuring instrument can sometimes give very closely grouped results centred a long way from the true target. A precise measuring technique gives better accuracy than an imprecise one if it is correctly calibrated. However, precise techniques may give the researcher a false sense of security if the calibration is inaccurate. It is quite legitimate to speak of the accuracy of qualitative studies, but the concept of precision is less appropriate in qualitative work.

Other criteria applicable to research methods are that they must be *reliable* and *valid*. Reliability refers to a method's ability to give the same result on different occasions. At first sight it seems similar to precision. However, reliability only asks for a similar *result*, whereas precision demands similar measurements. An elastic tape measure, which always gave the same spread of readings, would be reliable, but not necessarily precise, since the spread might be wide.

Validity is analogous to accuracy, reflecting a research technique's ability to give a true picture of the study subject. The concept of validity is related to the nature of reality itself, and hence to the relevance of positivistic as opposed to phenomeno-logical thinking (i.e. whether or not it is assumed that an independent absolute 'reality' exists). Three distinct kinds of validity are generally recognized: content validity, construct validity and predictive validity.

Content validity indicates that the technique assesses or 'measures' what it is supposed to measure. It applies both to measuring instruments and to more general methods. For example, a spelling test should measure how well people can spell; interviews which purport to gather or assess respondents' opinions about a service should do so in a clearly identifiable way.

Construct validity is concerned with the philosophical basis of methodology, rather than with specific techniques. It is present if the theories underlying the study are appropriate and the assumptions being made are true. For example, while it is acceptable to take spelling tests as an indication of people's ability to spell, it may not be appropriate to take them as an indication of overall language ability. Likewise, it may not be reasonable to interview people about the food in a restaurant and then to deduce from the results that they are satisfied with the service.

Predictive validity is the ability of a research technique to predict something about the sample, or about the outside world. In principle, a measurement which displays predictive validity demonstrates the existence of a 'natural law', i.e. a hypothesis which is generally true about the type of system under study. In practice, predictive validity tends to be hedged about with contingencies and preconditions. A more common instance of predictive validity is where a measurement is able to predict the fluctuations of another variable within the same system (e.g. in the same study sample). This type of validity is also known as *criterion validity*.

Authorities differ somewhat about appropriate criteria for research methodologies. For example, Skinner (1991) discusses internal validity: the extent to which the measured effect can be attributed solely to the variable which is being measured. He describes external validity as the extent to which the findings of research can be generalized to other situations. Both of these criteria assume an experimental and positivistic approach to research work, and imply that reliability, validity and accuracy only apply to quantitative studies. This is not the case. Accuracy and even precision are concepts applicable to qualitative studies, though precision is comparatively difficult to assess in this situation. Reliability and all three types of validity discussed in this chapter are applicable to both qualitative and quantitative work.

Project Management

Research is an expensive and time-consuming exercise, which must be carefully managed if the best value is to be obtained from available resources. It is therefore important to plan and schedule research activities. Planning the sequence and timing of research work is a useful discipline for an individual researcher and an essential activity where a team of several researchers must be coordinated. Bodies which sponsor research usually require the presentation of a research proposal in which at least the duration and sequence of the work is detailed. Often it is also necessary to detail the time inputs of specified individuals, in order to show how the research funding is to be spent. There are three basic ways in which this may be done: by timetabling, by means of a sequence chart or by using critical path analysis. All three involve identifying specific objectives which must be achieved during the period of the project. Other essential factors are the sequence of the activities and the time required for each one. The differences between the three planning techniques lie in the amount and accessibility of the information, the depth of the planning and the preference of the researcher.

A *timetable* should identify the tasks which must be carried out. It lists them in sequence and provides starting and finishing dates for each one. In joint project work the timetable may also indicate which individuals are involved at each stage and how much time each will input. A timetable is an important part of many research proposals. It is a very helpful device for fund-awarding bodies or research degree committees, because it permits a quick overview of the practical management of a project. However, it does not provide its information accessibly enough for the day-to-day management of projects. For example, it is difficult to show any overlap of activities, or to prioritize them in any way.

A *sequence chart* or Gantt chart shows the various tasks which make up the project in the form of blocks, superimposed on a calendar (see Figure 3.2). It indicates visually when each activity begins and ends, and also shows the durations of activities and phases of the work. As can be seen in the figure, such a chart can show the overlap between activities, as well as their sequence and timing.

In *critical path analysis*, the activities making up the research project are represented as a network. Figure 3.3 shows a network of this kind for the same activity sequence as is shown as a Gantt chart in Figure 3.2. The 'boxes' representing the various activities carry a variety of information, including the maximum and minimum possible time requirements. Although it is quite feasible to construct networks graphically by hand, probably the most effective way to do it is by using a suitable computer program, such as Microsoft *Project* or *Excel*. The computer program will also identify which activities are likely to slow or obstruct the progress of the project. Hence it identifies the 'critical path' and can calculate the maximum and minimum time required to complete the work.

PLANNING OUTCOMES

It is important to be clear about the outcomes of a research project, and to relate them to the purpose of the work. Although projects differ in their aims, objectives and overall purpose, outcomes can be broadly divided into three types: persuasion, publication and application. A project may aim to achieve all these outcomes. Indeed,

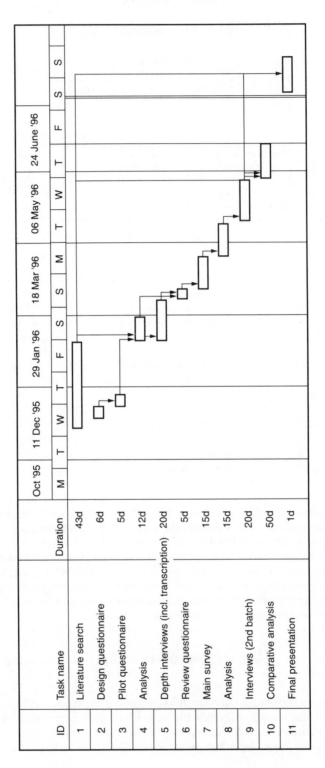

Figure 3.2 Gantt chart of research project

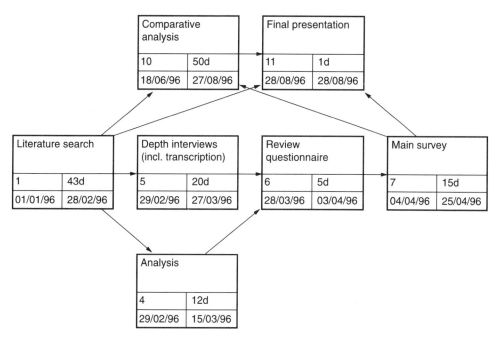

Figure 3.3   Critical path analysis/network of research project

it is important to extract the maximum benefit from every piece of research work, and achieving a breadth of outcome is one way of doing this. The three types of outcome are discussed below.

Persuasion

A common function of research is to gather information which will persuade others to accept a particular point of view. Commercial researchers may have high stakes in the outcomes of such research, and this may even interfere with the quality of the work or dictate the methodology to be used. For example, survey methods and statistical analysis are often used to gauge public opinion on a particular political issue. In principle, this is reasonable, because random sampling and large-scale questioning ought to give unbiased results. In practice, the accuracy and validity of the results may be determined by details such as the quality of the questions or the way interviewers are trained to ask them. Persuasion is to some extent a goal of all research. Graduate student work must persuade examiners and examination boards that new knowledge has been produced in appropriate depth. In fact, all academic studies are directed at audiences of other academics. These individuals must be persuaded that the work contains valid scholarship before they will add the knowledge to their teaching notes or build on it with their own research work. Industrial projects (in marketing research, for example) are often used to justify business strategy. The persuasive nature of research may be recognized at the initial stages of research, when aims, objectives or terms of reference are formulated for projects.

Publication

Practically all research is eventually expressed in written report form. Much commercial and industrial research is the property of particular organizations, and is frequently sensitive or confidential. The report is therefore not published as such, but it is nearly always disseminated to a selected audience, usually in order to persuade them of the value of some particular strategy or policy. Most government research and almost all academic studies are available to the general public. Publication provides the principal means of formulating and disseminating the results of such research. The importance of literature to the researcher has already been discussed in this chapter. The publication of research findings reflects this preoccupation with the written word. It adds a new chunk of knowledge to the growing pile and places the writer's findings and experiences in the context of others' work.

Publication can also serve to bring research to other people's attention and hence may enhance its persuasive powers. It is therefore important to plan publication carefully and to place project results in appropriate periodicals or volumes. Much academic research ends up in learned journals, which require all material to be refereed (scrutinized and criticized by other academics in the same field) before they will accept it for publication. The time scale from submission to acceptance and then to the actual appearance of the article in print may be very long – from six months to two years. Some disciplines (mostly in the sciences) have specialist journals which accept short reports of research work and arrange for rapid refereeing and publication. Although some journals in the service management field do invite short reports of work in progress, at the time of writing this by no means guarantees rapid publication.

A large body of research work (for example, an extended study) may also be published in book form, though it is sometimes difficult to interest a publisher in accepting this kind of work. Books tend to take even longer than journal articles between writing and publication – depending upon the publisher, the process requires between nine and twenty months. Other options for publishing academic research work include conference proceedings and edited collections of articles. Conference proceedings tend to appear quite quickly after submission, because the articles they contain have to be available for the event. However, they may be published only in small numbers by the organization which runs the conference. This may mean that the audience they reach may be limited to the delegates at the conference. Proceedings which are published as edited collections may take as long any other book to appear, but there is a tendency to speed up this kind of work by using camera-ready copy. In this case authors submit their work word-processed to a standard which can be simply photo printed, without going through the lengthy process of copy editing and typesetting. This may considerably reduce the delay between submission and publication.

Research work which is likely to appeal to practitioners within industry may be published in a trade journal. Such articles are intended for a wide audience and must therefore communicate the results and practical implications of the work in a simple, direct way. Research which has scope for practical application may be registered as an original invention and published in the form of a patent. Patents usually deal with machines, materials or other pragmatic topics, but it may also be possible to register other discoveries, at the discretion of the Patent Office. (For instance, processes, logical algorithms and even prime numbers have been submitted for patenting.) Once the patent has been issued, a written account of the invention must be filed, which can be viewed by interested parties at any time. Registration entitles the inventor to exclusive commercial rights for a specified period (usually fifteen years). After this time the patent rights lapse, but the published details are maintained on file at the Patent Office.

The publication of results is an important activity. It publicizes the work and at the same time presents the researcher with an opportunity to present a detailed account of it in a formal setting. Publication develops valuable research skills and should be included among the milestones of research planning: for example, in the schedule or critical path analysis. Publication should not be constrained by the format of the work or by its other planned outcomes. In fact, it is by no means necessary to wait to the end of a project before publication. It is often worth producing opportunistic articles as side issues arise during the course of a major study. External examiners look favourably upon postgraduate degree candidates who have published aspects of their work during their main period of study.

Application

Research work should always set out to fulfil some useful purpose. This may mean answering a topical question, or providing persuasive evidence to support a particular point of view. However, in a vocational subject such as service industry management, research should also aim to assist practitioners directly. Among the ways it can do this are:

- Providing new analytical insights into environmental situations and environmental change. For example, researchers may analyse existing information in detail, identifying likely changes and suggesting appropriate strategic responses.
- Developing organizational theory in a practical context. A good example of this is the intense work that has been conducted into quality improvement programmes since the 1980s. It is clear that services cannot adopt the systems developed by manufacturing industries without considerable redevelopment. Researchers can pinpoint and publicize examples of good practice and demonstrate how they fit with existing organizational theory.
- Investigating and clarifying essential human resource management issues, such as the availability of labour or worker motivation.
- Examining technical or technological issues of management, including the advantages and disadvantages of technological development and its impact upon operational effectiveness, or upon the organization as a whole.
- Developing or investigating new tools for measuring management activities. For example, there is a need for effective ways to measure managerial competence/ effectiveness and to benchmark progress (such as in total quality management or productivity management initiatives).
- Developing or investigating new tools for marketing services: for example, tools for measuring customer satisfaction or for gauging the appropriateness of a service product.

Chapter 1 identified four components of research activities: preparation, planning, process and product. Chapter 2 emphasized the iterative nature of the processes of generating and contextualizing research ideas. The eventual practical applicability of research should be at the forefront of research purpose and is a key consideration in the process of identifying and evaluating suitable research topics. It should also be considered in the planning process, since demonstrating an effective outcome may be as good a way to persuade others of the value of research as publication. This may be done in a number of ways, e.g.

- presenting work to industrialists;
- setting up practical trials to demonstrate a discovery;
- announcing research results in the trade literature;
- patenting, trademarking or copyrighting work.

Where possible, the planning process (including schedules and timetables) should allow for these activities as an integral part of the research programme.

PLANNING FOR CONTINGENCIES

Research is a creative activity dependent upon the vagaries of the human psyche. Often a breakthrough will only occur in a project when a discovery is made, perhaps after considerable trial and error. One discovery sometimes changes the whole direction of the research, by closing one topic or opening another more fruitful-looking one. Much research in the management field requires access to organizations or to busy individuals. This may be difficult to obtain, or may impose unexpected time constraints upon the work. Thus research programmes may go off course despite efficient scheduling and timetabling. A research plan must contain contingency arrangements for dealing with unforeseen events as they occur. Three kinds of activity are needed to achieve this: reviewing, evaluating progress and identifying possible ways forward.

Reviewing can take place on a number of levels. At the day-to-day level, researchers may meet and discuss their work. This activity is valuable whether or not the researchers are in the same group or working on similar projects. Research students often meet their supervisors daily in order to review progress and maintain contact. More formal meetings generally take place on a slightly longer time scale. For example, a research group may hold regular progress meetings. Many research institutions also arrange seminars and colloquia on a regular basis, which all researchers are encouraged to attend. Individuals may present their work, which is discussed by their colleagues. As well as being a useful way of reviewing one's work, this allows researchers to practise skills of expression, explanation, criticism and discussion, and further enhances the research process. National and international conferences are examples of similar events held on an even longer time scale. Presentations are more formal, and there is often an opportunity to discuss projects and findings with eminent researchers. The objective of such events is to encourage discussion and criticism among research workers and hence to improve the quality both of the research and of the way it is expressed. The same goals are achieved by academic publication, and this is another reason why it is a good idea to include interim publications as goals in longer research projects. Publications provide a forum for discussion and development (through the refereeing process). They also force authors to review and evaluate their work.

Evaluating progress means comparing the review with the original objectives. It cannot be done as informally as day-to-day reviewing, but an individual graduate student usually still achieves a level of evaluation during daily or weekly supervision meetings. This process is aided by building objectives of review and evaluation into the tutorial/supervision scheme. These objectives may even be systematized, by timetabling them and devising paperwork that must be completed at regular intervals to demonstrate that a review/evaluation process has occurred. Project groups involving several researchers need to hold regular formal meetings at which progress is reported and evaluated against the original terms of reference or the stated aims/objectives.

Possible ways forward must take account of most of the issues already discussed in this and the previous chapter. Any proposed change of direction must be justifiable in terms of the original research objectives and of progress so far. However, it may be wise to bear in mind the personal skills and preferences of an individual researcher, and some of the institutional and environmental issues discussed in Chapter 20. It is generally important to consider the progress of other researchers, gleaned from the literature, from conference participation and from personal contacts. The work of others is frequently a factor leading to a change of direction. Other researchers may unexpectedly publish results in the same area, so that the research project can no longer be claimed to be generating new knowledge. On the other hand, other researchers frequently publish new approaches and techniques, which may need to be built into existing projects. It may be necessary to review the scope of the research project, and thus to return to the focusing process, discussed under the heading 'developing a research idea' at the beginning of this chapter. In practice, the researcher is unlikely to need to identify new terms to qualify the area of interest. However, a change of direction may well involve narrowing the area of interest vertically (i.e. changing from an over-ambitious level to one which better suits the particular problem or the resources available). Alternatively, it might involve changing the sample size (i.e. narrowing the area of interest horizontally). It may be necessary to reconsider the methodological focus, in the light of research findings to date or of recent publications by other researchers.

SUMMARIZING THE PLAN: THE RESEARCH PROPOSAL

The most effective expression of an initial research plan is the research proposal. Proposals are usually produced for sponsors or for funding bodies, who require conciseness and clarity. Therefore, most proposals do not contain details of all the planning necessary for the successful completion of a project. Some of the issues and techniques discussed in this chapter necessarily belong to the personal or operational level of project planning. However, a successful proposal is likely to incorporate most of the areas discussed above, and a general structure is presented in this section as a means of summarizing and contextualizing the planning of research.

The actual structure of a proposal depends upon its purpose and its intended audience. Most proposals are produced as applications either for funding or for permission to carry out work. Most institutional research (e.g. government-sponsored work and/or academic studies) comes into the former category. Applications for higher degree registration and boardroom requests to conduct marketing or organizational studies come into the second category. Different universities, funding bodies and organizations have different ideas about structuring research proposals, which must be scrupulously followed if the application is to be successful. Despite this, all proposals have one primary purpose: to persuade their audience that the proposed research is worthwhile. Similarly, the following common elements can be found in most research proposals:

- title;
- abstract;
- introduction;
- aims and objectives/terms of reference;
- methods;
- timing;
- personnel;
- costing;
- references.

The following discussion aims to flesh out these components and to put them in a logical context.

Title and Abstract

The title of a project must reflect as closely as possible the intended content of the research work, but at the same time it should be as concise as possible. (Some recipients of proposals actually limit the number of words a title may contain.) It is often a good idea to make the title somewhat eye-catching, so that it stands out among its competitors (e.g. in a bid for research funding). These three objectives usually conflict, and this makes the formulation of titles something of an art. It is probably best to write down a number of possible titles and to discuss them with colleagues or with a research supervisor. It may be useful to divide the title into two parts, separated by a colon or semicolon. In this way an eye-catching opener can be followed by a more mundane statement telling the reader what the proposed work is about.

An abstract (sometimes called a summary) provides a brief overview of the proposed work. It should describe the work as fully as possible, but at the same time must be concise. As with titles, abstract lengths are sometimes specified, but usually it is best to aim for between 350 and 500 words. Abstracts should be composed after the rest of the proposal has been written, even though they usually appear near the beginning of the document. The first step to writing an abstract is to review the contents of the proposal and make brief notes, which can then be ordered and linked together to produce text. An effective way to do this is to use the subheadings as 'notes', editing and textualizing them as appropriate. The text of an abstract should always be edited several times, and as with titles it is best to discuss the content and wording with a colleague or supervisor.

Introduction

The purpose of an introduction is to make a convincing case that the proposed work is valuable and necessary. In order to do this, the introduction should be structured like a 'funnel'. It should begin by identifying the broad area of the topic and reviewing the work of other researchers. Once it has made clear what has been done already, the introduction should proceed to identify a conspicuous gap in the existing knowledge. This should be a specific piece of work which is clearly missing from the background picture. Finally, the introduction should state that it is the writer's intention to carry out this work, and that this is the subject of the proposal. Introductions to academic research proposals may justifiably include extensive references, but it is important to pitch the writing style at its intended audience. An audience of industrialists, for example, is unlikely to be impressed by a long list of references, and may become impatient with a wordy, dialectic style of writing.

Aims, Objectives and Terms of Reference

Aims, objectives and terms of reference are subtly different ways of stating the purpose of research work. An aim is a general statement of what is to be achieved overall, and is usually expressible in one single sentence. Objectives, by contrast, are practical goals which will be achieved as a series of steps in the fulfilment of an aim. Thus the work may be broken down into a number of different aspects, each corresponding to an objective which leads toward the overall aim. However, it may be counterproductive to break down the aim too far. It is probably best (and least confusing) to limit the objectives to a manageable number, perhaps four or five, at the proposal stage. The project can later be broken down into further subdivisions of work when the final schedules or critical path analyses are produced. Aims and objectives represent internal statements of purpose, chosen and owned by the researchers as suitable purposes for the work. Terms of reference perform a similar function, but are usually chosen by someone who has a stake in the research but plays no direct part in it. For example, the sponsors of an industrially funded research project usually specify what they want the research to achieve in the form of terms of reference. The same is generally true of contract research work. By contrast, academic research is usually the property of an individual researcher and must demonstrate its independence in the form of internal aims and objectives, rather than terms of reference.

Methods, Timing and Personnel

The 'methods' section of a proposal sets out the activities which will be used to obtain the results. It should be concise, yet provide sufficient detail for a funding body or awards committee to decide whether the approach is valid and cost-effective. A research proposal is no place for a long discussion of methodology. It may be necessary to justify the proposed methodology if it is novel, or if there is some reason why it might not be readily accepted by the proposal's audience (for instance, the proposed methodology may be contrary to current research fashions). Such justifications are a part of the background and scope of the research and should always be made in the introduction. A proposal should generally set down the order in which tasks will be undertaken, but schedules or lists should be kept to the minimum needed to satisfy the client, recipient or audience. It is generally important to indicate the timing of research activities. A proposal seeking funding must show how the money will be used; a proposal for a higher degree must usually indicate which activities belong to which phase of the work. Funding bodies also usually ask for a list of the personnel who will be involved in the project. Such a list should indicate who will do the work and what part the various personnel play in the research team. It may be necessary to specify the manager of the project as well as operational personnel. Frequently it is also desirable to give the curricula vitae of key project personnel, as this will give the reader of the proposal an idea of the suitability of the research team to carry out the work.

Costing

Research projects seeking funding must supply costings to show how the money will be spent. Funding bodies often require this information in a specific format, making it impossible to prepare one proposal which can be sent to a number of different committees. Costings should show all relevant costs, including:

- *materials* used in the research, such as questionnaires, cassettes or video tapes;
- *salaries* of research personnel, e.g. the total salary of a research assistant engaged full-time on the project, plus proportional salaries of individuals who contribute to it part-time;
- *general costs*, such as travel and subsistence and telephone calls;
- *overheads*, such as the services of an administrative assistant or typist, plus any overhead charges imposed by the institution;
- *management costs* (proportional time spent in coordinating the project by a senior member of the research staff) may or may not be chargeable under the regulations of the particular funding body.

References

The introduction to a proposal should generally be referenced, wherever it is necessary to substantiate a claim, or to place the proposal in the context of existing work. Referencing should take account of the proposal's intended audience. It is usually advisable to reference sparingly. The references should be listed in a standardized format at the end of the proposal. A further discussion of referencing can be found in Chapter 8.

CONCLUSIONS

This chapter has examined the process of planning research, from the formulation and development of an idea through to implementation and reporting. In order to do this, the planning process has been conceptualized in terms of a number of areas. The scope of a project is related to the number of terms or variables being considered and also to its sample size and comparative basis. In addition, these factors are related to the methodological basis of the work. All project development and planning thus has to take an iterative 'what if' approach, in order to refine the topic down to a size which is manageable and at the same time meaningful.

Project development involves planning the context. Chapter 2 outlined ways in which a research idea could be contextualized. However, it is important to build environmental awareness into a research project. This can be done by establishing good literature habits at the outset. Regular searching, reading, reviewing and referencing pay dividends as the project progresses, and the systematic scanning and analysis of subject literature is an essential research activity. This chapter has therefore outlined the types and sources of literature available, and their place in the research process.

At the heart of research planning is the scheduling of the work itself. Research techniques are all subject to questions of accuracy, reliability and validity, which must be considered before the implementation stage of the work can take place. Collecting and analysing data is often a complex process, with many different, interdependent stages. Scheduling is therefore always important in realizing the research process, and it may be critical to the final outcome of the work. This chapter has discussed various techniques which may be used to manage the implementation phase of a research project. Similar approaches can be used to integrate implementation with other phases of the work, such as literature scanning and report-writing.

It is also important to keep the intended outcomes of the work in mind at all stages of the planning process. Three different basic types of outcome have been discussed here: *persuasion, publication* and *application*; which may take different forms, depending upon the nature of the research. Identifying the outcomes of a project in this way is related to identifying the 'customer' at whom the research is aimed (discussed in Chapter 2 when the CATWOE procedure was explained). An essential characteristic of research is its unpredictability. For this reason, research plans should always allow room for contingencies, in case circumstances or unexpected findings suggest a change in the direction of the project. Three essential activities should be included in every plan: reviewing the work so far, evaluating progress against the original objectives and considering possible alternative ways forward.

Often the need to prepare a research proposal provides the impetus for the planning process. This chapter has therefore presented the elements of proposal structure as a way to summarize what has been said about the planning of research. A research proposal crystallizes the researcher's intentions into a verbal form, to which others can add ideas and offer constructive criticism. A research proposal can therefore be regarded as an initial summary of the planning process. However, a proposal only reflects part of the planning necessary for a successful research project.

REFERENCES

Lashley, C. (1995) *Improving Study Skills*. Cassell, London.

Ott, L. (1984) *An Introduction to Statistical Methods and Data Analysis*. PWS Publishers, Boston.

Parker, C. (1991) 'Using libraries: computer-based methods', in G. Allen and C. Skinner (eds), *Handbook for Research Students in the Social Sciences*. The Falmer Press, London.

Pinker, S. (1994) *The Language Instinct*. Penguin Books, Harmondsworth.

Poynter, J.M. (1993) *How to Research and Write a Thesis in Hospitality and Tourism*. Wiley, New York.

Ryan, C. (1995) *Researching Tourist Satisfaction*. Routledge, London.

Skinner, C. (1991) 'Quantitative research', in G. Allan and C. Skinner (eds), *Handbook for Research Students in the Social Sciences*. Falmer Press, London.

4

Quantitative Research Methods

INTRODUCTION

The *Concise Oxford Dictionary* (1990) defines 'quantitative' as 'concerned with quantity' and 'measured or measurable'. Thus, quantitative methods are those which involve analysis of quantities or measurements within data. The scope is wide. For example, governments use quantitative data (often published as volumes of statistics) to organize, plan and control society. Slattery (1986, p. 6) considers that quantitative methods 'present a manageable selection of statistical material relating to social policies which provides a picture of some of the ways our society is changing'. Service industry managers should be able to interpret published information of this kind. They may also need to undertake their own research at some stage, and must therefore be able to plan, implement and control their own quantitative research programmes. In other words, managers must be able to collect and analyse data in a way that is appropriate and valuable to their organization in order to optimize competitive advantage.

This chapter outlines the principles of gathering and processing quantitative research data. It endeavours to highlight methods of quantitative research appropriate to service industries. It discusses the identification of research ideas and the formulation of hypotheses, and explains the value of descriptive and inferential data. The chapter continues by outlining questionnaire design and introduces some techniques of quantitative data analysis using service industry-based examples.

STATISTICAL SURVEYS AND THE MANAGER

It is important that service industry managers understand the significance of quantitative data. Unfamiliarity with statistical techniques and quantitative interpretation leaves them at the mercy of 'statistical propagandists'. Surveys and statistical data should always be viewed at first with a sceptical eye. Quantitative data should never be accepted unquestioningly, and their value and utility can only be appreciated if there is an understanding of the underlying research situation. For example, it may be important to know who commissioned a research project and why, who collected the information, how many respondents there were and so on. The following list summarizes issues of which researchers and managers should be aware when analysing quantitative statistical data.

- Check the source. The more reputable and authoritative the source, the more reliable and trustworthy the data and conclusions.
- Check who sponsored the survey. See whether the statistics have been manipulated or only collected to support a predetermined case. Check the reasons why the statistics were collected and what use is intended for them.
- Check that interpretations and conclusions reached are fully supported by the data. Check that conclusions are reasonable and not mere conjecture.
- Check statistics themselves for error and distortion. See whether the terms used were valid and fair (that a rate or percentage has not been used to exaggerate the picture).
- Check the reliability and validity of the collecting or measuring instrument (register or survey, population or sample, questionnaire design, missing data).

Service industry managers should be familiar with a range of quantitative techniques. This enables them to plan and implement research programmes and to understand the work of consultants in this field. It may also prevent them from ascribing false or unrealistic expectations to the techniques used. Results are only likely to be meaningful if the techniques used are appropriate to the research situation. The quantitative techniques employed may also depend upon the type of information and the form in which it is required.

INFORMATION, QUANTITATIVE METHODS AND THE MANAGEMENT PROCESS

Kerlinger (1986) considers that industrial practitioners are aware of information in four ways.

- *Tenacity*: industrial 'folklore' which sometimes prevails despite new research suggesting otherwise.
- *Authority*: from management 'gurus', public acceptance or the government.
- *Intuition*: because something appears reasonable to believe.
- *Science*: by means of objective research.

For Kerlinger, 'science' involves questioning, and is systematic and empirical, and the results are dependable. The others may produce information which is correct, but this usually happens by chance. For certain topics, the opinion of key individuals is important. More generalizable research (applicable to large masses of population) requires questioning and testing of ideas, concepts and views in a structured way. However, it is inevitable that managers and researchers make mistakes when trying to explain why things occur. Careful research planning and design is an attempt to minimize this, but it is virtually impossible to eliminate all errors, which Babbie (1979) categorizes into seven areas.

- Inaccurate observation: looking without actually seeing.
- Over-generalizing from isolated incidents or from samples.

- Deduced information: having generalized from one observation, it becomes difficult to explain behaviour which may not 'fit'; thus behaviour may be ignored.
- Illogical reasoning: the exception does not always prove the rule.
- Ego involvement: manipulation of data as justification for long time periods engaged in research.
- Premature closure of inquiry.
- Mystification of residuals: researchers testing models which explain only some of the phenomena under study may be tempted to classify unexplained as random.

Quantitative methods of data collection and analysis are of enormous benefit to service organizations. They provide information about consumer behaviour, market trends, quality control, employee work attitudes and so on. Large amounts of data can be collected and analysed more efficiently than qualitative approaches allow. For many service organizations, speed is important to gain competitive advantage. Quantitative approaches allow this by providing data which can be quickly processed and analysed. Moreover, techniques used in quantitative analysis provide the researcher with some idea of the robustness and reliability of the findings (see Chapter 5). Deciding which quantitative method to use may be problematic because of the complexity of service provision. Some headway can be achieved if the manager has knowledge of the major elements of the management process, because they can be matched with the appropriate knowledge requirement. Table 4.1 provides a guide for this 'matching' process.

There is some overlap between stages of the management process and managerial

Table 4.1 Classification of research methodologies according to three dimensions of the management process

Stage of the management process	Level of management activity		
	Strategic	Managerial/tactical	Operational
	Policy research	Managerial research	Operational research
Analysis	Analysis of overall organizational situation with a view to formulating major policy proposals	Related to a specific problem of limited scope for which management has need of additional information	Range of quantitative/ analytical techniques designed to formulate and test decision rules which will permit management to optimize the relations between inputs and outputs of a given operational procedure
Planning			
Execution	Evaluation research	Action research	
	Formal, objective measurement of the extent to which a given activity has achieved its objectives	Continuous gathering and analysis of research data and the feeding of findings into the organization	
Control			

Source: adapted from Ritchie (1994, p. 15).

research elements. For example, 'policy research' requires 'analysis' and 'planning', whereas 'operational research' requires more 'planning' and 'execution'. The overlap is deliberate and reflects the realistic relationship between the management process and research procedure.

PREDICTION, DEPENDENT AND INDEPENDENT VARIABLES

In order for organizations to survive and develop, researchers and industrialists require key descriptive information. Organizations need to know who buys their product, how they are perceived by customers, whether the quality of their service is satisfactory, whether their employees are motivated and so on. Managers must also know how certain environmental/organizational elements or variables are linked. In other words, they need to be able to predict the effect of one variable upon another.

Some predictions are based on 'common sense' and others on complex theories. Everyone has his or her own idea about the 'truths' of human behaviour, and 'old wives' tales' abound. Suspecting a relationship, however strongly, is not the same as proving it to sceptics. For example, some managers may have an idea that low pay is linked with high employee turnover. In fact, predictions of this kind, which say that a change in one element will cause a change in something else, are common. For example, if the price of accommodation is altered, demand for it may change. If a particular type of lighting is used in a restaurant, customer satisfaction may be affected. In order to prove the relationship, it is necessary to identify the underlying features of this type of situation, namely the *independent* and *dependent* variables. The proposition is always that when the independent variable changes, the other variable changes with it in a dependent way. For example, it may increase when the independent variable increases, decrease when the independent variable increases or decrease when the independent variable decreases. In the first example above, the independent variable is the price and the dependent variable is the demand. In the second, the lighting is the independent variable and the proposition is that customer satisfaction is dependent upon it. Actual research situations may be more complex than those presented here, but the basic logic generally applies.

In practice, the issue of causality is very difficult to establish and care must be taken by the researcher when classifying variables as dependent and independent. It may also be the case that several independent variables all affect the dependent variable. Which elements the researcher holds important will depend very much upon the underlying theory upon which hypotheses are based. For causality to be established, Lazarsfeld (1955) suggested, the cause must precede the effect in time, the two variables in question must be correlated and the causal relationship between them must not be explainable through any other variable.

HYPOTHESES OR TESTABLE PROPOSITIONS

Research questions often begin life as vague, abstract generalizations. The issues inherent in a research situation must be considered carefully before the quantitative research process can be planned or implemented. For example, consider the study area of 'tourist drinking habits'. To begin, it would probably be useful to meet a group of people familiar with the situation, such as managers of hotels or tourist attractions, to obtain their general ideas about it. This process might produce thoughts about how to get the desired information. In addition, there could be informal observation of tourists, noting how often they go drinking when on vacation, with whom, where, what the expenditure tends to be and why. It may also be worthwhile undertaking a literature review to see what has been published on the subject. All these activities offer valuable insights into the overall research situation.

As a result of this initial work, the loose initial idea of tourist drinking habits may begin to crystallize into specific research questions or *hypotheses,* which for quantitative work should have a 'yes' or 'no' answer. A distinguishing feature of quantitative techniques is the methods used to see whether these hunches are plausible or *valid.* In other words, systematic data collection should assess whether the theory fits the behaviour. If it does not, the theory may be discarded or revised. It is therefore important that the design of the research instrument should not be carried out in isolation from the original hypothesis. Obtaining answers relevant to these hypotheses becomes the overall objective of the research.

The development of hypotheses is challenging, but fun. It is also a crucial part of the research process and should not be rushed. Examples of some hypotheses which might have been generated for the above study of tourist drinking habits are shown below:

- tourists who stay in unlicensed premises drink less often than those who stay in licensed ones;
- tourists who come from Glasgow drink less often than those who come from other areas of the country;
- tourists do not often drink on their own;
- tourists accompanied by children spend more on drink than those who do not have children with them;
- tourists think pubs in Blackpool town centre are generally overcrowded.

QUESTIONNAIRE DESIGN AND ATTITUDE MEASUREMENT

In order to test a prediction, a plan for collecting data must be devised. This is known as a research design. If a survey is being undertaken, the researcher will usually attempt to obtain as many responses as possible, so that the results are representative and statistically valid. One way to achieve this is by using a postal self-completion survey, rather than a series of expensive and time-consuming interviews. Ryan (1995) estimates the cost of a typical postal questionnaire as less than £2 per person, whereas the cost of undertaking individual interviews (even quite brief ones) is nearer £10 per person. Postal surveys also allow the researcher to specify large sample profiles using postcode databases, so that one individual can obtain a large sample comparatively quickly and cheaply.

Questionnaires should be designed carefully so that the respondent is not confused or misled. A survey is a question and answer dialogue between the questionnaire and informant, with the former posing a series of previously formulated questions. In order to elicit useful responses, researchers must be clear about the information they require and what the appropriate questions should be. If these issues are not carefully addressed beforehand, accurate answers cannot be expected. Questionnaire design also affects the response rate. As the number and complexity of the questions in a postal questionnaire increase, it becomes less likely that respondents will complete and return it. Therefore, the survey instrument must contain enough questions to be of value to the researcher, but not so many as to be off-putting to respondents. The questions must be long enough to elicit the information that is required, but short enough to encourage an optimum response rate.

A questionnaire must have a means of classifying respondents in a way that is appropriate to the study. Usually this is done by means of a biographical section which asks personal questions. These may appear threatening or prying to some respondents, and it is best to include them at the end of the questionnaire. In general, 'personal' questions deter respondents from responding. Putting them at the end allows respondents to be drawn into the less threatening part of the questionnaire and to become 'committed' to it. This may also help to improve the rate of response.

Postal and self-completion questionnaires must fulfil other criteria, which Ryan (1995, p. 127) summarizes as follows.

- Care should be taken over the sequence and wording of questions: for example, it is best to assess the frequency of an event before attempting to elicit an opinion about it.
- The questionnaire should accurately reflect the conceptual framework of the research.
- In the case of attitudinal research, questionnaires should use an analytical framework of attitudinal measurement within the context of the subject matter of the research.
- Questionnaires should permit detailed analysis, i.e. subsamples should be categorized in a way which permits comparisons, and scales composed so that they permit further analysis.

The questionnaire development process is outlined diagrammatically in Figure 4.1. All researchers will have an idea of the information they need to satisfy the survey objectives. Despite this, there are some common but avoidable pitfalls which await the unwary when questions are formulated. A common error in question wording is where the respondent is 'led' to answer in a certain way. This may occur if the informant is offered an insufficient range of answers and the preferred response is excluded. Certain people have a tendency to answer questions in a certain way. For example, respondents who think that the opinion of an 'authority' is more valid than their own will always tend to answer accordingly. They may view the author of the questionnaire as such an 'authority'.

THE PILOT STUDY

Self-completion questionnaires should always be subjected to a *pilot study* before the main survey takes place. In face-to-face situations, the interviewer can supply information or inquire further as necessary, but this is not possible with ques-tionnaires. Closed questions may not be correctly understood. Open-ended questions do not lend themselves to answer by self-completion, because respondents may use cursory phrases in reply. Therefore steps must be taken to minimize these dis-advantages.

A pilot study is an exploratory phase which aims to identify and eliminate problems before the full questionnaire survey is carried out. A common way to do this is to give a newly formulated questionnaire to a small sample of individuals who are similar to

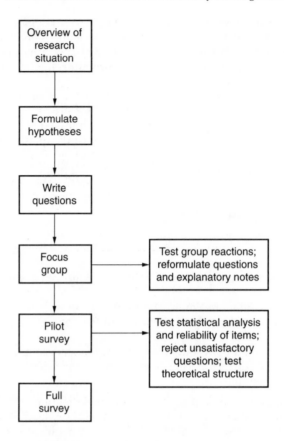

Figure 4.1   The questionnaire development process

the survey population. After this, a focus group (discussed in Chapter 6) is held, to find out whether people understand the questions and how they feel about them. Any misunderstandings or badly worded questions can be identified and corrected. The questionnaire is then reformulated and tested on a larger pilot sample. The results from this 'pilot survey' are subjected to statistical testing to check reliability and validity. Unsatisfactory questions can then be discarded before the full survey. A summary of reasons for pilot testing follows:

- to check whether questions are relevant to (all) members of the particular sample;
- to check whether respondents understand all the questions;
- to check the logic of the question order;
- to check whether any questions have double meanings, or lead or confuse respondents;
- to get an idea of the likely refusal rate;
- to find the best time of day to conduct the full survey;
- to suggest ways of rephrasing open-ended questions as closed or multiple choice ones;
- to show how long it takes to complete a questionnaire (or an interview);

- to indicate whether answers accord with design expectations;
- to check the reliability of questions using various statistical tests (for example correlation, Spearman–Brown, Cronbach's alpha);
- to indicate whether further instructions are necessary.

A helpful account of the development and purification of a standard questionnaire (the SERVQUAL instrument) can be found in Parasuraman *et al.* (1986).

For a questionnaire to be effective, questions must apply to respondents. For example, a questionnaire issued to an entirely male population (for example, tourists at the monastery on the Island of Athos, where no women are allowed) need not ask 'are you male or female'. Questions must also make sense to the respondent and be easy to answer, preferably in a way that generates respondent interest and involvement. Respondents must be told clearly how to enter their answers (for example, in an introductory section of the questionnaire). The following is a selection of common mistakes which questionnaire designers can make.

Imprecision	'When did you first work in the retail industry?' Should read 'At what age did you begin working in the retail industry?' or 'In which year ...?' 'How many children have you?' Should read 'How many children under the age of 16 do you have living at home with you now?'
Loaded questions	'Do you think you are being treated unfairly by your employer?' Should read 'How are you treated by your employer?'
Two questions in one	'Did you know that this hotel only accepts credit cards, and that there is a 5 per cent surcharge for every transaction?'
Double negatives	'Would you rather not stay in a non-recommended hotel?'
Hypothetical	'Would you like to work in a travel agency?'
Delicate and unclear	'Given that the recommended weekly intake of alcohol is twenty-eight units per week, how much do you drink?'
Convolution/vagueness	'If you thought that the government had caused mass unemployment, would you say that unemployment benefit payments should be increased?'
Insufficient detail	'What methods of cookery does the second chef normally use to produce complicated dishes during times of peak pressure in the kitchen?'
Colloquialism	'When working splits, do you find the time drags or not?'
Jargon	'Is this guesthouse registered with the ET?' Should read 'Does the standard of this guesthouse meet with that required by the English Tourist Board?'

Meaningless concept	'To what extent would you consider cider a substitute for lager?'
Doubtful communication	'Write the commencement month and year of your job (the former job if held during the last two years)', or 'If the former job has ended (if you were dismissed) write the month and year when it ended. If not ended, write NOT ENDED.'
Prior knowledge	A common oversight in questionnaire design is for the researcher to assume that the respondent has sufficient knowledge to answer a question. For example, a question may require respondents to rate their perception of the value for money of different airline tariffs. There is no guarantee that the respondent will have flown all the tariffs and there will be a tendency to circle the mid-point of the proffered scale, skewing the data towards the mean. There are two possible ways around this problem. One is to include a 'don't know' score of zero and the other is to ask a similar question elsewhere in the questionnaire to act as a cross-check.
Frequency assessment	A vague question asking 'How often do you use external financial services?' may be answered in a variety of ways. If a respondent puts 'often', it is probable that the actual perceived magnitude of this is quite different from someone else's 'often'. The question could be improved by including a time frame; perhaps it should be reworded to include 'over the past 12 months' or to give an actual date.

DESIGNING QUESTIONNAIRE FORMS

It is often convenient to design questionnaire forms on size A4 paper, but special processing or completion requirements may require different sizes. The typeface and legibility are important, especially where respondents might be visually impaired. Typefaces such as Serif, Times, Courier, Helvetica, New York, Arial and so on are equally legible, provided that other word processing conventions are followed. These include line length, word spacing, letter spacing, font size (8 point to 12 point are most suitable) and type of printer.

Paper quality may improve legibility and increase the chance that forms are returned. Coloured papers and inks may affect legibility, while textured paper conveys a feeling of quality and status, and hence may increase response rates. Table 4.2 shows a rough guide to colours and questionnaire legibility.

Graphics can aid form completion if information is too difficult or unwieldy to

Table 4.2 Colours and questionnaire legibility

Colour combination	Legibility loss
Green print on white paper	slight
Blue print on white paper	slight
Black print on yellow paper	slight
Red print on yellow paper	medium
Red print on white paper	medium

Source: adapted from Saville and Watt (1976).

express lucidly in words. It is likely that the careful use of graphics will improve understanding of the questionnaire and the response rate.

RATES OF RESPONSE

The potential advantage of large sample sizes using self-completion questionnaires may be lost if the response rate is low. Respondents must be given every encouragement to complete the questionnaires.

It is undoubtedly the case that researcher persistence increases the rate of returned questionnaires, because most people have to be cajoled and nagged into responding. Failure to send reminders almost always results in fewer questionnaires being returned. Often two reminder letters must be sent in order to achieve a usable number of responses. Other ways of increasing response rates include using stamps rather than prepaid envelopes, and recorded delivery for reminders. The individual effects of these factors on response rates may be minimal, but used together they can considerably increase the number of completed questionnaires. Figure 4.2 shows an approximate schedule for reminder by letter.

The precise shape, size and speed of response varies with the situation, but the graph's overall characteristics remain fairly constant for most surveys. Response rates should be plotted against time as shown in Figure 4.2, and reminders sent out when the curve begins to flatten. As a general rule, a good time for the first reminder is around ten days after the initial questionnaire has been sent out, followed by a second reminder on day 18. To encourage responses, the initial letter and reminders should emphasize three things: the importance of the study, the importance of cooperation and the need for a speedy response.

Response rates are higher when respondents are more involved in the survey topic. Government surveys generally have a higher response rate than those dealing with specialist issues, which are usually less relevant to the population as a whole. Respondents should be clear that the survey applies to them and that their opinions are valuable. This may be difficult under certain circumstances, especially where the purpose of the survey is to identify specific minorities. If this is the case, it is usual to include a few 'general' questions to encourage general identification with the survey. Response rates can be improved by offering respondents an incentive to complete the questionnaires. This can take the form of a gift or discount voucher sent to each respondent. A more cost-effective way to do this is to enter returned questionnaires in a prize draw.

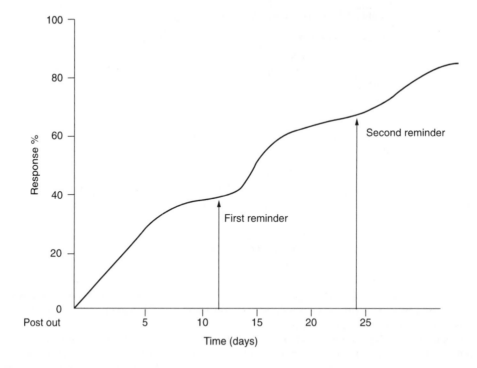

Figure 4.2 Approximate reminder schedule

QUESTIONNAIRE DESIGN AND STATISTICAL ANALYSIS

Statistical techniques have implications for questionnaire design. Careful wording of questions is important in eliciting data, but questions must also be linked with appropriate statistical techniques if the data are to be analysable. This is particularly important for the purposes of hypothesis-testing and prediction. In particular, it is necessary to understand the characteristics of different data types.

There are four basic types of quantitative data, usually known as *nominal, ordinal, interval* and *ratio* data. They have different mathematical properties, which affect their analysis. The four types are discussed below.

Nominal data are the simplest type to conceptualize, but the least conducive to statistical analysis, since they only describe things. An example is 'eyegaze', the movement of a subject's eyes during an observation session. It is not possible to quantify this movement from observation alone, but the positions of the eyes can be described. For example, the different movements can be assigned different number codes, with 1 to mean 'eyes right', 2 'eyes left' and so on. This procedure is attractively simple, but all that can be done with the resulting data set is to count it. This means that the only findings will be the numbers of times each movement occurred. The numbers assigned to the eye movements as codes cannot be used for mathematical calculations, because they only *indicate* the different behaviours. For example, an

Table 4.3 Example of some ordinal and actual values

Ordinal values of data	Actual values of data
1	40
2	23
3	22
4	10
5	5
6	4
7	1

'average' of the numbers in a data set would be meaningless. Other examples of nominal data are gender, socio-economic status and physical colouring of eyes or hair.

Ordinal data are ranked estimates of magnitude. In other words, ordinal data may be produced if respondents are asked to put things in order of preference, or to say what they like best. Ordinal data do not say anything about actual magnitudes of measurement, as can be seen by considering the two sets of figures in Table 4.3.

Interval data are measured on a scale which has regular intervals between its values. Thus the difference between any two points one scale reading apart is one, the difference between two points two scale readings apart is two, and so on. A typical example of an interval measurement is temperature. Most scientists would agree that a difference of one degree Celsius is exactly the same at one end of the scale as at the other, and that the difference between any two neighbouring scale points is one degree.

Ratio data are measured upon an absolute scale, which starts at zero. This means that scale readings are exactly proportional to the values being measured. Weights and heights are examples of ratio data. A measurement of 2 kg indicates a weight twice as large as 1 kg. A height of 2 metres is twice as tall as 1 metre. This is not generally the case for temperatures, because Celsius and Fahrenheit are not absolute scales (though Kelvin is). A temperature of 20°C is actually not twice as hot as 10°C.

Ratio data always have the characteristics of interval, ordinal and nominal data as well. Interval data have the characteristics of ordinal and nominal data (for instance, 7, 6, 5, 4 would also rank themselves in this order). Ordinal data possess the characteristics of nominal data, but, as mentioned above, nominal data possess none of the other mathematical properties.

Non-attitudinal data, such as temperature and height, can be measured with certainty using interval or ratio scales. This information is often termed hard data and lends itself to rigorous statistical analysis.

This is not true, or not true to the same extent, with attitude scales. A respondent may indicate the 'excitement' of a funfair ride on a scale of 1 to 7, where 1 is 'not exciting' and 7 is 'very exciting'. This information is fairly detailed, but it is impossible for the researcher to see whether the difference between the excitement of 1 and 2 is exactly the same as that between 6 and 7. Such data should strictly be treated as ordinal in nature. However, quantitative researchers often treat numerical attitude scales as if they were providing interval data. In fact, it is often possible to treat attitudinal data in this way, but it is important to bear in mind that the findings are at best an approximation to the actual underlying values. It is not justifiable to treat such scales as ratio data.

QUESTION STRUCTURE AND DESIGN

Question structure affects both the way respondents will view them and their ultimate analysis. Figures 4.3, 4.4 and 4.5 show some examples of measurement using *comparative rating*, *Likert* and *semantic differential scales*, which are discussed below.

Please rank the following modes of transport in terms of their attractiveness to you. Assign 1 to the most attractive, 2 to the next, 3 to the next and so on.

Private car	....
Bus/coach	....
Rail	....
Ship/boat	....
Hovercraft	....
Air	....

Figure 4.3   Comparative rating scales

Comparative rating scales are strictly ordinal in character. It is impossible to know the exact numerical interval between each rating, as all are individual value judgements. It would be methodologically wrong to treat the data as anything other than ordinal, because this is what the questions are designed to elicit.

Likert scales are the commonest type in general use for measuring attitudes or perceptions. There is some debate as to whether they should include a mid-point. Many psychologists argue that it increases respondents' confidence to have a 'neither good nor bad' value, and it is normal to include a mid-point on scales in academic work. However, in some practical situations (for instance, market research) clients may prefer to have an even scale, so that respondents must incline to one view or the other. Likert scales are frequently treated as interval scales in analysis, since the scale

---

Please indicate the quality of the service you received in our store:

Very good	= 5
Good	= 4
Neither good nor poor	= 3
Poor	= 2
Very poor	= 1

Figure 4.4   Likert scale

values one to five appear to be evenly spaced, one unit apart. However, there is no guarantee that the magnitudes of the feelings expressed by respondents are spaced like this, and there may be considerable variation between different individuals in this respect. Treating the data as interval in nature is at best an approximation, and it is much safer to treat the data as ordinal.

Semantic differential scale values are assigned in much the same way as Likert scales. However, the format (see Figure 4.5) makes it possible to position respondents' judgements on a preset bipolar scale. Opposing poles can be chosen by the

When describing the Island of Crete, would you say that it is:

Hot	1	2	3	4	5 Cold
Friendly	1	2	3	4	5 Unfriendly
Busy	1	2	3	4	5 Relaxing

Figure 4.5   Semantic differential scale

researcher rather than the respondent. Thus the 'opposite' of 'busy' could be set as 'relaxing', or 'too quiet', or even 'frenetic'.

GENERALIZING FROM RESULTS

The issue of generalizability is frequently debated by academics and industrialists alike. A dilemma for the researcher is what to deem irrelevant and what to include in a study. An increase in the number of variables makes it easier to claim 'generalizability' for results. However, at the same time they tend to mask one another, reducing the chance of obtaining meaning from the result. A study where the majority of variables are controlled gives a sensitive research design but makes the results less generalizable.

Research projects of this kind may make no claim to generalizability and therefore may say little about similar organizations elsewhere. In practical situations this is perfectly reasonable. Individual managers often have a limited interest in whether their findings are generalizable to other areas. Many research projects claim 'significant' findings, where the researcher believes that by the use of statistical tests, results may be generalized to a larger population. The actual generalizability of results is a matter for debate but researchers can certainly follow procedures which maximize this possibility. One of these is to use a rigorous sampling procedure.

SAMPLING

A *population* is a group of *cases* such as people, managers, organizations and so on. It is often too large for every case to be studied, so researchers usually try to take a sample. In other words, a smaller group which represents the whole population. They do this by assuming that the population is homogeneous and identifying a sub-population or *sample* which they hope reflects the composition of the population. Realistically achieving a perfectly representative sample in this way is unlikely. The best that the researcher can expect to do is to identify a few defining characteristics of population members and select the sample on this basis. For example, a study of bank customers might require a sample based on age, gender, socio-economic status and geographical location. However, this does not guarantee sample homogeneity, because, for example, members of a particular socio-economic group may enjoy several different lifestyles, and the latter may influence their purchasing behaviour more than their socio-economic status. Furthermore, 'bank custom' may include a number of different financial services. An overall sample of, say, 1000 customers may contain so many permutations of subdivisions (known as *population cells*) that each one holds only a few individuals, and in order to represent it homogeneity is lost.

The size of sample required for a particular survey depends upon three things: the *confidence level* to which the researcher wishes to work, the acceptable error range in the final result and the way the attribute that is being measured is distributed within the survey population. If these things are known, the sample can be calculated using the following formula:

$$n = \left(\frac{Z \times s}{E}\right)^2$$

where *n* is the sample size, *Z* is the number of standard deviations required to give the desired confidence level, *E* is the acceptable error and *s* is the standard deviation.

These statistical terms are explained in more detail in Chapter 5. Here, it is enough to know that standard deviation is a measure of the *spread* of measurements about the average value.

Example

Suppose we wish to survey holiday-makers to find out their patterns of expenditure while they are visiting a particular resort.

Z is the easiest value to find, because it depends on the level of confidence we require in a regular way. The values can be looked up in normal distribution tables (discussed in Chapter 5). For instance:

if we need to be 99.00% sure, *Z* has the value 2.58
if we need to be 97.50% sure, *Z* has the value 2.24
if we need to be 95.00% sure, *Z* has the value 1.96
if we need to be 90.00% sure, *Z* has the value 1.65

Generally, market research seeks to work to a confidence level of ±2.5 per cent. Therefore, the *Z* value is customarily 1.96.

Allowable error is based upon expenditure, since this is the main purpose of the survey. It is chosen entirely arbitrarily, based upon the requirements of the eventual findings. For instance, it might be decided that the allowable error will be £15.

The value of the standard deviation is often more difficult to ascertain. It can of course be calculated, but one needs data to do this with. If the survey has not been performed, there will generally be no data. In effect, one cannot know an accurate standard deviation until one has taken the sample. Therefore, it is often necessary to *estimate* a value for the standard deviation of the population. In the present example, an effective way to do this would be to ask hoteliers and attraction managers at resorts for their best estimate of the *range* of expenditure their customers are making per head.

If their estimates give a minimum and maximum of £200 and £2000, the range is £1800. The standard deviation can be estimated by dividing it by four, i.e. *s* = £450.

These figures can be entered into the equation above, as follows:

$$n = \left(\frac{1.96 \times 450}{15}\right)^2$$

$$n = 58.80^2$$

$$n = 3457$$

This must be considered in the context of the intended survey size, since response rates for many surveys are low. In this case, a survey which sent out only 1000 questionnaires would be wholly inadequate, and a survey of 10,000 people would have to show a response rate of 34.6 per cent. This is high by most survey standards. A postal survey is lucky to achieve 25 per cent, even with an inducement such as a prize draw. Questionnaires completed at hotels and attractions do better, but only if management and staff support the project and are prepared to remind guests to complete the questionnaires.

To be on the safe side, it would be best to calculate the survey size on a lower response rate than that expected, say 20 per cent. The calculation would then look like this:

$$\text{required number of questionnaires} = 3457$$

$$\text{response rate} = 20 \text{ per cent}$$

$$\text{survey size} = \frac{\text{required number}}{\text{response rate}}$$

$$= 17{,}287 \text{ (rounded} = 17{,}500)$$

There are several ways to select samples. Simple random selection attempts to ensure that every unit in the population has an equal chance of being picked. This usually means selecting from a *sampling frame*, which is a list of individuals (for example, from an electoral register or a list of previous customers). A number is assigned to everyone on the list and the sample individuals are drawn by using random numbers obtained from tables or a computer program.

A more practical technique is known as 'random interval sampling'. The population is first divided by the size of the required sample to provide the *interval* (X). The sample is selected by selecting every Xth name on the list, beginning at a randomly selected starting point. For example, if the size of population is 500 and a sample of 50 is required, the interval will be ten. Starting from a randomly chosen number between one and ten, say two, the 12th, 22nd, 32nd person on the list will be selected, and so on.

Stratified sampling is used when the population is known not to be homogeneous. For example, visitors to a particular attraction may be from different customer segments. If the proportion of each type of visitor is known, a random sample can be taken from each type, weighting the actual numbers taken to the proportions in the original sample.

CODING QUESTIONNAIRE DATA

Quantitative data must be *coded* in order to extract meaning from them. Coding is comparatively straightforward, and aims to convert the data that have been obtained from respondents into numbers. There are three main elements to this:

- coding to identify each item of data;
- coding to identify each type of respondent;
- coding to identify each response.

Identifying Data Items

It is essential to be able to identify specific questionnaires or interview pro-formas once analysis has begun. Some questionnaires may have been spoiled, certain questions may have been answered ambiguously or perhaps certain individuals may answer a particular question in an interesting way. Whatever the reason, it is always valuable to be able, if necessary, to check back to particular data items.

The best way to do this is to assign each questionnaire a serial number when it is returned. The number should be written on the paper itself, and the questionnaires should be kept in serial order, so that individual ones may be found again easily if necessary.

Some survey designs may make it necessary to serialize questionnaires before they are sent out. For example, a prize draw may be offered as an inducement to respondents to return the questionnaires. In this case, each questionnaire must be numbered to prevent forgery and to facilitate the draw. In order to reach all employees in an organization, it may be desirable to use the payroll as the sample frame, and to precode questionnaires with employees' personnel numbers. It is generally best to record questionnaire serial numbers as the identification code. However, it may also be necessary to add a new serial number to each returned questionnaire, in addition to the one that was on it when it was sent out. Under certain circumstances the order in which the questionnaires were returned may be important survey information in its own right: for instance, it may indicate individual enthusiasm about the object of the survey. However, this may become confusing unless it is strictly controlled. An effective procedure is to put the questionnaires into serial order as soon as they arrive and (if desired) to add the 'returned' serial after this. The key thing is that it should be possible to find specific questionnaires if they are needed, and serial numbering systems should be designed accordingly.

Identifying Each Type of Respondent

The purpose of a survey is usually to find out how many people are doing what. For example, the aim may be to find out who are visiting a particular hotel, and what services they use while they are there. A questionnaire used for this purpose needs to ask for details about each hotel user. It may be of interest to know the numbers of males and females, their age range and their socio-economic status. Such data are often called 'base data', or 'bio-data' and are coded by assigning a number to each category, as shown in Table 4.4.

It considerably aids coding if aspects such as age are requested in a closed format,

Table 4.4   Typical bio-data coding

	Category	Code
Gender	Male	1
	Female	2
Marital status	Married	1
	Unmarried	2
	Partner	3
Age	Less than 18	1
	18–25	2
	26–35	3
	36–45	4
	46–55	5
	56–65	6
	66 and over	7

with tick-boxes against specified age ranges. The same applies to questions which ask, for example, how far the respondent lives from the establishment. If respondents are allowed to enter a number of their own choice, much time and effort may have to be spent simplifying responses and putting them into categories. However, sometimes it is necessary to calculate the average age of respondents or the average distance they live from a service establishment. If this is the specific requirement, an open numerical answer format may be the most satisfactory.

Bio-data are nominal in character and the category codes given to them are 'dummy numbers'. They are not usually subjected to calculations, as their function is to identify questionnaires from particular individuals. For example, supposing it is desired to know the response from men aged 26 to 35 to a particular question, all questionnaires with 1 against 'gender', and from these all the ones with 3 against 'age' must be sorted out. Responses from these questionnaires represent the views of this segment of the population.

Identifying Each Response

In order to analyse response patterns, each question must be given a code, identifying how each respondent answered it. Survey instruments often contain a variety of questions. Some lend themselves easily to the process of coding, others less so. Figure 4.6 shows examples of two types of question. The first, which asks informants to indicate their responses on a numerical scale, is comparatively easy to code, since the possible responses are already numbered. The second question asks for information which is potentially wide in scope. One way to deal with such questions is to anticipate what the respondent might put: for example, to cash a cheque, to open an account, to make a complaint. This will hardly ever cover all the possibilities, and there should always be a box labelled 'other'. When the questionnaire is pilot tested, it may turn out that there are a substantial number of unforeseen 'other' possibilities. If this is the case, it may be better to use an open format like that shown in Figure 4.6. Coding must then be applied as the data are recorded, by treating each new reason that appears as a new category and giving it a new code. This is time-consuming, as it is

Question 1. How would you rate the overall service quality in this bank?

Very poor			Neither poor nor good			Very good		
1		2		3		4		5

Question 2. Please give your main reasons for coming to the bank today.

....

....

....

Figure 4.6 Two types of response and coding

necessary to write down every new category. Otherwise, the same response may end up with two or more identifying codes.

DATA ENTRY AND PROCESSING

The most practical way for researchers to manage vast quantities of survey data is by using a computer. After data have been coded, they should be entered into a suitable software package which allows the codes to be counted and subjected to statistical analysis. Most such packages visualize the coded responses in the form of a data matrix (or data block), like that shown in Table 4.5. Matrix columns are termed *variables* because the data they contain vary from respondent to respondent. In Table 4.5, each question or part of a question has its own column, in which its data are entered. Each row represents an individual respondent, called a *case*. It is helpful to enter the serial numbers of the cases down the left-hand column as shown in Table 4.5.

Table 4.5　Part of a survey data matrix

Serial	Gender	Age group	County of origin	Question 1	Question 2	Location
9	2	2	Cambs.	1	5	3
10	2	2	Kent	1	4	1
11	2	1	Norfolk	3	3	1
12	2	1	Norfolk	3	1	1
13	1	1	Norfolk	3	1	2
14	2	1	Essex	3	1	3
15	2	1	Lincs.	1	3	1
16	2	1	Worcs.	2	3	2
17	2	1	Herts.	2	4	2

'County of origin' is an example of a question which is too wide to be set as precoded categories. In this case, the actual responses have been entered into the matrix. Some computer packages can handle entries in this form, either as text or by recoding them, but it would have been better to code these counties with numbers, either as they were entered or using a 'search/replace' facility.

An essential part of questionnaire design is how to process data once the completed forms have been returned. Inadequate planning at the design stage could result in chaos, because there might be hundreds of completed and returned questionnaires. When inputting coded data, the researcher should check each questionnaire to see that it has been fully completed. A decision must be made about how to deal with incomplete questionnaires and data, e.g. to retain or discard them. The judgement will depend upon the research situation, but it is usual to discard questionnaires which have a substantial proportion of missing questions. Omission of one or two questions is not usually problematic, but the researcher must be clear how missing data are recorded in the matrix. A non-reply may be an important piece of information in its own right.

Some researchers opt for the middle numeric value whenever data are missing from a questionnaire response, but this has an impact on the returned values. Others include a 'no response' category and code it as zero. If this category is chosen by the respondent, it could be excluded from subsequent analysis.

CHECKING DATA

Ideally, every cell of the matrix should be checked before the data are analysed, but this is very laborious and generally prohibitive in terms of time and expense. A quick way to check a data matrix on a spreadsheet is to calculate the maximum and minimum of each column. This immediately shows up any rogue entries: for instance, it might show a maximum of 6 or higher in a scale which only goes from 1 to 5. Another common problem is the addition or omission of a digit in a figure. A respondent's age given as 6 may in fact be 16, 26 or 60, for example. Manual data entry is tiring, and it is easy to become confused. If there are a lot of questions with a similar format (for instance, a 1 to 5 scale), it is possible for the entry to 'slip' if a respondent skips a question. Thus data from question 3 can be entered under question 2, question 4 under question 3 and so on all along the columns. Good questionnaire design should be aware of such problems and occasionally insert questions of a different format (a much higher or lower answer, for example), which can be used to check column alignment.

SOFTWARE FOR MANAGING QUANTITATIVE DATA

Several software packages are available for handling quantitative data, and all have their strengths and weaknesses. There are two main types, those based upon a spreadsheet and those based upon a database. In fact, standard office software for either spreadsheet or database work can be used quite effectively for quantitative analysis. It is also comparatively straightforward to enter data into a spreadsheet package such as *Excel* or *Lotus 1-2-3*, using the format shown in Figure 4.5. However, the person who enters the data must be familiar with the spreadsheet, and the package will not correct errors. If non-numeric characters are entered into a cell which should contain a number, an error will result during analysis. This sounds simple and obvious, but take, for example, the following two cells:

A	B
500	'500

Cell B is very difficult to pick out from a large mass of data, yet it can occur quite easily if, for example, the typist presses <'> instead of <enter>. As described above, it is comparatively easy to identify errors in a spreadsheet, and they can then be pinpointed using a search facility and corrected. Thus spreadsheets are easy to use, but have to be checked carefully for errors. They are relatively memory-inefficient and may be prone to delays or errors if large quantities of data are used.

Database packages (for example *Access*) can be programmed to reject data that do not fall within set parameters. For example, non-numeric characters will not be permitted in a designated 'numeric field'. They make it possible to specify ranges, so that, for example, values of zero, or six and above, cannot be entered under a question which is scaled from one to five. Standard database packages thus provide more accurate data entry, but they are time-consuming to program for each new questionnaire job, and it takes longer to train personnel to enter data into them. Once the data have been entered, they can be checked, purified and analysed as with a spreadsheet.

Several packages are available specifically for conducting questionnaire surveys. An example is *Snap*, published by Mercator Ltd. It uses a database principle, and questionnaires can be written simultaneously while the database is being programmed to receive the data. *Snap* can be preset to admit particular types of response to particular questions, and it is possible to specify the permissible values in answer to each question. This makes data entry quick and accurate. The package is capable of simple statistical analysis: for example, counting the frequencies of responses and returning them as percentages. It can also produce basic statistics, such as means, standard deviations, maxima and minima.

Data can be entered still more reliably and quickly using scanning techniques. Questionnaires are fed page by page into a scanner, which reads the responses and records them automatically in a data matrix. The most cost-effective way to do this is *optical mark reading* (OMR). Questionnaires have to be preprinted in such a way that the response boxes are at designated positions on the pages. Respondents must also mark them in a specified way (sometimes with a specific colour of ink), so that the scanner can read them. There have been considerable advances in scanner technology in recent years. Modern machines can often accept photocopied black and white questionnaires, crumpled papers and responses in different coloured inks (though red is almost always invisible to them). OMR is only able to read marked responses to closed questions, but at the time of writing, software is being developed which can read hand-printed comments and convert them into ASCII text. Such equipment is currently relatively expensive and inefficient. It cannot recognize joined handwriting, or writing that has been entered at an angle or squeezed into margins. There are similar problems to those with OMR equipment with coloured inks, particularly red. Nevertheless, this represents an interesting way forward for questionnaire analysis in the future.

A number of packages are available for performing statistical analysis on data once they have been entered. These include *Minitab*, *SPSS* and *GenStat*. *SPSS* is probably the package most used by social researchers. It has three working areas: data, output and log. The data area displays the data in a matrix form similar to a spreadsheet, where they can be inspected, corrected and manipulated as necessary. Calculations on the data are reported in the output area, where they can be inspected, manipulated, saved and printed. The log area records operations that have been carried out. It is possible to program the package to perform specific functions and to customize the way findings are reported.

BASIS OF QUANTITATIVE ANALYSIS

Quantitative information can be used by the researcher in two ways. The first is for description: for example, managers can express how many people visit a tourist attraction, how long they stay, how much they spend and where they come from, using numbers and percentages. Numerical data are described by statistical parameters. For example, the central tendency of the data can be expressed as a *mean* value and the variability or dispersion as the *standard deviation.*

Further analysis may attempt to prove relationships between different aspects of the data, and explain, for example, why people use a particular service. This is done by deriving further parameters, known as *inferential* statistics, which attempt to explain links such as causality. Chapter 5 discusses the use and value of both *descriptive* and *inferential* statistical analysis, using service industry examples where appropriate.

CONCLUSIONS

Quantitative research can provide useful and important management information because it can target specific areas and uses large, representative samples. It generally adopts a positivistic stance, starting from a fairly simple hypothesis, which can be answered with a 'yes' or a 'no'. Once the research area has been identified, a considerable amount of qualitative work is required to understand the important issues and to refine the issues down into a simple overall question.

Quantitative data can be gathered through structured interviews or self-completion questionnaires. The latter are efficient in terms of cost, but the questions must be very carefully formulated and tested before the actual survey commences. The best way to do this is through a piloting process, in which typical respondents complete the questions and comment on them. The pilot survey is also an opportunity to check the validity of the questionnaire using statistical techniques. Questions should be designed using scales which lend themselves to statistical analysis.

Data from questionnaires and interviews are best analysed statistically, using a computer. In order to do this, they must be entered into a data matrix so that the respondents and responses can be clearly identified. The matrix can be analysed by a variety of computer packages, based upon either spreadsheets or databases. Statistical analysis is a complex subject in its own right, and is discussed in the next chapter.

REFERENCES

Babbie, E.R. (1979) *The Practice of Social Research*, 2nd edn. Wadsworth Publishing, Belmont, CA.

Churchill, G.A. (1991) *Marketing Research: Methodological Foundations*, 5th edn. Dryden Press, Hillsdale, IL.

Gunn, C. (1994) 'A perspective on the purpose and nature of tourism research methods', in J.R.B. Ritchie and C.R. Goeldner (eds), *Travel, Tourism and Hospitality Research,* 2nd edn. John Wiley and Sons, New York.

Kerlinger, F.H. (1986) *Foundations of Behavior Research,* 3rd edn. Holt Reinhart & Winston, New York.

Lazarsfeld, P. (1955) *Survey Design and Analysis*. Hyman, Herbert, Free Press, New York.

Parasuraman, A., Zeithaml, V.A. and Berry, L.L. (1986) 'SERVQUAL: a multiple-item scale for measuring customer perceptions of service quality', Marketing Science Institute, *Working Paper Report No. 86–108* (August).

Ritchie, J.R.B. (1994) 'Roles of research in tourism management', in J.R.B. Ritchie and C.R. Goeldner (eds), *Travel, Tourism and Hospitality Research,* 2nd edn. John Wiley and Sons, New York.

Ryan, C. (1995) *Researching Tourist Satisfaction: Issues, Concepts, Problems.* Routledge, London and New York.
Saville, E. and Watt, R. (1976) *Ask a Silly Question.* Sheffield City Polytechnic, Sheffield.
Slattery, M. (1986) *Official Statistics.* Tavistock, London.

5

Analysing Quantitative Data

INTRODUCTION

Chapter 4 discussed the preparation, piloting and administration of questionnaires, and examined the problems of obtaining and recording data in a form appropriate for analysis. Although it dealt briefly with the nature of quantitative analysis, it did not discuss the numerical basis of analysis in detail. This chapter completes that task.

Quantitative analysis begins by counting the frequencies of responses (i.e. the numbers in each category). For example, the starting point for analysing responses to a question scaled from 1 to 5 would be to count all the 5 responses, all the 4s, 3s and so on. It is often valuable to rank the responses in order of their frequencies and to calculate percentage frequencies. Statistical analysis further aims to reduce the data to a few numbers (sometimes also known as *parameters*). These describe the basic features in simple terms and enable decisions or deductions to be made about the data. Further simplifications may be achieved by rendering the data visual, through graphs and diagrams. Statistical techniques are the tools which make these things possible.

Quantitative research problems often seem quite simple at the outset, then become more complex as the questionnaire and survey develop. When they reach the analytical stage, the researcher may suddenly be faced with an apparently impenetrable morass of statistical concepts. This chapter aims to set out statistical analysis in a straightforward way, to refresh the memories of readers whose statistics have grown rusty and to provide a working basis in quantitative analysis for those who are encountering practical statistics for the first time.

RAW DATA

Quantitative data start as 'raw' data, where nothing has been done to extract any meaning from the numbers. The first step is often to count the numbers of respondents who answer a question in a particular way. For example, consider the following scaled question from a staff questionnaire relating to a total quality management (TQM) programme:

	Agree strongly					Disagree strongly	
I know what my internal customers need from me	1	2	3	4	5	6	7

Managers typically wish to know the number of individuals who answered 1, 2 or 3. They may also need the percentage who answered in this way. Both are useful indicators of employee attitudes.

Sometimes the data from individual questions are pooled into overall scores, and these can be analysed by counts and percentages. Table 5.1 shows job satisfaction scores obtained from two groups of hotel workers. Each score is obtained by pooling four scaled 1 to 5 questions, giving values up to 20. One group of workers was subjected to an 'autocratic' style of management and the other to a more 'participative' style.

With twenty scores in each set it is difficult to get the 'feel' of the data by mere inspection. Nine is the lowest and 15 the highest score in the sets, but it is still difficult to see how the scores are distributed between these two numbers, i.e. whether they are spread evenly or 'bunched'. Percentages may sometimes give a clearer view, but where many scores exist even this approach is problematic, so a more comprehensible format is needed.

Table 5.1   Raw job satisfaction scores of workers exposed to two different styles of management

1 (autocratic)	2 (participative)
5	15
12	11
13	12
10	13
7	10
9	14
10	12
12	13
8	9
6	11
10	13
9	14
14	12
8	12
11	10
9	11
11	13
13	9
10	12
12	14

Table 5.2 Job satisfaction scores of workers reorganized as frequency distributions

Group 1			Group 2		
Score	Frequency	%	Score	Frequency	%
5	1	5	5	0	0
6	1	5	6	0	0
7	1	5	7	0	0
8	2	10	8	0	0
9	3	15	9	2	10
10	4	20	10	2	10
11	2	10	11	3	15
12	3	15	12	5	25
13	2	10	13	4	20
14	1	5	14	3	15
15	0	0	15	1	5
Total	20	100	Total	20	100

FREQUENCY

The first stage in all quantitative analysis is to count (the *SPSS* package calls this 'enumerate') how often particular scores appear. Some values occur several times, but others only once. For example, Table 5.1 shows that, in group 2, four subjects achieve a score of 13. Thus, the frequency of occurrence of 13 is four. This is a more economical way of organizing the data, and is known as the *frequency distribution*. Table 5.2 shows the frequency distribution of the data from Table 5.1.

A frequency distribution gives a clearer impression of the characteristics of each set of scores, and of the relationship between the two sets. The scores of group 1 fall in the range 5 to 14, but tend to be bunched in the centre of this range. The scores of group 2 are higher, occupy a narrower range (9 to 15) and are even more closely bunched around the central values. It is always worthwhile calculating the percentages as shown here. However, in the present case, the small numbers make the percentages less meaningful.

If there were more scores in each group (for example, 100), and if the range was much wider (e.g. between 1 and 50), the data could be reclassified into groups or *classes* (1 to 5, 6 to 10, 11 to 15). The frequency of scores falling within each class interval could then be recorded, producing a *grouped frequency distribution*, like that shown in Table 5.3.

Some information is lost when data are grouped in this way: for example, the raw data cannot be recovered from the frequency table in their original form. On the other hand, data are more manageable for manual calculation than would have been possible otherwise. It is generally agreed that the total range of scores should be divided into between 10 and 15 classes of equal width, which give an accurate representation of most data distributions.

It is conventional to indicate the mid-point of each class of scores, as it represents the 'numerical value' of all scores in that class for the purposes of further analysis. This is necessary when working with grouped data, because the individual scores in each class are unknown. The same approach can be used to calculate averages and other values where codes are used to indicate specified ranges, e.g. of age or distance. A question that had been coded as shown in Table 5.4 would require this treatment.

Table 5.3 Job satisfaction scores of workers arranged into a grouped frequency distribution

Class interval	Mid-point	Frequency
1–5	3	1
6–10	8	0
11–15	13	5
16–20	18	12
21–25	23	20
26–30	28	32
31–35	33	23
36–40	38	5
41–45	43	1
46–50	48	1
$N = 100$		

Table 5.4 Example of data coded by ranges

Code	Range (miles from store)	Mid-point value
1	1–5	3
2	6–10	8
3	11–15	13
4	16–20	18
5	21–25	23

Data can be displayed graphically by representing the interval frequencies in graphical form, as a *histogram* or a *bar chart*. Figure 5.1 shows the frequency data from Table 5.2 as two histograms. These show at a glance that the scores of group 2 tend to be higher than those of group 1 (further towards the right-hand end of the axis) and are more closely bunched around the centre of the range.

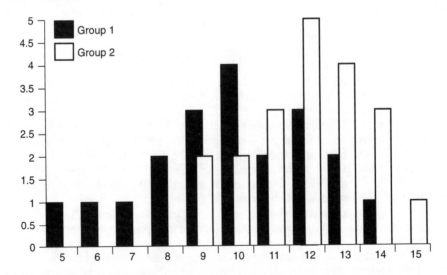

Figure 5.1 Histograms of job satisfaction scores

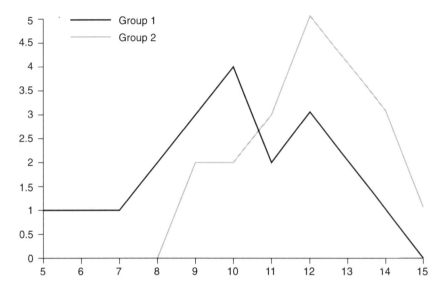

Figure 5.2 Frequency polygons of job satisfaction scores

The columns of a histogram can be replaced by dots plotted at the mid-point of each bar, to give what is called a *frequency polygon*. The heights of the dots on the vertical axis represent the frequencies of the scores shown along the horizontal axis. Joining up the dots produces a visual effect analogous to that of a histogram. Frequency polygons sometimes have the advantage of clarity when two or more sets of data need to be compared. This is illustrated in Figure 5.2.

Histograms and frequency polygons both give a clear impression of the main features of the data, and it is largely a matter of personal preference which is used. The main requirements are that data are displayed concisely, in a clearly labelled form, and that the reader can easily comprehend the pattern of results.

SUMMARIZING QUANTITATIVE DATA

The next step in the statistical treatment of data involves summarizing them in two ways. A measure of the most representative score for the whole set, known as the *central tendency*, is obtained. The spread of scores on either side of the central value, known as the *dispersion* or variability of the data, must also be measured. Other features of the distribution may also be significant (the maximum and minimum values, for example, and whether or not the data fit a symmetrical curve). However, for the purposes of describing the results and drawing inferences from them, *central tendency* and *dispersion* are the most important descriptive parameters.

MEASURES OF CENTRAL TENDENCY

The central tendency of a set of quantitative data can be expressed as the *mean* (also called the *average*), the *median* or the *mode*. The mean is calculated by adding together every score and dividing this total by the number of scores, using the equation:

$$\bar{x} = \frac{\Sigma x}{N}$$

where $\bar{x}$ is the mean, x represents the other scores, the symbol Σx indicates the sum of all the scores and N represents the number of scores.

The median is defined as *the value which has as many scores ranked above it as below it*. For example, in the set of scores 2, 3, 3, 5, 7, 9, 13, five is the median score, because there are three scores above it in the rank order and three below it. If there are an even number of scores, the median is the mid-point between the two middle scores.

The mode is *the most frequently occurring value in a set of scores*. It is found by simply inspecting the data. If there are not many scores it reveals little, but with large numbers of observations the mode becomes quite a useful index of central tendency. A set of data can have only one mean and only one median, but it can have more than one mode if several values have the same highest frequency.

Mean, median and mode can be calculated either from the raw scores or from a frequency distribution. Table 5.5 shows raw quality scores obtained from 100 visitors at a particular tourist attraction. Table 5.6 shows the same data as a frequency distribution.

The mean is calculated from frequency data by multiplying the scores by their

Table 5.5   Tourist attraction quality scores

42	53	54	47	54	47	50	50	51	52
49	50	52	50	53	49	53	50	45	51
51	46	52	49	48	46	47	47	51	48
52	53	51	50	45	51	50	49	43	53
46	50	49	48	51	50	49	51	50	48
50	43	50	46	50	49	51	52	49	50
49	45	52	50	49	54	50	48	45	52
48	51	50	52	48	51	49	52	49	48
51	49	51	48	47	53	50	52	48	52
50	47	48	48	50	49	46	47	52	51

Table 5.6   Frequency distribution of tourist attraction quality scores

Score (x)	Frequency (f)	Cumulative frequency	fx
42	1	1	42
43	2	3	86
44	0	3	0
45	4	7	180
46	5	12	230
47	7	19	329
48	12	31	576
49	14	45	686
50	20	65	1000
51	14	79	714
52	12	91	624
53	6	97	318
54	3	100	162
	Total (Σ) = 100		$\Sigma fx = 4947$

frequencies, totalling the values thus produced and dividing by the total number of cases. The equation for this is:

$$\bar{x} = \frac{\Sigma fx}{N}$$

where x represents each score, f is frequency, Σfx is the sum of scores times frequencies and N is the number of cases. Using this formula, the mean score for the data shown in Table 5.6 can be calculated as follows:

$$\bar{x} = \frac{4947}{100}$$

$$= 49.47$$

The median can be obtained from the frequency distribution shown in Table 5.6 as follows. All the scores are ranked in order from the lowest to the highest. There are 100 scores in total, so the middle position in the series falls between the 50th and 51st scores. The median is therefore the mid-point between the 50th and 51st scores. The observations ranked 46 to 65 all have a score of 50, which thus straddles the mid-point. Thus the median score has a value of 50.

The mode can be read directly from the frequency distribution, as the most frequently occurring value. Thus, the mode of the data in Table 5.6 is also 50.

When data in a series are fairly symmetrically distributed about the central tendency, the mean, mode and median have similar values and one could reasonably use the value which is easiest to compute, i.e. the mode. However, if further analysis of the data is required (e.g. to test whether the scores of one group of respondents are significantly lower than those of another), the mean is the preferred measure of central tendency. The mean summarizes all the data from which it is derived, so a change in any one score changes its value. This makes it a more reliable index of the underlying features of the data. The mean also has mathematical properties which make it suitable for more advanced statistical analyses. However, if scores are asymmetrically distributed about the central tendency, the mean will differ significantly from the mode and the median. It may therefore be less appropriate as a measure of central tendency for some purposes.

THE NORMAL DISTRIBUTION

One single, basic shape recurs in distributions of many different sorts of quantitative data: the bell-shaped curve known as the *normal distribution* (shown in Figure 5.3). It is symmetrical, with most values falling in the central region of the curve, near the mean. The frequencies of scores form a broad peak near the central value and fall off rapidly on either side. Because the shape is symmetrical, the mean, median and mode of a perfect normal distribution all have the same value. The perfect 'bell' shape of the normal distribution is never achieved in practice, because it requires an infinite number of observations. The frequency polygons shown in Figure 5.2 demonstrate this. They do not conform to the smooth curve shown in Figure 5.3, because the data are based on a limited number of observations.

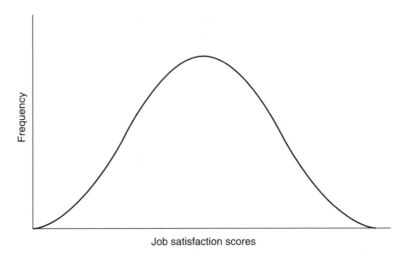

Figure 5.3   A normal distribution curve

Satisfaction scores, quality rating scores, individuals' heights and weights are just a few examples of data types which tend to have normal or close-to-normal distributions. The normal distribution also has some useful properties which help in the description of data and underlie the formulation of many statistical tests.

THE NORMAL CURVE AS A FREQUENCY DISTRIBUTION

The area of each bar in a histogram is proportional to the frequency of the observations within the interval represented by the bar. In an exactly parallel way, the area beneath a normal distribution bounded by two vertical lines represents the proportion of cases falling within those limits. This interpretation of the area under a curve is very important in quantitative analysis and is used repeatedly in statistics.

ASYMMETRIC DISTRIBUTIONS

An asymmetric distribution of scores, distorted from the normal distribution, is said to be 'skewed'. It can be skewed either *positively* (right-hand tail extension) or *negatively* (left-hand tail extension). Skewness separates the three measures of central tendency. The mode always stays at the central point of the distribution, irrespective of its shape. The mean moves in the direction of the extended tail and the median falls somewhere between the mode and the mean. This effect is shown in Figure 5.4.

In the first symmetrical distribution shown in Figure 5.4, the mean, median and mode all have similar values. The mean in the positively skewed distribution increases in value because there are some very high scores. The median is also higher, but this increase in value is not influenced by the values of the high scores, only by their effect on their rank order. The negatively skewed distribution shows the opposite effect.

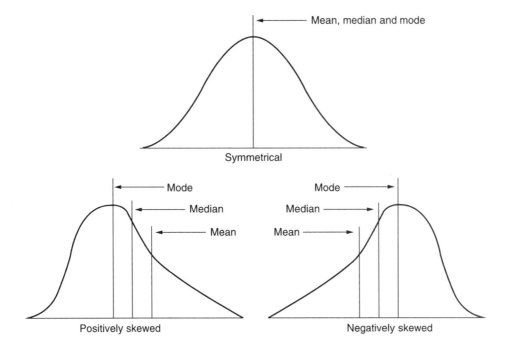

Figure 5.4 Skewness and central tendency

The median's insensitivity to extreme values (i.e. highly skewed distributions) is helpful in that it retains the characteristic of being a 'typical' value. The mean gives a misleading picture of the typical value because it is very sensitive to the value of extreme scores. Hence, for highly skewed distributions the median is the preferred measure of central tendency.

The mode is sometimes useful as a quick but approximate index of the central tendency, but its value depends on just a few scores and it is not a very stable way to describe the features of the data. It is also possible for distributions to have more than one mode, and for these reasons modes are infrequently used in research.

SPREAD OF THE DISTRIBUTION

Another important feature of a set of data is the 'spread', or *dispersion* of scores on either side of the central value. Figure 5.5 shows two distributions of hypothetical job satisfaction scores which have the same mean but different dispersions. From the figure it is clear that this has no bearing on the dispersion of the two sets of scores. They have the same mean, median and mode, and cannot be distinguished from one another unless the dispersions are also known. A narrow dispersion means that individual scores are quite similar to one another and the distribution is fairly homogeneous. A wide dispersion indicates that the data diverge considerably from the mean score, which consequently is less representative of the distribution. Thus it is important to have some measure of how the data vary within the set.

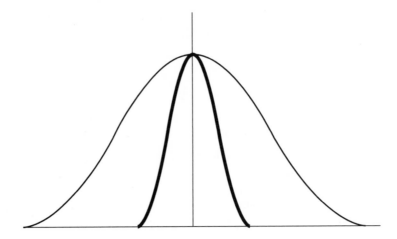

Figure 5.5 Two different dispersions of job satisfaction scores around the same mean score

The simplest index of spread is the *range*, defined as the *difference between the maximum and minimum scores*. For example, if a group of scores has a maximum value of 14 and a minimum value of 5, the range is 9 (14 − 5). The range is easy to understand, but may be misleading if just a few of the scores are unusually high or low. Thus the range is sensitive to extreme values and says nothing about the way the scores vary in between.

The *interquartile range* is the range of the 'middle half' of the scores. It is calculated by ranking the scores in order from the lowest to the highest and then subtracting the score that is located 25 per cent of the way along the series (the first quartile) from the one 75 per cent of the way along (third quartile). These scores are found in the same way as the median (i.e. by ranking and counting the scores). The interquartile range is a more stable measure of dispersion than the overall range, but uses only a small proportion of the available information, and lacks the mathematical properties needed for more complex statistical analysis.

The *variance* is defined as the *sum of the squares of differences between data points and the mean*. It is a useful measure of dispersion because it reflects the distance of every observation from the mean of the scores, rather than just two arbitrarily chosen points. The reason for squaring the differences is that about half of them are negative, and for normal distributions the simple sum of the differences always approaches zero. The formula for calculating the variance is:

$$\text{Variance} = \frac{\Sigma(x - \bar{x})^2}{N}$$

where x represents each score value, $\bar{x}$ the mean value and N the number of scores. Thus the variance is in effect the *mean squared deviation* of all data from the sample mean.

The most widely used measure of dispersion is the *standard deviation*, which is defined as the *square root of the variance*. Thus the variance can also be expressed as the square of the standard deviation. Formulae for calculating the standard deviation are based on this property, i.e.

$$s^2 = \frac{\Sigma(x - \bar{x})^2}{N}$$

and

$$s = \frac{\sqrt{\Sigma(x - \bar{x})^2}}{\sqrt{N}}$$

Both the standard deviation and the variance take account of every individual score in the data set. In principle, they both measure the amount of spread in the same way and it does not matter which is used, as long as there is no confusion between the two. Both measures increase with the amount of spread in the data, and become zero when there is no spread. In practice, the standard deviation is the most used as a measure of dispersion, and it is important for testing differences between sets of scores. It is an extremely robust measure in mathematical terms, and can be used for a variety of other statistical purposes. For example, it can be used to calculate the proportion of scores in a distribution that falls between any given pair of values.

AREAS UNDER THE NORMAL CURVE AND THE STANDARD DEVIATION

If the mean and standard deviation of a normal distribution are known, the height of the bell-shaped curve (y) can be found for any particular point on the horizontal axis (x). This makes it possible to describe the whole distribution and specify the proportion of observations falling between any two points precisely. For example, approximately two-thirds of scores in a normal distribution fall within one standard deviation of each side of the mean. Because the curve is symmetrical, a vertical line drawn a certain distance (1.5 standard deviations, for example) below the mean cuts off the same proportion of scores as one drawn that distance above the mean.

The standard deviation provides a basis for calculating the proportion of scores that fall within particular limits, provided a distribution is approximately normal. The symbol Z is generally used to express fractions of the normal distribution in terms of numbers of standard deviations from the mean. For example, suppose job satisfaction scores obtained from service staff by questionnaire are normally distributed, with a mean of 68 and a standard deviation of 2.5. The proportion of employees scoring 70 or more may be found by using the formula:

$$Z = \frac{x - \bar{x}}{s}$$

where Z is the number of standard deviations corresponding to this proportion of the employees, x is the score, $\bar{x}$ the mean and s the standard deviation. Entering the actual data into this formula gives the following:

$$Z = \frac{70 - 68}{2.5}$$

$$= 0.8$$

This question may be stated as 'what proportion of a normal distribution falls beyond 0.8 standard deviations from the mean?'

From the Z score, the proportion of employees can be found by using *normal*

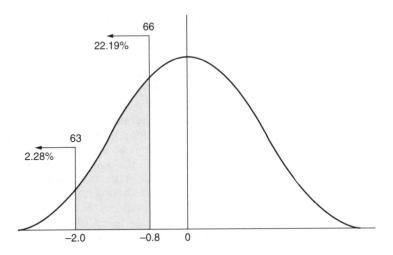

Figure 5.6 Proportion of visitor attraction quality scores falling between two values in a normal distribution

distribution tables. These are available in most statistical textbooks (for example, Miller, 1986). They show the total area under a normal curve in terms of the corresponding Z scores (i.e. distances from the mean measured in numbers of standard deviations). In this case, the tables give the proportion of a normal distribution falling 0.8 standard deviations or more from the mean as 21.19 per cent.

As another example, the manager of a theme park might wish to know how visitors rate a particular attraction, with a view to upgrading it, repositioning it within the park or closing it down. One way to find this is to calculate the proportion of visitors who give the attraction a quality rating of between 63 and 66. It is possible to do this using a normal distribution curve, as shown in Figure 5.6.

The quality rating scores shown in Figure 5.6 are approximately normal, with a mean of 68. The proportion of scores between 63 and 66 can be found by subtracting the first proportion (obtained from normal distribution tables) from the second. Sixty-three is two standard deviations from the mean because $63 - 68 = -5$ and $-5/2.5 = -2$. Normal distribution tables show that 2.28 per cent of cases fall below this value of Z. A score of 66 is 0.8 standard deviations below the mean (i.e. $(66 - 68)/2.5 = -0.8$). According to the tables, 21.19 per cent of cases fall below this value of Z, so the proportion of people scoring the attraction between 63 and 66 will be $21.19 - 2.28$ per cent, which is 18.91 per cent.

Managers might also want to know the score that is so high that only 10 per cent of visitors rate an attraction above it. In this instance it is necessary to work backwards from the general properties of the normal distribution. Tables may be used to find out how many standard deviations above the mean will cut off the upper 10 per cent of cases. The appropriate Z value is 1.28. Since the standard deviation of scores is 2.5, the 10 per cent of visitors enjoying the attraction more than anyone else will have scored it at least 1.28×2.5 (3.2) above the mean, so the value of the 'extreme' score will be $68 + 3.2$, or 71.2. Another way to express this result is to say that there is a 10 per cent chance (a probability of 0.1) that a person picked at random from the population of visitors will give the attraction a score of 71.2 or more.

INFERENTIAL STATISTICS

Descriptive statistics often do not provide all the necessary information about a research situation. Researchers also often need to draw *inferences* from data about market position, customer satisfaction, the motivation of workers and so on. Inferential statistical analysis is used when ideas, hypotheses or predictions need to be tested. Inferential statistics can relate to a pair of variables (bivariate) or to a larger number (multivariate). The mathematical complexity of the calculations increases with the number of variables that are involved.

BIVARIATE STATISTICS: STATISTICAL TESTS

Two general types of statistical test are available for research. *Parametric* tests assume that the data being analysed are taken from a normal distribution. Data are assumed to be measured on an interval scale (see Chapter 4) and the test populations are assumed to be comparable in terms of variance. *Non-parametric* tests make none of these restrictive assumptions. They can be used with ordinal data, with skewed distributions and for samples with widely divergent variances (or standard deviations).

Parametric tests are considered more powerful and can detect more subtle differences between sets of scores. Parametrics are still commonly used by researchers on data which violate one or more of the restrictive assumptions mentioned above. For example, they are often used with scaled response data from questionnaires, which are seldom demonstrably 'interval' or normal in nature. If researchers are uncertain about whether to use one or other type of test, they should use both and compare the results. As a rule of thumb, scaled data may be treated as though they were measured on an interval scale. At the same time, researchers must be constantly alert to the possibility that parametric approaches might give inaccurate results.

Statistical tests are available for a variety of situations. For example, a researcher might wish to study the impact of supervisory styles upon staff motivation. As long as the data can be converted to a numerical form, statistical tests can be used to test a prediction that 'autocratic' management styles motivate employees differently from 'participative/supportive' ones. A statistical test calculates the possibility that observed results are owing to the proposed hypothesis (i.e. that a particular dependent variable is influenced by an independent variable) or to chance fluctuations. If the test suggests that differences between groups may be due to the independent variable, the results are said to be *significant*. Statistical tests also seek to put a figure to significance, expressing it as a *level of confidence*, i.e. a percentage likelihood that the hypothesis is correct.

The acceptable level of confidence for most research work is 95 per cent. Thus, if the level of confidence (sometimes written as the *probability*, p) turns out to be less than or equal to 5 per cent ($p \leq 0.05$), the chance explanation must be rejected. The level of confidence is calculated by converting the difference between two sets of scores into a standardized measure of deviation known as the *test statistic*. The test statistic is then converted into a probability, using published tables analogous to the normal distribution tables discussed above. The lower the level of significance, the more convincing the outcome of the survey (or experiment). A researcher testing an already 'proven' theory of consumer behaviour might decide to work to a more stringent level of significance: 1 per cent or even 0.1 per cent.

t TESTING

The *t test* is used to establish whether there is any significant difference between the means of two sets of scores. It does this by calculating a *t statistic*, which effectively consists of the difference between the two means divided by the mean of the two standard deviations. The formula for this is as follows:

$$t = \frac{\bar{x}_1 - \bar{x}_2}{\sqrt{\left(\dfrac{N_1 s_1^2 + N_2 s_2^2}{N_1 + N_2 - 2}\right)\left(\dfrac{N_1 + N_2}{N_1 N_2}\right)}}$$

where $\bar{x}_1$ and $\bar{x}_2$ are the means of the two samples, s_1 and s_2 are the two standard deviations and N_1 and N_2 are the sizes of the two samples being compared.

The *t* test procedure consists of comparing the calculated value of *t* with the *t* value that would have been obtained if the two samples had been drawn from the same population. These 'null hypothesis' values can be found from published tables analogous to those for normal distribution values, which are available in many statistical textbooks. The tables give the level of confidence as a percentage likelihood that the test samples are not the same.

It is possible for the difference between two test groups to be 'directional'. For example, it is widely assumed that a participative/supportive approach should produce greater worker job satisfaction than an autocratic one. An attitude survey could be conducted with two groups of workers, one under a 'participative/support-ive' management and another under autocratic management. The researcher might expect the first group to exhibit a higher level of job satisfaction than the second, and therefore to have a higher mean score. The experimental hypothesis would be:

> Workers experiencing a 'hands-off' style of management will be more satisfied with their jobs than workers experiencing an autocratic approach.

The null hypothesis would be:

> Workers experiencing a 'hands-off' style of management will be no more satisfied with their jobs than workers experiencing an autocratic approach.

This kind of hypothesis is directional because it proposes that 'hands off' is only associated with higher satisfaction. The alternative 'non-directional' hypothesis would simply propose that the two samples would show demonstrably *different* satisfaction levels. This would be 'proven' even if autocratic management were associated with higher satisfaction. The directional hypothesis is more specific and more rigorous than the non-directional one. When hypotheses are specific or directional, the type of *t* test conducted should be a 'one-tailed' test. If the directionality is not important a 'two-tailed' *t* test is used.

A distribution showing critical values of *t* at both 5 and 2.5 per cent confidence levels is shown in Figure 5.7. Both tails of the distribution represent extreme cases, i.e. on the right-hand side of the diagram the mean $\bar{x}_1$ is significantly larger than $\bar{x}_2$. On the left, $\bar{x}_2$ is much larger than $\bar{x}_1$. If the test is two-tailed, the most extreme 2.5 per cent of cases at either end of the distribution will be of interest; if the test is one-tailed, 5 per cent of cases at one end of the distribution will be of interest. In the motivation/

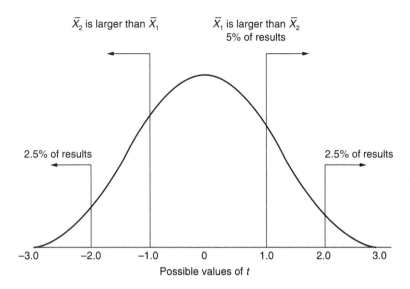

Figure 5.7 *t* distribution showing critical values of *t* at the 5 per cent level for one-tailed and two-tailed tests

management style example, the researcher is interested in the most extreme 5 per cent of cases contained in the right-hand tail of the distribution. In other words, the mean of the 'hands on' group ($\bar{x}_1$) will be higher than the mean of the other ($\bar{x}_2$). The results are significant if they produce a *t* value in the upper 5 per cent of the distribution. If the hypothesis were non-directional, the results would be significant if they produced a *t* value in the upper or lower 2.5 per cent of the distribution.

Z TEST

The Z test, or normal distribution test for independent samples, can also be used to compare the mean scores of two independent samples. Like the *t* test, it compares the means and standard deviations of two samples, but it converts them to a Z value, from which a probability can be derived using normal distribution tables. The Z test and *t* test are similar in outcome, but the *t* test is better suited to smaller samples (30 or

Table 5.7 Meal duration for customer experiencing two different types of interior restaurant illumination

Sample 1 Reaction times of subjects responding to red light ($N = 35$)	Sample 2 Reaction times of subjects responding to green light ($N = 32$)
5, 4, 5, 5, 6, 4, 7, 6, 5, 6, 6, 5, 5, 5 6, 8, 4, 6, 5, 7, 7 5, 5, 6, 5, 6, 5, 6 8, 6, 5, 5, 4, 6, 4	6, 7, 6, 5, 6, 7, 7 7, 6, 5, 6, 8, 6, 7 8, 6, 5, 7, 6, 8, 9 6, 7, 5, 5, 6, 7, 7 6, 5, 8, 6

fewer). The samples for a Z test need not be exactly the same size, but it is assumed that the two sets of scores come from normal populations with equal variance. However, slight violations are not usually critical.

The Z test can be illustrated by the following example. A manager predicts that restaurant customers will eat their food more quickly in red light than in green. She notes the duration of each customer's stay by representing each ten minutes' duration as one increment on a numeric scale, i.e. one hour is noted as 6. Table 5.7 shows the results of her experiment.

The first step is to calculate the mean scores for the two samples using the formula:

$$\bar{x} = \frac{\Sigma x}{N}$$

This gives the results

Sample 1   Sample 2
$\bar{x}_1 = 5.6$ $\bar{x} = 6.438$

Next, the two sample variances $s_1{}^2$ and $s_2{}^2$ are calculated using the formula:

$$s^2 = \frac{\Sigma(x - \bar{x})^2}{N}$$

This gives the results

Sample 1   Sample 2
$s_1 = 1.040$ $s_2 = 1.052$

The values of $\bar{x}_1, \bar{x}_2, s_1{}^2, s_2{}^2, N_1, N_2$ are then substituted into the formula for Z:

$$Z = (\bar{x}_1 - \bar{x}_2)\bigg/\left(\frac{s_1{}^2}{N_1} + \frac{s_2{}^2}{N_2}\right)$$

This gives the result $Z = -3.352$

Z is converted into a probability that the difference in the means arose by chance, using normal distribution tables as described earlier in this chapter. If the hypothesis is not directional and the test is two-tailed, the probability shown in the tables must be doubled. If the probability obtained from the table is less than 0.05, the null hypothesis must be rejected and the experimental or alternative hypothesis accepted.

Using the table, -3.352 corresponds to a probability smaller than 0.0005 (one-tailed test). (The negative value of Z can be ignored. It arises because the mean score of the second group is larger than that of the first group. If the samples had been set out in a different order, the Z score would have been positive.)

The independent variable (restaurant lighting) is presumed to have caused the difference between the sample means. The probability that these two samples could have been randomly selected from the same population is very low. Therefore, the null hypothesis is rejected at 0.05.

NON-PARAMETRIC TESTS

The non-parametric equivalent of *t* and Z tests is the Mann–Whitney test. Non-parametric tests make no assumptions about the normality or variance of statistical data, so they apply equally well to all types of data. The Mann–Whitney test could equally have been used to analyse the data in Table 5.7. Its rationale and procedures are somewhat different from t and Z testing, and it is conducted as follows.

All scores from the two test samples are combined into one large group and ranked from lowest to highest. If scores from one sample are ranked on average lower or higher than those from the other, it may be suspected that the two samples were not drawn from the same population. The test determines the probability that a given separation between the ranks of the two samples could have arisen by chance.

Application of the Mann–Whitney test can be illustrated using the hypothetical data shown in Table 5.8. A manager predicts that there will be a difference in effectiveness between two 'customer care' staff training packages (A) and (B). Effectiveness is measured by asking the receptionists to rate their feelings about it. (Note that this simple example ignores many other important elements, such as prior skill and experience of employees, skill of trainers and so on.)

Table 5.8   Effectiveness of two customer care training packages on hotel receptionists

Ratings of group by method A ($N = 6$)	Ranks	Ratings of group by method B ($N = 8$)	Ranks
5	6.5	4	5
7	10.5	6	8.5
7	10.5	3	4
6	8.5	5	6.5
9	13	2	2.5
10	14	1	1
		2	2.5
	$R = 63$	12	

The procedure is as follows:

1. Let N be the size of the smaller group
2. Rank the combined set of $N_1 + N_2$ scores from the lowest to the highest value. Use rank 1 for the lowest, 2 for the next lowest and so on.
3. Find the sum of the ranks for the smaller group and call this R.
4. Substitute the values of N_1, N_2 and R in the following formula:

$$U_1 = N_1 N_2 + \frac{N_1(N_1 + 1)}{2} - R$$

5. Substitute the values of U_1, N_1 and N_2 in the following formula: $U_2 = N_1 N_2 - U_1$
6. Find the critical value of U needed for significance at the desired level from tables. The critical value will depend on the values of N_1 and N_2, and whether the prediction was directional.
7. If the observed value of U_1 or U_2 (whichever is smaller) is less than or equal to the critical value of U, reject the null hypothesis.

Applying this procedure to the set of figures given in Table 5.8:

$$U_1 = (6 \times 8) + \frac{(6 \times 7)}{2} - 63 = 6$$

$$U_2 = (6 \times 8) - 6 = 42$$

Using published tables for $N_1 = 6$, $N_2 = 8$, the critical value of U for 5 per cent significance (two-tailed) is 8. Therefore, as the smaller obtained value (U_1) is less than the critical value of U for 5 per cent significance, there is a significant difference between the two groups.

Statistical testing with complex formulae appears convincing, but researchers must remember that they can never prove beyond *all* doubt that the differences between two groups are not caused by chance alone. It is a consequence of hypothetico-deductive methodology that one can only ever show for certain that a hypothesis has been *falsified*. One can never prove it to be the truth. Misinterpretation of results could lead to organizational disaster. For example, an organization could make major changes to its policies, to discover later that the hypothesis on which the thinking was based was incorrect. Hypotheses must be realistic and based on experience in order to reflect organizational situations accurately.

MORE RELATIONSHIPS

Another important way to study quantitative data is by *relating* variables to one another. In real-life commercial situations, variables cannot be manipulated as in the hypothetical 'restaurant lighting experiment' discussed above. Nevertheless, it is often desirable to see whether relationships exist between variables. This procedure does not seek to explain *causality*, and is probably the most common form of analysis in service industry situations.

Correlation aims to relate one variable to another by calculating the extent to which one increases as the other is increased. For example, it might be possible to correlate customers' hotel accommodation preferences with their tendency to drink champagne. In order to do this, both types of buying behaviour must be measured using some kind of numerical scales.

A numerical value known as a *correlation coefficient* can be calculated to describe the relationship between the two variables. The most common measure of correlation is the *Pearson coefficient of correlation*, usually represented as the letter r. This is a parametric measure, which can take values between -1 and $+1$, and represents the strength of the linear relationship between two variables. A value of $r = +1$ indicates that points relating to the two variables fall on a perfect straight line with a positive slope (i.e. from lower left to upper right). A value of $r = -1$ means that the two variables have a perfect *inverse* relationship: that is, as one increases the other decreases proportionately. The perfect straight line in this case slopes from upper left to lower right. A value of zero means that the two variables are not correlated, and values in between indicate varying degrees of linear correlation.

A useful way to present the results of such a study is to envisage the two variables (for instance, room price and number of bottles of champagne consumed) as the axes of a graph. The data points can then be plotted on scattergrams. Figure 5.8 shows four hypothetical data sets. The coordinates on the x and y axes can be considered to represent four different groups of customers' scores on room price and champagne consumption.

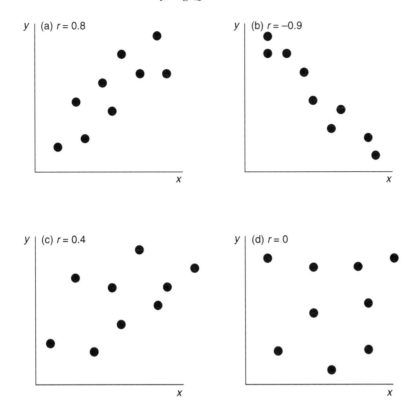

Figure 5.8 Scattergrams of four different types of relationship between two variables

In Figure 5.8, each scattergram gives an impression of how variables are correlated with each other. The first (a) shows a 'high' correlation, with the dots tightly clustered around an imaginary line sloping upward from left to right. The second scattergram (b) also shows a high degree of correlation, but this time the imaginary line slopes downwards from right to left. This indicates a negative correlation between two variables. Scattergram (c) shows a weaker positive correlation, while (d) indicates none at all.

The correlation coefficient conveys two important pieces of information. It is a *measure of the spread of points* about an imaginary line. As shown in Figure 5.8, the closer the points are to this line the larger the value of r. Alternatively, if r is squared, it indicates *how much of the variation in the y scores can be explained by knowing x*. For example, scattergram (a) in Figure 5.8 has an r value of 0.9. Thus, 81 per cent $(0.9^2 \times 100)$ of variation in y can be predicted by knowing x.

It may be important to know whether a correlation coefficient is significant or not. A rough guide to this can be seen in Figure 5.9. Significance varies with the amount of data used in the computation, i.e. the number of pairs of data. In addition, the boundary between significance and non-significance is comparatively broad and diffuse. Thus, interpretation of correlation coefficients should always proceed with caution. A significant value for r does not mean that a causal relationship can be

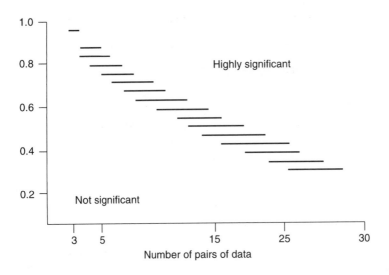

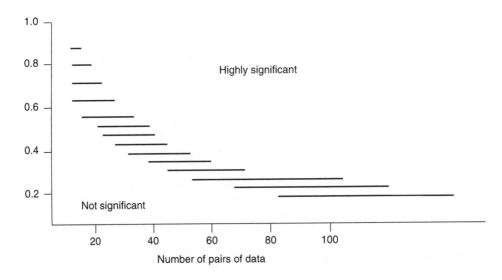

Figure 5.9 A guide to the significance of the correlation coefficient

assumed, but neither does an insignificant value indicate that no causal relationship exists.

Correlation analysis can be applied to non-parametric data by using *Spearman's rank correlation* procedure. As the name suggests, this is based upon the rank orders of two sets of data. If they are the same, the rank correlation coefficient (known as *Spearman's rho* or ρ) is +1.00. If they are exactly reversed then ρ = −1.00. Values in between indicate degrees of partial correlation. Most statistical packages can be programmed to calculate Spearman's rho, but not all of them come with it as standard, and it is not generally available on spreadsheet packages. Pearson's *r* is often used, even with non-parametric data, as an approximate indicator of correlation.

REGRESSION ANALYSIS

Correlation seeks to discover how well the data from two variables correspond to a straight line. However, it says nothing about the slope of this line or its intersection with the y axis. Both of these things might be important in studies where a theoretical model is being tested against real data. *Regression analysis* carries correlation one stage further. It determines whether two sets of data fit a straight line graph with the standard mathematical formula $y = ax + c$. However, in regression analysis the constants are usually represented by β, and the equation is written:

$$y = \beta_1 x + \beta_0$$

This can be represented graphically as shown in Figure 5.10. As with correlations, regression analysis is best carried out using a computer program. Most spreadsheets and all statistical packages have the facility for doing this. It is usually necessary to specify which data set is to be taken as y (the dependent variable) and which is represented by x (the independent variable). Most programs then produce at least three outputs:

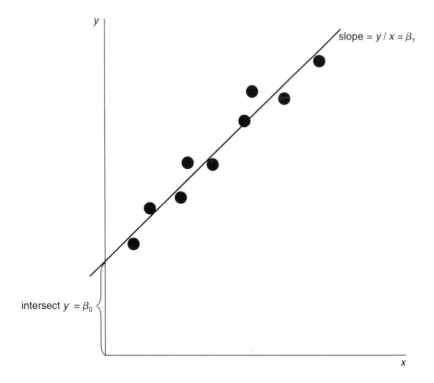

Figure 5.10 Regression model in the form of a graph

- the value of the y axis intersect ($x = \beta_0$);
- the slope of the line (β_1);
- a measure (usually denoted R) of how well the data fit the linear model.

Regression can demonstrate a relationship between two variables, but like correlation it cannot *prove* causality. This issue is more easily confused with regression, since it is necessary to designate the dependent and independent variables. In order to get a clearer picture of what is going on, the researcher should always reverse the roles of the variables and see what happens to the regression line. It is a good idea to draw regression lines on graph paper and ask oneself what happens to one of the data points when the other is equal to zero, where the first will move if the other increases and so on.

MULTIVARIATE ANALYSIS

Multivariate procedures represent a type of inferential analysis which deals with several variables at the same time. They include testing by analysis of variance, multiple regression, and factor, cluster and discriminant analysis, which are all outlined below.

Analysis of Variance and the *F* Ratio

Z and t tests are based upon the difference between the mean scores of two data sets. However, group differences can also be detected by the *analysis of variance* (ANOVA). This process has the advantage that several data subsets and several variables can be examined at once. For example, it is possible to test whether different customer segments have different perceptions of service quality. Customer questionnaires can be differentiated into groups by demographic characteristics such as age, gender, income or marital status. A difference between the responses from any one subgroup and those of the population as a whole is indicated by a difference in variance, which can be converted to a single test statistic, the F value. However, further testing (for example, t testing) is necessary to find which and how many subgroups are significantly different from the rest.

The value of F is calculated by first ascertaining the values of the two or more subgroup means and the total population mean. Next, the differences between each subgroup mean and the population mean are calculated, squared, multiplied by the number of scores in that subgroup and then added together. The total of these values is divided by the number of *degrees of freedom* (the number of subgroups minus 1), providing the *between variance*.

The difference between each score and its own subgroup mean is then calculated and squared. The sum of these values is divided by the degrees of freedom (i.e. the total number of scores minus the subgroups) to produce the *within variance*. The F ratio is calculated by dividing the between variance by the within variance and compared with a 'chance' value of F, obtained from published F tables.

Multiple Regression

Multiple regression seeks to model data into a relationship between a dependent variable and independent variables. Unlike simple linear regression, it allows more than one independent variable to be considered. The form of the multiple regression equation is:

$$y = \beta_0 + \beta_1 x_1 + \beta_2 x_2 + \beta_1 x_3, \text{ etc.}$$

where y is the dependent variable and x_1, x_2, x_3, etc. are the independent variables. β_0 is the value of y when all independent variables are zero and $\beta_1, \beta_2, \beta_3$, etc. are the coefficients which relate the independent variables to the dependent variable.

Multiple regression programs typically need to be given the designations of dependent and independent variables and then compute the β values for the model.

Factor Analysis

The objective of factor analysis is to simplify data by identifying relationships between variables in the data set. The variables are then grouped together into a smaller number of 'factors', bringing out patterns within the data. Factor analysis proceeds in two stages: *principal components analysis* (PCA) and *rotation*.

Principal components analysis aims to group the variables, usually through correlation. High correlation coefficients between any pair of variables are taken to indicate a relationship between them. The PCA procedure thus involves calculating all possible correlation coefficients and identifying and grouping the relationships. Raw variables can be envisaged as protruding from a central point at irregular angles, like a 'hedgehog' with projecting 'spines'. The PCA operation rearranges these spines, so that they project outwards in identifiable 'tufts', rather than bristling randomly.

'Rotation' is a mathematical procedure in which the list of principal components is compared with regular geometrical arrangements of factors. Visually, it is like taking the now tufty 'hedgehog' and rotating it until the thickest 'tuft' is uppermost, and then gauging the angles of all the other tufts and of the individual 'bristles'. The objective is to identify the exact geometrical position of each variable relative to each factor. The output of rotation consists of a matrix of correlation coefficients which relate every variable to every factor and (if necessary) relate the factors with one another.

Of the two types of rotation available, *orthogonal rotation* assumes that the factors are all at right angles to one another. *Oblique rotation* assumes that the factors are angled in other ways, and calculates the correlations between them. Researchers normally use orthogonal rotation unless there are good grounds to do otherwise. However, oblique rotation may be desirable if the factors themselves are likely to be interdependent.

For example, the results of a questionnaire which aims to measure service quality might factorize into aspects such as the quality of the physical surroundings, the smartness of staff, the speed of service and so on. However, one would expect all these factors to correlate quite closely with customers' overall experience of service quality. It is unlikely that they are independent of one another, as would be implied by assuming them to be at mutual right angles. They are more likely to resemble the spokes of a half-opened umbrella, i.e. pointing approximately in the same direction (that of overall quality), but diverging slightly outward. Oblique rotation is preferable in a case like this, because it allows the development of a non-orthogonal model.

Various rotation procedures are available, all of which are very complex in mathematical terms. The one generally used for orthogonal rotation is known as the VARIMAX procedure. Researchers may use a variety of oblique rotation routines, named, for example, MAXIMIN, OBLIMAX, OBLIMIN. *SPSS* commonly uses OBLIMIN.

Cluster Analysis

The objective of cluster analysis is to identify groups of respondents who give similar responses to two or more variables. Its principle can most easily be seen using two variables, as shown in Figure 5.11. Data points are plotted against the two variables as if they were coordinates in a planar space. Spatial distances between each pair of points are then calculated using Pythagoras' theorem. In principle, clustered points can be identified by their proximity, but in fact they are seldom straightforward to identify. The computer output therefore shows a tree of spatial relationships, called a *dendrogram*, an example of which is shown in Figure 5.12. From the dendrogram it is possible to identify which points are close to one another and which are far apart and (with luck) to assign them to clusters.

Cluster analysis often needs to use more than two variables. If three are employed, the computer must calculate inter-point distances in three-dimensional space. If more than three variables are used to fix the positions, the computer must envisage the distances in a space of more than three dimensions, i.e. in *hyperspace*. Although hyperspace is impossible for humans to visualize, distances separating points can be

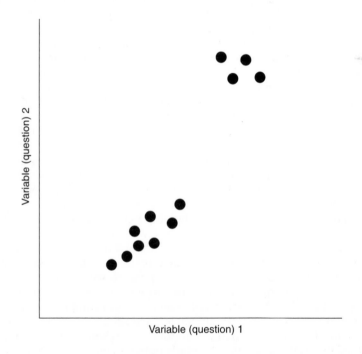

Figure 5.11   Clusters formed by plotting points against two variables

Figure 5.12   Dendrogram

calculated by Pythagoras' theorem in just the same way as in two- or three-dimensional space.

Discriminant Analysis

Discriminant analysis is comparable to factor analysis, in that it aims to relate variables together into similar groups called *discriminant factors*. The difference between factor and discriminant analysis is the basis of the grouping. Factor analysis relates variables together on the basis of their correlation coefficients. In contrast, discriminant analysis groups variables on the basis of their ability to discriminate within the data. For example, Lewis (1985) used the technique to differentiate between guests' perceptions of different hotels. From questionnaire data, he used the *F* test to find out which variables (i.e. questions) differentiated most strongly between the hotels. Then he used discriminant analysis (a series of complex mathematical procedures performed by a computer) to group the variables in terms of discriminating power. Discriminant analysis is less used in research than factor analysis, but offers an alternative means of grouping variables, and hence a fresh insight into data structure.

CONCLUSIONS

The first step in quantitative analysis is to count and rank the responses on the basis of their frequencies. The second is to calculate percentages. After this, descriptives such as the mean and standard deviation are derived and the data from each variable are examined to ensure that they have approximately the characteristics of a normal distribution.

Inferential statistics can be used to test relationships within the data: for example, to test whether different age groups or genders have responded differently to the questions. Bivariate tests may be parametric or non-parametric. Parametric tests may only be applied to normally distributed data, whereas non-parametric tests can be applied to all data types. Parametric tests are often easier to comprehend and use than non-parametrics, and for this reason are more often used. As a general principle, a non-parametric version exists for every bivariate test.

Multivariate statistics are derived from several variables at once. They may seek to differentiate between sub-populations (e.g. ANOVA), to group variables together (factor analysis, discriminant analysis) or to group respondents together (cluster analysis).

This chapter has attempted to present sufficient information to refresh readers' statistical knowledge and to place statistics in a service industry context. It is impossible to do justice to subjects such as multivariate analysis in such a short space. The reader is referred to the section entitled 'further reading' at the back of this book, and recommended to read widely before tackling statistical analyses of quantitative data in depth.

REFERENCES

Lewis, R.C. (1985) 'The market position: mapping guests' perceptions of hotel operations', *Cornell Hotel and Restaurant Administration Quarterly*, August, 86–99.
Miller, S. (1986) *Experimental Design and Statistics*, 2nd edn. Methuen, London and New York.

6

Qualitative Research Methods

INTRODUCTION

The *Concise Oxford Dictionary* (1990) defines qualitative analysis as 'detection of the constituents' of something. In the social science context, qualitative research usually aims to find out the characteristics of a research sample, in terms of behaviours, perceptions, values, attitudes and so on. It does not seek to quantify attitudes or behaviours like quantitative research. However, the distinction is not as clear as might be supposed. For example, a questionnaire can identify attitudes, show strength of feeling and provide a general description of a sample. Qualitative research is described by Hammersley (1990, p. 1) as:

> [investigations] using unstructured forms of data collection, both interviewing and observation, and employing verbal descriptions and explanations rather than quantitative measurement and statistical analysis.

Qualitative research has the potential to probe deeply, uncovering subtle and complex issues, but this takes time, and therefore small sample sizes are generally used. There are fundamental differences in the assumptions underlying the methodology. A questionnaire usually starts from a known theoretical position. Its questions are fixed, and they generally conform to an existing hypothesis. Thus, questionnaire techniques always adopt a hypothetico-deductive outlook. The major criticism levelled at them is that they always presuppose to some extent the situation that they are supposed to be researching. Qualitative techniques can take a more flexible approach, adapting their questions to the data as they go along. In this way they permit an inductive view of the situation, in which hypotheses arise from the data, rather than the other way around.

Although qualitative social research uses smaller samples, it tends to spend more time on data gathering from each one. Often it provides a partial view of population, rather than a broad and truly representative one, but it can achieve a much deeper portrayal of individuals' feelings, attitudes and behaviour. Qualitative research mostly gathers its information using interviews and observation. Its methods may seem less structured than quantitative techniques, but this does not mean they are less effective or that less planning is involved. A variety of skills are needed to perform effective qualitative research, summarized by Strauss and Corbin (1990, p. 19) as follows:

> to step back and critically analyse situations, to recognize and avoid bias, to obtain valid and reliable data, and to think abstractly.

Thus qualitative researchers have to be able to maintain distance between themselves and the phenomena under investigation, and to draw upon practical and theoretical knowledge to interpret what they see. However, in the interests of methodological rigour, this interpretation needs to conform to some agreed criteria. Ryan (1995, p. 97) lists the following criteria for research to be generally accepted.

- *Credibility*: researchers' interpretation must be acceptable to others (other researchers, managers of service organizations, etc.).
- *Transferability*: results must be relevant to other organizations and situations.
- *Dependability*: findings must permit forecasting or extrapolation (for example, to support related theories).
- *Confirmability*: similar groups in similar organizations should also be able to duplicate the research findings.

These criteria are similar to those of Strauss and Corbin (1990), who have developed a formal qualitative analysis process known as *grounded theory*. This seeks to validate qualitative research through systematic processes of data collection, development, analysis and verification. Grounded theory procedures are discussed later in this chapter.

Opponents of qualitative research, such as Wells (1991), consider that qualitative findings lack factual data-based validity. They assert that qualitative research should be conducted systematically enough to render it valid in the sense that quantitative research is valid. This view ignores the flexibility of qualitative research and its ability to cope with the needs and exigencies of organizations. Research projects in service organizations often need to be dynamic, because organizational and environmental conditions change continually.

Service organizations are not scientific laboratories with controlled conditions, nor are individuals always willing to take part in research projects. Research programmes conducted within them are always subject to practical constraints and researchers must have contingency plans. Most service organizations are labour intensive, with personnel interacting with customers much of the time. (Indeed, this 'service encounter' is a crucial element of service 'products'.) It is therefore generally important to assess the attitudes of employees, customers and managers. This usually involves tailoring research flexibly to organizational needs. Qualitative research provides an effective way to do this, and it is important that both researchers and managers understand the basic techniques available.

Qualitative research techniques tend to be more adaptable and flexible under practical organizational conditions. The glimpses they provide of the research situation are often very helpful to managers in practical terms. However, from a methodological standpoint, it is often advisable to use more than one research technique, so that findings may be compared and a definitive picture obtained. Using a variety of qualitative techniques also increases flexibility. For example, a series of interviews may have been scheduled only to be cancelled by the interviewees at the last minute. In this instance, interviews may have to be replaced by some other qualitative approach.

The use of qualitative research in service organizations is not new. Authorities such as the Automobile Association use qualitative methods to grade hotels and restaurants. Speaking with clients and employees is a crucial managerial role in service industries, and managers are ideally positioned to gather valuable information about markets, customers and workers. Even informal conversation may be viewed as a qualitative research technique, provided its data can be structured in some way. Information elicited through interview or conversation is usually practical and can be actioned immediately. Thus, qualitative techniques are frequently used by managers, but not recognized as such. One of the reasons for this is that an analytical framework is usually lacking. In order to convert conversation into valid research it is necessary to learn the skills of scrutinizing data for concepts and structuring them in different ways to form hypotheses.

This chapter discusses the role of qualitative research and its practical value in service organizations. It reviews various qualitative data gathering methods and shows how they can contribute to research projects. The chapter also discusses the coding and analysis of data both manually and using computer software.

SCOPE OF QUALITATIVE RESEARCH

Qualitative techniques can be used in various ways, depending upon the nature of the research problem and the preference of the researcher. Some prefer to begin a research programme with a qualitative study. As discussed in Chapter 4, interviewing and observation are good ways to begin the development of a questionnaire, and focus groups may play an important part in piloting and purifying a questionnaire. However, it is possible to *begin* a research project with a quantitative survey and to use qualitative studies to shed clearer light on the findings of the questionnaire. This may particularly be the case if a tried and tested questionnaire instrument already exists. It is also possible to design integrated studies, which use an interplay between quantitative and qualitative methods. For example, the research programme may be structured into quantitative and qualitative stages in such a way that each stage provides a sharper focus than the one before. An example of this type of design is the *case study*, discussed in the next chapter.

Qualitative research methods are useful for longer investigations such as higher degree studies, because they provide flexibility and a chance to develop areas of interest. Interviews may also unearth unforeseen aspects of the research. In a motivational study of seasonal hotel workers (Lee-Ross, 1996), interviews with managers revealed that unemployment benefit had a strong impact upon the behaviour of workers. This issue had not been foreseen at all in the original research schedule, but was explored in detail during later stages of the investigation.

Qualitative research may also improve communication between the researcher and respondents. It provides researchers with information about the attitudes and values of informants, but equally may give employees insight into the researcher's perceptions. On the other hand, managers, customers and employees frequently all use language in different ways, ascribing different meanings to common words and phrases. Researchers may need to learn how to communicate clearly and effectively with informants, with both parties having full understanding of the dialogue.

Misunderstandings could have devastating effects upon the value of the data and ultimately of the research.

BASIC TECHNIQUES

Research can be considered to contain three elements: gathering data, coding them and analysing them. Gathering data not only consists of collecting them from the sample under study, but also 'fixing' them for later study. *Quantitative* data from questionnaires have the virtue that the evidence is in written form and hence secure. It is more difficult to do this in qualitative research, where the data may come in the form of interview notes or audio or video recordings. As with quantitative work, there must be some way of coding the individual respondents, different parts of their responses and recurring features within them. Unlike quantitative data, qualitative material may be coded in a number of possible ways. It is mainly for this reason that qualitative research finds itself a source of controversy. The researcher must choose the analytical framework, which necessitates a clear understanding of whether the approach to be taken is phenomenological or positivistic. Ultimately this will dictate whether an existing theory will be tested or new theories allowed to emerge from the data. Thus, qualitative analysis stands directly at the crux of the positivist/phenomenologist, inductivist/hypothetico-deductivist debate.

DATA COLLECTION TECHNIQUES

Data collection techniques available to the qualitative researcher fall into three basic categories.

- *Interviews:* verbal responses to questions are gathered from individuals or focus groups of respondents.
- *Observation:* respondents' words and/or actions are recorded without (necessarily) asking them questions.
- *Documents:* written materials, such as archives, legal statutes, minutes of meetings, letters, memos, communications.

All these basic approaches can have many variations and considerable overlap is possible. For example, an interview may be highly structured, or the interviewer might just start with an objective, adapting the questions to the drift of the conversation. Group interviews may 'focus' upon a designated topic (they are often used to discover what people think of a new service product). They might also 'focus' on what people *don't* say in the group context (even when challenged), or upon the way individuals interact with one another. The research objectives dictate how the group is handled and the data are recorded. Observation is perhaps subject to the most variations in style and content. Data may be recorded as written notes, photographs, or audio or video recordings, and, in addition, each technique may contain elements of the others. For example, it is often meaningless to observe without also recording dialogue. During a focus group, individuals may provide 'interviews', or members' behaviour may be observed. Documentation may be related to the statements of individuals or to observations of behaviour. Minutes of meetings and company policies sometimes provide good examples of both of these.

INTERVIEWS

Qualitative research is much less formally structured than quantitative work. The researcher may have comparatively little control over the situation, sometimes acting only as a facilitator or passive data-gatherer. Question phraseology is less important because conversations often develop between researcher and respondent so that issues or misunderstandings can be explored. However, there are opportunities for bias, because there is no anonymity in face-to-face situations and respondents may feel bound to say the 'right' thing.

Arranging interviews with individuals has numerous practical implications. Contact must first be made with individuals to explain the nature of the research, to propose interview dates and to assure confidentiality. Individuals should be invited to respond and the researcher may send them a list of questions or areas to be covered during the interview. Afterwards the researcher should send informants a letter of thanks, assuring them of confidentiality unless any specific agreement was reached between them during the interview.

Unstructured or in-depth interviewing is perhaps the most common qualitative technique used for gathering data. The interviewer starts with a plan indicating the areas to be covered, and the interview is allowed to proceed at its own pace, in a conversational style. Thus the interviewee is guided, but also permitted and even encouraged by the interviewer to make 'detours'. This makes it possible to identify issues which are important to the interviewee but unforeseen by the interviewer (an essential part of inductive hypothesis-building). The free format often makes it possible to gather striking comments that shed light on the way interviewees view the research area. However, it requires considerable interviewing skill to cover the essential points and at the same time allow respondents sufficient expressive freedom.

As discussed in Chapter 4, a structured interview has closed questions similar to a questionnaire, but is administered verbally. *Semi-structured interviews* contain a combination of open and closed questions. Closed questions are coded and analysed in much the same way as questionnaire data (see Chapter 5). Open format questions allow respondents considerable freedom to express their opinions and may be analysed in a similar way to in-depth interview material. Being shorter and more focused than unstructured interview responses, they are particularly suitable for keyword coding, although other types of analysis may also be appropriate. Closed questions can add a wealth of data about respondents and allow direct comparisons between interviewees. They also make it possible to compare the responses of different samples.

Closed question data from structured and semi-structured interviews are gathered by the interviewer on preprinted forms, by ticking boxes. Longer responses are written down in full, or (more usually) as notes. Data from unstructured interviews may be gathered in several ways. The interviewer may make written notes, expressing the drift of what the respondent says, and taking down the most expressive comments in full. Alternatively, the whole interview can be recorded on audio cassette. Later it can be transcribed in full, or the interviewer can make notes and select particularly interesting passages for transcription. Interviews can also be recorded on videotape, which provides a still greater depth of information. After recording, it is important to allow sufficient time to transcribe data. This can be a very lengthy process, as a recorded interview of 30 minutes may take anything up to four hours to transcribe *verbatim*. It is advisable to word-process all notes and transcriptions, as this permits computerized searching and can substantially help the process of analysis.

FOCUS GROUPS

Group interviews make it possible to compare the views of a number of individuals at once and to achieve synergy of expression. Group interviews usually concentrate on one particular topic at a time and seek to identify the ways in which different individuals react to it. For this reason they are often called focus groups. Focus groups are used widely in marketing research to gauge individuals' responses to new products or to new advertising campaigns. Focus groups are a good way to identify research issues for developing a questionnaire and can also be used in the piloting of questionnaires.

Focus groups normally consist of between eight and ten individuals who discuss a topic under the guidance of a trained researcher. Sessions should start with general issues and develop into specific areas. Refreshments are usually provided and the researcher should aim for an informal ambience. This relaxes individuals and predisposes them to introduce their own ideas with minimal prompting. The ways in which the topic is introduced are limited only by the imagination of the researcher. Discussions may be stimulated by using 'opening' questions, quotations, pictures, video extracts and so on. Focus group facilitators may also use explicit objectives to stimulate conversation. Some objectives which might be used in a focus group discussion of the potential for a new tourist attraction are:

- generate ideas for new tourist concept;
- evaluate ideas for new tourist concept;
- assess how to position an existing tourist concept in a new geographical market;
- determine consumer attitudes towards an attraction's 'product' and 'atmosphere';
- evaluate new tourist attractions or changes in existing attractions;
- generate questions that can be asked in follow-up research;
- identify variables used by tourists to evaluate and select attractions;
- monitor an attraction's effectiveness in meeting consumer needs and expectations;
- test advertising copy;
- determine consumers' reaction to promotional ideas.

Members of focus groups should not have previous experience or they may dominate discussions and bias group responses. The researcher's objective is to allow all members the same opportunity to speak in order to obtain a wide range of attitudes and opinions. However, if individuals have a limited knowledge of the area, or the conversation is becoming exhausted, the researcher may need to prompt the group or change the topic. Focus groups are subjective and there are no hard and fast rules for conducting them. They are most effective if the researcher allows the ideas of all the members to emerge.

Researchers must also have the required skills to manage the subtleties of the discussion process. They must understand the subject well and be sensitive to the implications of various responses, without intimidating respondents. Researchers must have empathy and patience and allow individuals the time for full expression. Agreement *and* disagreement should be encouraged from participants, but control of the group should be maintained at all times. However, the group must not be led or biased by the researcher/facilitator in any way.

Focus groups are more than just research tools. They may be used to influence social dynamics in the workplace and to motivate employees as a group. This teamwork goal can be exploited in quality circles, which are in effect focus groups aimed at identifying opportunities for process improvement. A variety of tools are available for identifying, classifying and using these new ideas in this way (see Johns, 1994). Entrepreneurs and local tourist authority officers may decide to promote their holiday resort jointly, creating a 'partnership' with shared responsibility for marketing the holiday destination. In such a situation a focus group may enable both private and public sector representatives to identify common themes and ideas in the interest of the holiday trade in the area. However, approaches of this kind belong to the domain of *action research*, discussed in Chapter 7.

Marketing strategies are also better understood and developed after involving focus group discussions. It may be useful to make up a focus group of service customers, providing a mechanism through which managers learn to understand their customers' needs more effectively. For example, restaurant customers might be asked how they would improve on the service they have received and what other restaurants they use. They could also be asked something about their 'ideal' restaurant.

Focus groups also provide a comparatively simple and informative way to assess the effectiveness of advertising. Managers need to know the message that customers are receiving about the organization and its services. Clearly this information is crucial if managers decide to differentiate their product for different market segments. For example, if a hotel is close to a number of golf courses or in an area visited by rare birds, advertisements must communicate this to the intended market. However, marketing messages often contain subtle nuances, some of which may be off-putting to potential customers. Focus groups provide a good way to identify such problems before an advertising campaign gets under way.

These suggestions by no means exhaust the range of ways in which focus groups can be used. They are appropriate for any research situation where people's reactions *as a group* to a particular phenomenon are of interest. An important advantage of focus groups is that of time. More ideas may be elicited and discussed during a one-hour group session than in several hours of interviews. In addition, focus groups are said to engender a feeling of security or 'social ease' among members of the group, reducing defensiveness and insecurity. Group members tend to stimulate one another and this results in spontaneous responses and synergy among the group.

Data from focus groups can be taken down in note form, but usually it is more effective to record them in some way. Even then, if several people make comments at the same time on to audiotape, it may be difficult to hear what is happening and to transcribe the tape. The situation can be improved by using a stereo cassette recorder, so that voices may be distinguished from one another by their direction. It can also be worthwhile to videotape focus groups, but it may be quite difficult to seat the group so that everyone can be seen at the same time. Transcriptions may take substantially longer than those of one-to-one interviews. Notes and transcriptions should be word-processed wherever possible.

Table 6.1   A summary of observational roles

Type I: Complete participant	Type II: Participant as observer	Type III: Observer as non-participant	Type IV: Complete observer
Participant, similar age, interests, activities, covert	Participant, overt or covert	Overt, non- participation but present among subject groups	Observation at a distance, non- participation

OBSERVATION

As the word suggests, observation is about watching the behaviour of individuals, or groups of people. The scope is very wide, because observation may take place on a comparatively broad, general scale, such as watching how people behave as they enter a shop. On the other hand, it is possible to observe the *minutiae* of people's behaviour close up, recording facial expressions, body language and gestures. Researchers engaged in such work can adopt one of several roles relative to the individuals they are studying. The choice (particularly in busy service organizations) depends partly on what is practically feasible, but there are also ethical considerations. The four basic observational roles are summarized in Table 6.1.

Observation is an everyday reality in many service industry settings, particularly in large service organizations. For example, a mystery guest in a hotel or a mystery shopper in a retail outlet is a type I 'complete participant', usually with a brief to act covertly. In contrast, a 'time and motion' researcher of operational efficiency is a type IV 'complete observer', observing openly, and clearly differentiated from the workers themselves. A trainee is often a type II 'participant as observer', doing part of the job while observing. An outsider engaged in job shadowing is a type III 'observer as non-participant'.

Covert observation, or 'going native', in research situations is effective because the researcher is unknown to the subjects. The observer can pose as a work colleague of equal status, so that the observees are more likely to behave 'normally'. However, covert observation raises ethical issues and researchers should consider whether it is morally acceptable to occupy a covert or type I position. This is particularly the case if the findings may be used to manipulate or exploit the subjects. In addition, if covert observers are 'discovered' by observees, results may be compromised and violent situations may even develop (for example, see Mars and Nicod, 1984).

Observational researchers should not project their own motivations or preferences upon their subjects. This may be particularly easy to do if the researcher is totally immersed in the social context. Neither should observers allow their personal experience to focus their attention erroneously upon or away from certain social phenomena. Observers with background experience of the research situation are in a strong position to gather data, but they may inadvertently ignore aspects they have grown accustomed to regarding as 'unimportant'. In addition, the relationship between researcher and informant may affect attitudes and behaviour. Research subjects often respond better to an observer of a similar age and gender. This is also true of other characteristics, such as upbringing, dialect or race.

Observations can be recorded in note form, but it may be difficult to identify a suitable nomenclature or code with which to do this. It is usually more effective to videotape them. Even so, the information may be so rich that several recorders must be used at once, and this can present a problem of synchronizing the recordings, identifying views and angles and so on. It is best to consider the recording process carefully at the outset in order to minimize such problems. The analysis of observational data usually follows a rigorous inductive procedure such as the grounded theory approach, discussed later in this chapter.

Ethnography

Ethnography is an anthropological approach, which uses a rigorous style of participant observation. It allows the researcher to use participants' socially acquired and shared knowledge to account for observed patterns of their behaviour. Ethnography focuses on the ways in which people interact with one another in their everyday situations. Ethnographers attempt to learn about the culture of their subjects and to interpret it in ways compatible with the way the members of the group see it. This research approach considers that social interactions cannot be studied under artificial conditions of experiment or interview, but only in their natural situation in 'the field'. Studies such as that of Mars and Nicod (1984) have a strong element of ethnography, and this approach is also proving a fruitful way forward in tourism research.

DOCUMENTS

Almost all researchers use literature in their work to some extent. In particular, the work of other researchers – papers, books, statistics, reports and so on – makes up the *secondary research* which underlies the writing of research proposals, and the development of ideas (see Chapters 2 and 3). Qualitative research also *generates* documents: for example, the notes and transcripts of observations and interviews. However, in addition to these considerations, documents are qualitative research sources in their own right.

For example, *public archives* can provide information about events in the past, where the original subjects are dead or cannot be reached. They may contain useful visual materials such as photographs, sketches or maps, which can enhance and illuminate data that have already been collected from live sources. Archives can also give clues to behaviour, either directly, by describing it, or indirectly. For example, advertisements, instructions, notices and codes of practice may provide evidence of how people once lived and behaved.

Another useful source of data may be provided by *administrative documents*. These include minutes of meetings, letters, memos and financial records. Administrative documents have a similar status to archives, but are usually privately (often informally) held, and for this reason may be incomplete, with access to them having to be negotiated.

It is often necessary to photocopy appropriate sections of archive material, whether publicly or privately held. Copies must always be carefully labelled and dated, and annotated as soon as practically possible after they have been collected.

ETHICAL CONSIDERATIONS

Quantitative research frequently adopts a positivistic philosophical position, similar to that of science. The researcher assumes that there is an unambiguous, objective 'truth' which the research will uncover. This 'truth' is imagined to be independent of the researcher and of the subjects, and even implies some obligation on the part of the research subject to provide it. There may be a feeling that it is somehow in the 'interests of science' for the subjects to provide the information that will unlock the 'truth'. In one form or another, this argument is often used to legitimize the collection and analysis of data about research subjects who may be given little or no say in the process.

In contrast, qualitative research usually takes a phenomenological perspective which acknowledges the subjective position of the researcher to a much greater extent. To suppose that a researcher's subjective position is somehow 'superior' to that of research subjects is not justifiable. Therefore, the research subjects must have a right regarding both the privacy of the information gathered and the way it is used. In fact, as has been discussed in earlier chapters, the 'scientific objectivity' of quantitative social research is itself spurious. Considerations of privacy and ownership are equally relevant to quantitative research, though this is not always acknowledged.

It is impossible to guarantee anonymity to most types of qualitative research. It is therefore usual to ask interviewees' and other subjects' permission at every stage of the research and to discuss with them how the research is to be reported and used. It is also good ethical practice to give subjects access to transcripts of interviews and other data. An area of particular concern is the type I observation situation discussed above, in which the researcher makes covert observations of the subjects.

DATA CODING AND ANALYSIS

Qualitative data are generally complex. They are also highly dependent upon the timing and circumstances under which they are gathered. Thus they should be recorded instantly, or as soon as possible after observation. Inexperienced researchers often believe they can record data accurately some considerable time after the event. This is a mistake, because only the most colourful statements or incidents are generally remembered. It is also important to record contextual information and subtle nuances of speech and behaviour if the full value is to be extracted from the situation. Respondents frequently reveal information which seems irrelevant at the time, but later gains in significance. They may also come up with something important that the researcher had not considered and that changes the whole basis of the analysis.

CODING DATA

Before they can be analysed and used, qualitative data must be *coded*. The coding process ensures that the data are managed methodically, and that the researcher can access all the material they contain. As in quantitative research, coding is a way of marking information for later use, and there are three levels at which it should be done:

- identifying all pieces of data and respondents;
- identifying units of analysis (sections and subsections within the data);
- identifying features of the data for analysis.

Data Identification

Data items should be linked methodically to the specific research project or phase. Both numbers and letters can be used, but in qualitative research it often preferable to use a coding system based on an acronym or a shortened version of the project name. The coding system should also make it clear what each item is and where it came from. The more easily data can be identified, the more efficiently they can be managed. Computer files should be stored in a dedicated subdirectory, so that they are accessible and updatable. It is worth giving some thought to data management at the outset of a project and learning to maintain systems methodically, until this becomes just a way of life.

It is essential to identify categories of data, and interviews, focus groups, observations and documents must all be separately identified by coding with numbers or letters. This is not always as simple as it seems, as each type of data-gathering event may give rise to several different forms of data. For example, an interview may start life as an audio recording and then give rise to both notes and a transcript. A standardized code should be used to identify each type of information. Audio and video recordings should be labelled carefully and preserved until the end of the research project, and so should transcripts and other documents. Computer files should always be dated.

Individual respondents should be identified clearly, ideally by a number, as a name may breach anonymity. Sometimes pseudonyms are used in this type of research, particularly at the time the work is reported. There may be an advantage to using such pseudonyms right from the start, keeping individuals clearly identified as 'people', but concealing their true identity. The main objective of codes and pseudonyms is to prevent data from different individuals becoming mixed up.

The coding ideal is to render all the identifying information about a piece of data into a short sequence of letters and numbers that can be attached to the file in a computer or a filing cabinet. In practice it is virtually impossible to do this satisfactorily for all the information. For hard copy files, tapes and diskettes it may be preferable to prepare preprinted sticky labels. Each label should show a code, together with a variety of other necessary information. This may include the date and time the data were collected, the circumstances (for example, who collected them and where), the particular phase of the project and so on. It is usually important to record information about the research subjects, particularly if they are to be designated only by reference numbers or pseudonyms. This information will differ from project to project, but it may include the respondent's gender, age and position or role within the organization. Other data may also be important: for example, a project about smoking at work may need to identify interviewees as smokers or non-smokers.

Computer files should be headed with a few lines of text showing the item code, the individual code and basic biographical information. A good practice is to set up word processor templates for different types of document (e.g. transcripts, notes, minutes), which prompt the typist for details of respondents before the business of entering data begins. This kind of precoding is particularly important if specialist software is to be used to analyse the qualitative data.

Units of Analysis

Before data can be analysed they must be broken down into units, so that the positions of important findings can be located. A whole document may be considered the unit of analysis and particular ideas or key words counted if this is the only aim of the analysis. However, this may make it difficult to find respondents' specific comments again in order to quote them or to examine their context. Therefore, it is often best to identify particular lines or paragraphs of the text. Audio- and videotapes can be broken down into subsections on the basis of footage meter readings. An interview may change in emphasis as it proceeds, making it necessary to identify specific phases within it. It is possible to divide up interviews and observations into phases, to make identification and analysis of highlights easier. For example, a videotape of employees' and customers' behaviour during a service encounter may contain phases where employees greet customers and put them at their ease, customers express their wishes, employees deliver the core part of the service and so on.

Coding Interesting Features of the Data

Inductive approaches to analysis aim to draw hypotheses from qualitative data. In order to do this, it is necessary to go through data in detail, picking out elements from which theory can be constructed. These elements must be sorted into types, coded and *indexed* (i.e. referenced against a particular section of a particular document), so that they can be found again when they need to be quoted, counted, or have their context checked. Coding must also be done if a hypothetico-deductive stance is taken towards the research. However, in that case the hypotheses and their constituents are known before the coding is undertaken, and it is comparatively easy to go through the data identifying specific elements. Most qualitative research uses an inductive approach, and the researcher must usually go through the data several times, developing and revising hypotheses and reconsidering the structures which seem to be appearing. A typical example is as follows:

- identify possible relevant structures within the data;
- assign codes to them;
- draw out possible hypotheses (and perhaps rationalize and recode structures identified in the data);
- test and revise hypotheses (and perhaps reconsider and recode structures.

Thus the coding process often plays a much more integral part in qualitative than in quantitative analysis.

ANALYSING DATA

The procedures used to extract information from quantitative data are essentially mathematical and well-defined, and they flow from the original assumption that the research hypothesis is quantifiable. The researcher begins by counting the numbers of responses and follows this by ranking the data, deriving percentages and descriptive statistics. The final stages of analysis often involve rigorous testing procedures, together with bivariate and multivariate analysis.

In contrast, there is no such defined procedure available for analysing qualitative data. This is partly due to the fact that different research programmes may be based from the outset on different assumptions and partly because the inductive process requires the researcher to take a phenomenological stance. This in turn means that the analysis of data also has a subjective element.

The phenomenological basis of qualitative analysis puts a strong onus upon researchers to validate qualitative findings as rigorously as possible. This is particularly true where qualitative results are intended to reflect the views of a whole population. In such cases, the structure and composition of the interview sample may be almost as important as in survey work. Arguably, it may be even more important, as samples are smaller and their composition (at least in principle) is more critical. Baseline details about individual respondents discussed in the previous section – age, gender and so on – should be coded and tabulated as frequencies and percentages in the same way as with quantitative data.

Keyword Analysis

One way to analyse qualitative textual data is to identify *keywords* and to count the frequencies with which they occur. This can be done with complete interview transcripts, but it is quicker and more efficient if the responses themselves have been made in a simple format. For example, keyword analysis is the basis of the *profile accumulation* technique of Johns and Lee-Ross (1995). Guests' free responses about a service experience are elicited on single-sheet forms, which ask for positive comments with the prompts: 'The things I liked best about my experience at **** were ...' and 'The reason I liked this aspect is ...' on one side. On the other side of the forms, respondents can write negative comments against: 'The things which I found least satisfactory about my experience at **** were ...', and 'The reason this aspect was unsatisfactory was ...'. In Johns and Lee-Ross's (1996) work, the free response forms were customized with the name of the service establishment and a few lines of introductory text.

The data thus obtained were analysed by identifying two categories of key words: 'aspects' (elements of the service, such as food, service, etc.) and 'attributes' (descriptors which the guests used about each aspect of the service, such as 'delicious' or 'polite'). The assumption underlying the technique is that service customers refer most frequently to the element of their experience that they perceive to be the most important. In the same way, the keywords they use most frequently to describe the elements of their experience are regarded as the most important. Therefore, counting up the keywords and analysing them numerically provides insight into the elements customers perceive within a service 'product', the importance attached to them and the ways in which customers characterize them.

A similar frequency-based approach can be used with other features of interview data. For example, researchers count and analyse pauses in conversation or frequently repeated conversational mannerisms. It is of course necessary to establish a clear case for the meanings of these frequencies. For example, pauses may be taken as a sign that the respondent is momentarily under stress caused by the emotive nature of a particular question that has been asked. However, this position cannot be taken unless evidence is offered that this is in fact true. Otherwise, no meaningful inference can be made from the analysis.

Non-verbal Communication

Non-verbal communication is potentially as important as the spoken or written word. It is possible to note down examples of non-verbal communication as they occur in either written or dictated form, but such recordings necessarily omit much important information. Note-taking also tends to distort data records. What is noted depends upon the personality of the researcher, and once it has been noted down, neither the original researcher nor another individual can go back with fresh insight to the original event. Therefore, video recording is probably the best way to capture non-verbal communication for analysis. Behaviours (i.e. different types of non-verbal communication) can be analysed for frequency, like words in text. The more frequently a behaviour occurs, the more meaningful it is likely to be to the subject who exhibits it. Often, however, the subject may be unaware of the behaviour and its significance.

Some common gestures (forms of non-verbal communication) made by research subjects are:

- smiling;
- frowning;
- open palms;
- handshake;
- hand over mouth;
- lower lip between forefinger and thumb;
- pulling the collar;
- rubbing forehead;
- clenched fist;
- arms folded;
- rocking forward and backward;
- pointing with finger;
- shrugging;
- chin resting in palm;
- fingers in mouth;
- looking downward;
- gaze with eye-to-eye contact often broken;
- hands in pockets with thumbs outside;
- hands in pockets with whole hand inside;
- standing with hands on hips.

The researcher is faced with the problem of identifying the meaning of each gesture as captured on a video recording. There are further difficulties. Individuals *feel*, rather than seeing their gestures, so that the meaning is unconscious and often quite different from their intention. In any case, the feeling, intended expression and outwardly visual effect all vary between individuals.

Gestures possess tacitly agreed meanings within particular cultures. It is possible to catalogue gestures by discussing them in a group with other researchers and identifying commonly agreed meanings. For instance, it is generally accepted that folded arms indicate a protective pose, figuratively fending off some threat. Video-tapes can be coded with named gestures plus their agreed interpretations. Another way to tackle the problem is to watch the videotapes with the subjects and ask what each gesture and behaviour trait means to them. In effect, this process converts the video recording into a textual form in (it is hoped) the respondent's own terms, and the resulting transcript can be analysed like any other text.

GROUNDED THEORY

Although there is no universally accepted approach for analysing qualitative data, that of grounded theory comes closest to this ideal for research in service industry management. The approach has several advantages. For example, it is:

- capable of handling all kinds of qualitative data, i.e. those from observations and documents as well as from interviews and focus groups;
- flexible enough to suit a wide range of situations and variations in personal style;
- inductive in concept, so that it makes no presuppositions about the data or the research situation.

The grounded theory approach is essentially phenomenological. It aims to derive concepts inductively from raw qualitative data (taped/transcribed interviews, videoed/annotated observations, annotated documents) and to develop them into theories. Relationships between these hypotheses are explored systematically in order to provide coherent patterns of understanding about the research situation. Thus, theories (hypotheses) spring from concepts, which in turn arise from observations. They have been 'grounded' empirically in the data and can be supported by actual, demonstrable evidence.

The grounded theory approach is systematic, and can be envisaged as the series of stages shown in Figure 6.1. Theory is to be developed during the research process, so the research question needs to be open enough to allow this to happen. Instead of the hypothesis/null hypothesis required by the positivist approach, qualitative research should start with a clear statement of the research situation. Using this, a work schedule is drawn up, and the data are collected. Three types of coding are then employed to extract meaning from the data: *open* coding, *axial* coding and *selective* coding. The objective is to produce theories which are grounded in empirical data, are conceptually dense (i.e. related to the data through many justifiable generalizations) and are well integrated (i.e. have common themes and support one another).

Open coding involves looking through the data in order to identify concepts. Grounded theory takes the view that raw data contain only specific anecdotes and that subjective insight must be used to convert these into generalistic concepts from which theory can be derived. This stage of the analysis therefore requires a considerable level of skill from the researcher. It cannot be regarded as 'final', because new ideas and questions will almost certainly spring up as the analysis progresses. The open coding stage is effectively a first 'filtering process' to which the data are subjected. At this stage it is generally helpful to begin indexing the statements, incidents and anecdotes from which the concepts are drawn. The end product of open coding is a list of concepts, indexed to specific passages of documents (lines, paragraphs, pages) or recordings (audio or video footage). The most persuasive anecdotes should be identified in some way, as many of these will need to be presented as evidence in the final report.

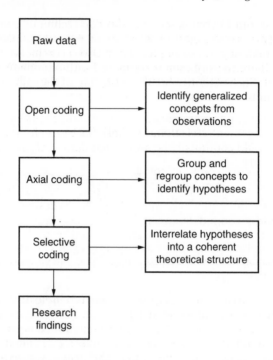

Figure 6.1   Model of the grounded theory process

Axial coding is the next stage of the analysis, in which patterns are identified within the data. As Strauss and Corbin (1990, p. 96) put it:

> [Axial coding consists of] a set of procedures whereby data are put back together in new ways after open coding, by making connections between categories. This is done by utilizing a coding paradigm involving conditions, context, action/inter-actional strategies and consequences.

In other words, the concepts identified during open coding are assembled to form new patterns and to identify relationships (exclusions, generalizations, causal links, etc.) between them. The effect is to produce new hypotheses inductively from the concepts that are embedded in the raw data. Protagonists of grounded theory insist that researchers must possess *theoretical sensitivity* (i.e. the ability to spot causal or relational patterns among the anecdotes and concepts in the data) in order to do this adequately. It is claimed that theoretical sensitivity can be developed by practice. Strauss and Corbin (1990) recommend the following activities for increasing one's sensitivity to the theoretical structures present within data.

- *Questioning:* asking why, what, where, when, who, how, and how much/many of each concept and proposed theory in turn.
- *Analysis* of words, phrases or sentences: listing the underlying meanings and connotations of words and of the way the respondent has put them together. This renders researchers more sensitive not only to the data, but also to the wording (and hence understanding) of the concepts and theories they derive from those data.

- *Changes:* Strauss and Corbin describe a 'flip-flop technique', where the researcher reverses some aspect of the research situation (imagines a large company as a small one, for example). They also recommend 'far out comparisons', where the situation is compared with one that is apparently very different from it. Such activities break up the line of thought and refresh the way the problem is viewed.

These three activities bear a resemblance to the formalized problem-solving methods taught by some management consultant groups (for example, see Allen and Allen, 1997). The reader should continually be aware that data analysis is basically a type of problem-solving activity.

Open and axial coding aim to identify the main concepts inherent in data and to develop theories from these. *Selective coding* takes this development one stage further, and aims to integrate and interrelate the hypotheses which have been produced. Strauss and Corbin define selective coding as:

> The process of selecting the core category, systematically relating it to other categories, validating those relationships, and filling in categories that need further refinement and development.

Like axial coding, selective coding requires theoretical sensitivity. It also demands that the researcher stand back from the problem, in order to see its theoretical underpinning in a clearer, more holistic way. For example, it is possible to argue that people's values and orientations are either expressive or instrumental, and to produce a theoretical structure based upon one or the other. However, in a tourism situation they can reflect the same thing (Ryan, 1995). For example, tourist activities are *expressions* of wish fulfilment but they are also *instrumental* in living out the expression.

A well-constructed grounded theory, developed with the aid of these coding processes, must meet the following criteria.

- It must fit, i.e. faithfully reflect the researchers' and subjects' views of the research situation (the phenomenon being studied).
- It must be mutually understandable: both to the researcher(s) and to the people who were studied.
- It must be general, i.e. sufficiently abstract to allow it to be applicable in a variety of contexts.
- It must be capable of directing any management action that plans to intervene in the situation, after the research has been completed.

COMPUTER-AIDED ANALYSIS

Several software packages are available to assist the analysis of qualitative data. Most have been developed for specific needs or to support specific styles of qualitative research. For example, *Ethnograph* enables stored material from interviews, notes and observations to be analysed using an anthropological framework. One of the most flexible packages is perhaps *NUD-IST* (**N**on-numerical **U**nstructured **D**ata – Index-ing, **S**earching and **T**heorising), published by Qualitative Solutions & Research Pty Ltd, Melbourne, Australia. This software reflects the grounded theory principles discussed above, and for this reason it is discussed here at length. However, it is highly versatile and can be used in a wide range of qualitative analytical work. This includes analysis of keywords and pauses in written data, analysis of non-textual materials such as video recordings, photographs and maps, and analysis of documents. The package is also helpful for analysing and reviewing subject literature produced by other researchers.

NUD-IST is a database system which contains two working areas. Document details can be entered into one area and concepts, links and hypotheses can be built up graphically in the other. Indexing (i.e. linking the two together) makes it easy to carry out various types of coding and to retrieve evidence from the documents to support and illustrate the hypotheses.

Data are entered into the package in ASCII text format, providing a low-memory way of storing large quantities of data. This usually just means saving files of data as text from a word-processing package. Once the data have been entered, *NUD-IST* can be programmed to search for particular words and contexts. The package is very powerful and searches can be progressively refined by adding more keywords and by using Boolean terms such as 'and', 'or' and 'not' to add and exclude terms from the context. The package can also capture the results of searches as single lines of text, or expand them up to three lines above and below the selected words, and it can index captured text against concepts and hypotheses. This speeds up the selection of text considerably, but does not dispense with reading through it. Each item highlighted by the software must be reread, and selected or rejected according to its relevance. A very wide search (e.g. with only a few common keywords) usually highlights a large number of items, many of which are irrelevant and must be sorted manually. On the other hand, a sophisticated, narrow search may miss important passages because they happen not to contain particular keyword combinations. Some of these may only be found through a manual search. In addition to this, *NUD-IST* can support other types of analysis. For example, it can count the occurrences of keywords and phrases or (if they are clearly coded in the text) of pauses or gestures.

It is not necessary to enter all documents as full text. *NUD-IST* distinguishes between 'on-line' documents (i.e. those which are entered as full text) and 'off-line' documents. Only the titles and baseline data of 'off-line' documents are entered into the package, so these are not limited to text documents. As long as some suitable system of position coding is identified (e.g. footage of audio- or videotapes, map references, areas of a photograph), almost any kind of item may be used.

The indexing/theorizing area of the database allows concepts to be identified and labelled. The package terms the concepts 'nodes' and represents them as boxes, interlinked in tree or 'root and branch' structures. An example of a typical structure is shown in Figure 6.2. The root and branch structure makes it possible to display hierarchies of different concepts and show the linkages between them. Nodes can be indexed to passages in documents and tree structures can be continuously pruned and rearranged as the analysis proceeds. Thus the package can facilitate open, axial and selective coding and support the complete development of grounded theory from a variety of raw data. *NUD-IST* can be used to structure theory in many ways, and may be used in other research contexts, such as in anthropological or linguistic studies.

CONCLUSIONS

Qualitative research asks 'what?' 'how?' and 'why?' rather than 'how much?' It works from a narrower, necessarily less representative, base than quantitative surveys. It is

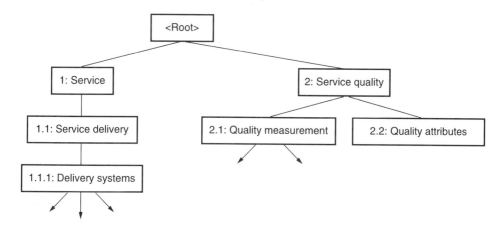

Figure 6.2 Example of how *NUD-IST* structures hypotheses

predominantly phenomenological in outlook and aims to provide a deep insight into a limited area of study. This essentially subjective stance has raised objections from some authors about the reliability of qualitative findings. However, it is generally agreed that qualitative research provides useful and valid results as long as data collection and analysis are rigorously carried out.

The collection of qualitative data is wide in scope, and all kinds of documents, visual or audio materials may be appropriate. Data items need to be coded according to type, source and origin. There should also be a way of identifying specific parts of research materials: for example, going through documents line by line, or through recording tape in defined sections.

Numerous approaches are available for analysing qualitative materials. For example, keywords, concepts and other features may be counted. However, most qualitative work is based upon inductive analysis. A good way to tackle this is by using the grounded theory approach. This is a systematic procedure, in which concepts are derived inductively from raw data and linked together into theories; the theories are then tested to maximize their coherency. Qualitative analytical procedures can be enhanced and accelerated by using analytical software. The *NUD-IST* package is one of the more versatile, and allows the coding and indexing of concepts and theories in a flexible way, suitable for grounded theory and other approaches.

REFERENCES

Allen, R.E. and Allen, S.D. (1997) *Winnie-the-Pooh on Problem Solving*. Methuen, London.

Glaser, B. and Strauss, A.L. (1967) *The Discovery of Grounded Theory: strategies for qualitative research*. Aldine, New York.

Hammersley, M. (1990) *The Dilemma of Qualitative Method: Herbert Blumer and the Chicago Tradition*. Routledge, London and New York.

Johns, N. (1994) 'Managing quality', in P.L. Jones and P. Merricks (eds), *The Management of Foodservice Operations*. Cassell, London, pp. 245–61.

Johns, N. and Lee-Ross, D. (1996) 'Profile accumulation: a quality assessment technique for hospitality SMEs', in R. Teare and C. Armistead (eds), *Services Management: New Directions and Perspectives*. Cassell, London.

Lee-Ross, D. (1996) 'A study of attitudes and work motivation amongst seasonal hotel workers', doctoral thesis, Anglia Polytechnic University, Chelmsford.

Mars, G. and Nicod, M. (1984) *The World of Waiters*. London, Allen and Unwin.

Ryan, C. (1995) *Researching Tourist Satisfaction: Issues, Concepts, Problems*. Routledge, London.

Strauss, A. and Corbin, J. (1990) *Basics of Qualitative Research: Grounded Theory Procedures and Techniques*. Sage, London.

Wells, S. (1991) 'Wet towels and whetted appetites or a wet blanket: the role of analysis in qualitative research', *Journal of the Market Research Society*, 33(1), 39–44.

Witt, C.A. and Witt, S.F. (1989) 'Why productivity in the hotel sector is so low', *International Journal of Contemporary Hospitality Management*, 1(2), 28–34.

7

Integrative Research Approaches

INTRODUCTION

Integrative approaches combine two or more different research techniques to obtain multiple data about a single situation. For example, a quantitative technique such as a questionnaire survey can be used to provide a representative overview of a research situation, followed by in-depth interviewing to gain a more detailed view. At the same time, the qualitative study verifies the quantitative findings. The scope for integrating research techniques is wide, and includes combinations of two or more different qualitative methodologies: for example, interviewing and observation.

Integrative approaches make it possible to focus on a particular situation in depth and to combine the benefits of several different research viewpoints. It is also possible to integrate research with professional development, or with actual management intervention, so that the situation is actually changed while it is being researched. Thus integrative approaches tend to be pragmatic in outlook, and very attractive from a practitioner point of view.

Unfortunately, the integration of different techniques raises objections from the point of view of academic rigour. As has already been discussed in other chapters, quantitative work is generally conducted within a hypothetico-deductive, positivistic framework, which is incompatible with the phenomenological stance of qualitative research. Besides this, integrative research is often aimed at narrow study situations, and it is reasonable to question whether the results comprise academic knowledge if they are not applicable to other systems elsewhere. The practice of integrating research and action is also questionable on the basis that it is difficult to identify clearly how much of a project is research and how much is action.

Although there is a wide range of possible techniques from which to choose, the essence of much integrative research is to combine quantitative and qualitative data collection and analysis. There are several reasons for doing this. For example, two independent techniques can be used to support (or test) each other's findings. A mixture of quantitative and qualitative techniques is also a pragmatic way of going about research, because it mirrors the way individuals go about making sense of their everyday environment. It is therefore likely to appeal to service industry managers, because in general it reflects the way they understand and manage their organizations. The integration of methods may seem 'natural' compared with the academicism of rigorously applied quantitative research. Managers are sceptical of rigour, because in order to achieve it, research questions have to be honed very finely. It is relatively easy (and rigorously achievable) to be sure of a tiny piece of knowledge. However, managers tend to see such rigour as 'nit-picking'. They may feel that they need a broader overview, and can afford to dispense with some certainty or precision to get it.

Alternatively, integrative research can take an overall phenomenological stance. Under this circumstance its validity may be similar to that of any other qualitative research approach. As long as the methodology is the centre of focus, it will generally be possible to defend the research on academic grounds. However, under these circumstances any related survey work must be regarded as applying only to the specific situation under study. This means that the resulting findings may not be transferable to other situations, and therefore may not constitute new knowledge in an academic sense. None the less, they may be of great value in practical management terms.

Research projects have to negotiate these considerations in principle, but in reality the situation may be more complex. For instance, what is the methodological position if a tried and tested, positivistically verified, questionnaire instrument is used to verify some qualitative findings? It is also possible to conduct integrative projects where the 'findings' are not the main outcome of the formal research. For example, it is possible to help a group of managers to carry out their own research and to reflect more effectively on their professional practice. In such a case, the managers' research, and more especially its rigour and validity, are of secondary importance. The main findings relate to the managers' ability to reflect upon and improve their practice. The researcher could stand outside the managers' approach and concentrate on assessing their ability to reflect on their work, and any improvements in their professional practice. However, this approach brings problems. One might reasonably question whether such an exercise is actually research, or something else: education, training or project management, for example. The phenomenological stance becomes confused by the question of whose viewpoint the phenomenon is being considered from. The question of ownership also becomes more complex, as the research may be 'owned' by several individuals (or even several *groups* of individuals) to different extents and in different ways.

Integrative research approaches may take a variety of forms. In this chapter they are discussed within a framework of three basic types. *Triangulation* is the term applied to the use of two techniques in order to check each other's results. *Case study research* concentrates on a specific study situation and may use any available technique as long as its appropriateness as a tool can be justified. *Action research* aims to empower active professionals to research their own work situation in order to reflect more effectively upon their practice.

TRIANGULATION APPROACHES

Triangulation is a term derived from land surveying, where it is used to fix the exact positions of topographical features (such as mountains). The principle of triangulation

Figure 7.1 The principle of triangulation

is to take bearings upon an unknown point from two known ones. This makes it possible to establish exactly the angle between the two known points and the unknown. If the compass bearing between the known points is certain, the bearings and the position of the unknown point can be defined (see Figure 7.1). The term triangulation therefore means 'making triangles', from two known points to an unknown one.

In social research, triangulation usually involves comparing the data from two different techniques in order to check the accuracy of each set of results. Frequently this involves comparing quantitative and qualitative data. The objective is to provide a clearer idea of the research situation. Triangulation sometimes takes the positivistic stance that there exists an 'actual picture' which can be measured and described. Qualitative findings may thus be used as a means of checking and even of falsifying a hypothesis, but such a position needs careful justification in philosophical terms.

In principle, there are two main bases for integrating qualitative and quantitative research methods into a single project. A qualitative study may be used to provide insight into a specific research situation prior to proposing hypotheses and drawing up a questionnaire. This approach has already been discussed in Chapter 4. It is also possible to follow a quantitative study with a qualitative one, where the objective is to build upon survey findings by examining the sample in greater depth.

Either of these rationales can be applied in a triangulative approach, but neither represents triangulation *per se*. The essence of triangulation is that techniques are used in a parallel sense, so that they provide *overlapping* information. This is what makes it possible to check results from more than one viewpoint, analogously to geographical triangulation. The techniques used should be carefully selected with this goal in mind. However, the overlap between techniques does not have to be perfect. Many of the benefits from triangulative approaches result from the fact that different techniques cast different lights on a research subject.

Triangulation is commonly employed in commercial research projects. The use of overlapping, mutually supporting, research techniques is often the most effective way to assess the feasibility of a new marketing strategy, or to evaluate a new management initiative. Evaluations of this kind usually need to survey a large sample of people, in order to provide an overview of the research situation. They usually also include an element of interviewing, which allows the researcher to check the survey findings. This enriches the data available for the evaluation, and also allows the survey findings to be verified through an independent research approach.

Qualitative findings used in this way should be linked to 'hard' data about the interview sample. In other words, interviews in the qualitative phase should ask for the same personal details about the respondent as the questionnaires used in the survey. The details required may vary depending upon the purpose and rationale of the survey, but often include gender, age, occupation, family status and geographical location. The first step in triangulation is to compare the survey sample with that used for the interviews. Any other data that have been gathered will be meaningless unless a comparison can be made.

The next stage is to check correspondence between the information provided by interviewees and that obtained from the survey. The survey must already have been subjected to some analysis, enabling an outline picture of the responses to be drawn up. The qualitative findings are then compared with this picture. For example, consider the question from Chapter 5, concerning employees' perceptions of a TQM programme:

	Agree strongly					Disagree strongly
I know what my internal customers need from me	1	2	3	4	5	6	7

Suppose analysis reveals that 80 per cent of the survey sample have indicated a 1, 2 or 3 response. As long as the sample of interviewees corresponds to that in the survey, one would expect interviewees' comments to reflect the same picture. They might simply answer 'yes' to a direct question or generalize a little more by saying something like 'most of them, yes'. Both of these responses show that the individuals understand who their internal customer is, and that in general they feel they know what their internal customers require. If approximately 80 per cent of interviewees answer in this way, the survey result is confirmed. However, this is an over-simplification, since triangulation generally relates to a web of interrelated hypotheses.

In such a case, qualitative results do not *only* confirm or refute the survey findings. Usually they also give a clearer picture of the research situation, by providing further information which the survey could not have obtained. Some respondents may comment in more depth about the phrase 'I know what my internal customers need from me'. For example, they may say that the people who supply *them* in the TQM chain do not seem to have understood the internal customer concept. Or they may say that they distrust management's motives in introducing the TQM initiative. Or it may transpire that the individual feels that he or she knows what the internal customer requires, but that the internal customer does not. All of these findings make valuable contributions to the research. However, they may be quite difficult to interpret in the black-and-white context of the original question. Triangulation frequently calls for interpretation and perhaps further data-gathering.

The use of qualitative methods in an essentially quantitative research programme overlaps to some extent with the processes of questionnaire development and piloting, discussed in Chapter 4. A period of qualitative work is often necessary before a questionnaire is drawn up, in order to clarify hypotheses, and to identify the most appropriate questions to ask and the best way to ask them. Before any questionnaire is issued to the full survey sample, it should be tested with typical respondents and feedback obtained, in the process known as 'piloting'. This usually involves interviews or focus groups at the start, progressing to a limited survey with quantitative analysis. The purpose of piloting is to check whether questions are appropriate and relevant and whether respondents understand them.

Thus, a qualitative research element of some kind is generally included in survey work. Its purpose is to get in close to the respondents and identify their feelings and concerns in sharper focus than can be provided by the questionnaire. In particular, it allows the researcher to access the individual characteristics which a survey seeks to 'smooth out' as random 'noise' using statistical methods. This can be very illuminating, since most surveys assume that their wording is understood in similar terms by all respondents. In fact, every respondent may interpret the wording differently.

Qualitative techniques can be used to study this phenomenon. For example, Johns and Tyas (1997) used interviews to study the way restaurant guests understood questions in the standard SERVQUAL instrument of Parasuraman *et al.* (1986). Respondents completed the questionnaire and were then interviewed to discover why they had responded in the particular way they did. Two of the response sequences were as follows:

Interviewer: 'Premises are convenient to get to in the time available'. You gave this question 4 [out of seven]. Was the restaurant difficult for you to get to?

Respondent 1: That depends on where you are coming from. Yes if you're coming from the city, no if you're coming from out of town. I was with a group of friends and after we had been shopping we happened to go that way. Supposing we had gone the other way?

Respondent 2: ... It's next door to where I live. It might have been different if I'd had to drive, because it's difficult to get in and out of the car park. But I put a 4 because I don't know who you meant. [Pause] And anyway I don't like all these people coming to **** and parking in the street outside my house.

This question had been piloted by a number of research groups, including Johns and Tyas, before it was administered. Yet despite this it was clearly still not being understood in the sense or context that was intended.

Johns and Tyas (1997) proposed that mythologies become attached to different service contexts, and that these mythologies define the language in which the service is understood. Mythologies (and hence the language in which they are couched) vary across cultures and contexts. They have profound effects upon the way questions should be asked and the answers interpreted.

A simple example of a mythology at work is apparent in a question such as 'Do you like to eat cornflakes?' Cornflakes are regarded in our culture as a breakfast food, typically eaten at home (British people notoriously tend to have the full English breakfast while staying away from home). Cornflakes also have overtones of vegetarianism (i.e. they do not contain meat) and health (they are associated with added vitamins and with fibre). In order to elicit the most precise information, the question needs to include or exclude these overtones of meaning. This could be done, for example, by asking 'Do you like to eat cornflakes for breakfast ... when you are away from home ... when you are on a diet?' Yet each of these modified versions carries further connotations, the implications of which may not be clear from questionnaire responses. It is in such circumstances that triangulation may shed fresh light on the research situation and challenge assumptions about it.

Triangulation is not restricted to comparing quantitative and qualitative results. It may also employ different qualitative techniques to provide a more meaningful view of a research situation. For example, observation can be used to verify or challenge information provided during interviews. It is quite common for people to say, and even believe, that they behave in one particular way when actually they do something quite different. Triangulation can be used to check the truth of informants' statements. Frequently it also provides useful insights which suggest new lines of enquiry and new interview schedules. For instance, it may be worthwhile to challenge interview subjects to explain the observations and to comment on the differences between what they say and what they actually do.

In addition, triangulation may use documentary evidence to check interview or observational findings. For example, minutes of meetings, letters, memos and official records all provide opportunities to check actions, intentions and statements. Documentary evidence is usually dated and allows a sequence of events to be analysed in a way that would be impossible (or at best highly subject to error) on the basis of interview information.

CASE STUDIES

Case study research typically employs multiple sources of information to study a single, limited situation through one particular contemporary period of time. It is somewhat different from triangulation, which regards the research techniques it uses as parallel, employing them in such a way that they counteract each other's weaknesses and reduce bias. In contrast, case study research is a *focusing* approach. As it proceeds it examines an ever smaller portion of the research situation (the *case*) in ever greater depth and detail. Case study method thus has a different philosophy and emphasis from triangulation. Rather than seeking to optimize a configuration of research methods, it aims to view a research situation from *as many sides as possible*, in order to build up a rich data picture about it. In principle, each stage of the case study focusing process may require a different research technique. Case study method undoubtedly offers benefits similar to those of triangulation, because at root it is still a collection of different research methods which may complement one another. In addition, the case study research process is flexible, developing as it proceeds to account for unexpected issues which may arise or which are deemed important by participants.

MANAGING COMPLEXITY

Case study research is particularly useful where areas of perceived complexity exist. For this reason it is increasingly being recognized as having a distinctive place in evaluation research (see Cronbach *et al.*, 1980). Yin (1989, p. 23) provides a useful summary of case study research as:

> an empirical enquiry that ... investigates a contemporary phenomenon within its real-life context; when the boundaries between phenomenon and context are not

clearly evident; and in which multiple sources of evidence are used. The approach attempts to explain causal links in real-life that are too complex for surveys or experimental strategies, in situations where a description of the real-life context is necessary.

Complexity is generally recognized to be a feature of service organizations. Case study method is therefore ideally suited to pragmatic studies of actual service management situations. Its freedom to use a variety of techniques to obtain its data is likely to appeal to managers. However, from the viewpoint of methodological rigour, it is correspondingly difficult to defend.

A useful tool for the study and analysis of complex situations is soft systems methodology, discussed in Chapter 2, which is particularly useful for case study research. It provides a framework for identifying the case as a system with a more or less permeable boundary. Interaction between the case and its environment (i.e. its supersystem) can be identified and described. Features present within the case can be defined as subsystems and their interactions studied and recorded. Soft systems methodology also provides a tool for looking at 'what if' scenarios and hence for developing a coherent theoretical framework with which to model the case.

ANATOMY OF A CASE STUDY

Case study research should start from a clear strategy, firm enough to provide a basis to start the work, but flexible enough to allow further adaptation as the research proceeds. An example of a case study strategy is shown diagrammatically in Figure 7.2. Continuous arrows in the figure show the relative contributions from each research method, while the broken arrows show the influence of the methods on each other.

This particular study set out to investigate the work attitudes of hotel employees in a seaside tourist resort. The case 'boundary' was defined geographically as the seaside town and its travel-to-work area. The first step in the study was a survey of employees' attitudes, using a standard questionnaire instrument (Hackman and Oldham's 1980 Job Diagnostic Survey). In this way it was possible to sample a reasonable proportion of the whole employee population and to access rich data about variations in work attitudes between different categories of employees.

Thereafter, the methods tended to be more qualitative and exploratory in order to focus progressively upon the research situation and build an increasingly rich picture of the case. The latter stages of the research were concerned with exploring employees' views of their world and with integrating hypotheses. Each research method is discussed in some detail below, in order to demonstrate how different techniques may be used together in a typical case study approach.

Survey Phase

Hackman and Oldham's Job Diagnostic Survey (JDS) is a well-documented questionnaire instrument, known to give reproducible results. Its three sections allow the job attitudes of employees to be measured and the measurements internally checked. It has been used with employees from a number of industries, job types and geographical locations, and Hackman and Oldham (1980) have published a detailed model relating its findings to work motivation and employee satisfaction.

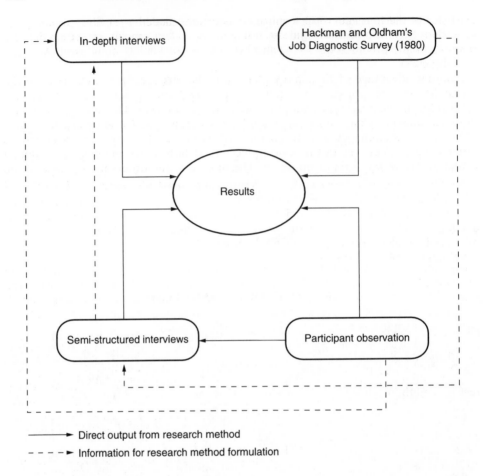

Figure 7.2 Research design

The JDS seemed a suitable starting point for the case study because it could be used with a large number of employees. This would provide an overview of attitudes, which could be segmented into different employee subgroups and compared with published information. The questionnaire would thus have three functions:

- a normative view of a large sample of the employee population;
- a means of studying any segmental variations within the sample/population;
- a means of comparing the case population with other industrial, social and geographical situations.

When the survey was carried out it showed few identifiable differences between demographic segments (based on gender, age, and education). However, the sample could be divided into four clear segments in terms of employment aspirations and behaviour. Four subgroups were identified. There were those who aspired to year-round (permanent) work but lived at their place of work, those who aspired to year-round work but lived at home, those who aspired only to seasonal work and 'lived in' and those who aspired to seasonal work but lived at home. The demonstrated existence of the four subgroups confirmed assertions made by previous authors. The subgroups became a basis for understanding the prevalent subcultures within the case population and provided questions and hypotheses for further study using the other techniques.

Another advantage of the survey phase was the 'distance' it placed between the researcher and the subjects. It was felt that there might be a tendency for 'blind spots' to develop if the researcher was too close to the subjects. The survey phase was intended to identify and clarify the main features of the case situation and to suggest ways for the focusing process to go forward. However, this 'distance' also had its disadvantages. A survey of this kind reduces its data to a few numbers, providing a broad overview, but little or no detail. The interview and observation phases of the research provided this detail, but brought the researcher into close contact with the subjects, possibly jeopardizing objectivity.

Observation Phase

Observation is the second stage of the research strategy. In practice, it continued on an *ad hoc* basis throughout the study, and whenever hotels were visited for the purposes of interview. Wherever possible, observational information was used to design and interpret interviews. Observation represented a simple way to build an overview of what was happening within the case situation.

In order to fulfil this phase, the researcher worked as a hotel manager in the seaside resort during part of the research period. This permitted 'type II' observation (see Chapter 6), where the observer acted as a participant, was known to the subjects but was distanced from them. It gave the researcher access to a variety of sources which would not otherwise have been available. For instance, it was possible to establish working relationships with the managers of other tourist facilities in the town, and also with the local office of the Department of Social Security, which played a significant part in the lives of many seasonal employees.

Participant observation is said to be holistic, searching for 'realism' by looking at a range of activities and their interconnections, rather than focusing on a single activity. In the present case, observations provided a great deal of valuable anecdotal evidence which supported and tested other findings. The four employee segments identified by the survey were clearly differentiated by their lifestyles and behaviour, particularly their leisure and community activities. For example, aspirants to seasonal work all tended to spend a great deal of time drinking, gambling and joking with their fellows. Aspirants to full-time work did the same if they 'lived in' at their place of work. If they lived at home they were mostly concerned with home-making and with their family life.

Participant observation in the role of hotel manager enabled observations to be made continuously, and information could be gathered in a relatively stress-free, unhurried fashion. Observational data suggested a number of concepts that were used to build up hypotheses about the case. For example, the observation phase explored the idea and influence of an 'occupational community' in which 'surrogate family relationships' developed. These appeared to have a marked effect upon employees' attitudes. The researcher spent enough time in hotel jobs and with employees outside the workplace to identify whether worker attitudes changed systematically during the time they spent at a particular establishment.

Observation is a relatively straightforward and unsophisticated way of gathering data, yet it permits a very close study of the complexities of a case. For this reason, it allows the researcher to appreciate the situation in a wider view than may be possible with other methods. In the present case it allowed the attitudes and motivation of employees to be understood in ways that would not have been possible by interviews or questionnaires alone.

Observation may affect the behaviour of research subjects, due to the presence of the researcher. This acknowledged drawback may be controlled in two ways. The researcher can act covertly (as Mars and Nicod (1984) did in their study), changing the research style to one of 'type I' observation. Alternatively, the researcher can develop and maintain a rapport with the participants. In the present study, the researcher occupied a role that brought him into contact with employees, yet also kept him apart from them to some extent. The employees undoubtedly became accustomed to his presence, and it was not necessary to act covertly, or to overplay the researcher's role.

Semi-structured Interview Phase

Semi-structured interviews were used to gather information about work attitudes, work history, leisure activities and employee qualifications. These results were compared with the findings of the questionnaire survey, which they generally supported. Semi-structured interviews consisted of a mixture of precoded and short-answer, open-ended questions. They elicited biographical data about the respondents, such as age, gender and marital status, as well as attitudinal and behavioural details.

Some interview questions were based on employees' responses to the JDS questionnaire, and others were centred on the researcher's observations. Another series of questions was adapted from the work of other authors in a similar research area. Open-ended questions allowed respondents to supplement the data they gave with opinions and attitudes about their work. Demographic questions allowed direct comparisons to be made across worker subgroups and made it possible to check the representativeness of the sample. The data obtained in this way overlapped with both survey and observation findings. They could therefore be used to check results that had been obtained previously, substantiating and explaining data from the first two phases of the research strategy. Semi-structured interviews also provided further attitudinal information and were used to contextualize and explain data from the other sources.

In-depth Interviews

The final stage of the focusing procedure used in-depth interviews. They were structured as 'guided conversations' in which the researcher steered respondents around specific topic areas in whatever order seemed appropriate at the time. The objective was to ensure a free response so that the informant could discuss issues or add anything important. In this responsive situation a particular reply could be re-examined during the interview itself in the context of the interviewee's other replies. In this way, the in-depth interviews were able to provide a high level of contextual understanding.

In-depth interviews reduce the 'distance' between interviewer and interviewee. In this case interviewees were more willing to reveal details about themselves and their

Table 7.1 Summary of samples

Phase of research	Sample size	Time required per respondent
Survey	168	About 30 minutes
Observation	Various, including casual comments of workers, discussions with other managers and DSS personnel	Various
Semi-structured interviews	30	45 minutes
In-depth interviews	16	90 minutes

organization because they did not perceive the interview situation as threatening. Like the semi-structured interviews, in-depth interviews noted demographic details of respondents, so that their findings could be correlated with the other results. In-depth interview results correlated well with the results from other phases of the study, but also provided further insight into the lives and attitudes of the employee subgroups. This took the form of anecdotes and comments, which were presented as evidence when the research was reported.

A summary of the samples used for the four different research techniques is presented in Table 7.1. Data from the four phases of the study were systematically examined for concepts. Concepts were also identified when the results from different phases of the case study were compared with one another. The concepts were assembled into hypotheses which were successively tested until a coherent, integrated theoretical structure emerged. This structure formed the basis for understanding the case.

ACTION RESEARCH

Triangulation and case study methods are forms of research in which the researcher is an external agent looking at a research situation from (more or less) an external viewpoint. In action research an attempt is made to work from within the research situation itself, through the perceptions of members of an organization, i.e. managers or employees, in order to enhance operational practice. This brings advantages to both researcher and researched, and can provide very interesting and stimulating research situations. It also brings further difficult questions of methodology and research ethics.

The idea of an external researcher is common to most forms of social and management research. The researcher, often a consultant engaged by the organization that is being researched, comes from outside the research situation, and looks in upon it. This is true even where an anthropological or ethnographic stance is adopted. For instance, in the example presented in the previous section, observational data were obtained by working within the case situation as a manager. However, the researcher came from outside the case situation, and made observations of employees without himself being an employee. The data were used for preparing a doctoral thesis (Lee-Ross, 1996) rather than for informing other practitioners within the case situation.

Action research (e.g. Sanger, 1989) aims to set up a team of practitioner-researchers with a rigorous, research-based orientation. In principle, the 'researcher' is independent of the research that is occurring, and only acts as a facilitator. (In organizations, this function is normally associated with management consultants.) The facilitator may select the members of the action research team, with the help of the management of the organization which is being studied. He or she accustoms members of the team to the action research philosophy and may provide advice: for instance, suggesting appropriate research techniques. The research facilititator may also gather or analyse data when requested by the team. The facilitator generally summarizes the findings and may chair or advise the meetings.

The action research process can be represented as shown in Figure 7.3. It begins with the induction of team members into the philosophy of the action research approach. Alternating phases of planning, data collection and data analysis then take place, producing a progressively richer picture of the research situation. The action research model demands rigorous reflection after each data collection phase, and a progressive focusing on the research problem from the action team's standpoint. In this sense it resembles the case study method. Like the case study method, it is usually used in research situations which are limited in terms of the organizations, geographical area and time scale involved. Action research adopts a phenomenological stance and generally aims to describe the research phenomenon from the viewpoint of the participant team, rather than that of the researcher/facilitator.

Hypotheses are generated in an inductive way through the action research team's discussions as the data collection and reflection occur. They are progressively developed, tested, modified and reformulated. In essence this process is an informal version of the enhanced model of scientific enquiry shown as Figure 1.8 in Chapter 1, where successive observations may give rise to hypotheses (induction), test hypotheses (hypothetico-deduction) or act as anecdotes to suggest new lines of enquiry. However, the testing of hypotheses in action research situations is inevitably less rigorous than that in the natural sciences.

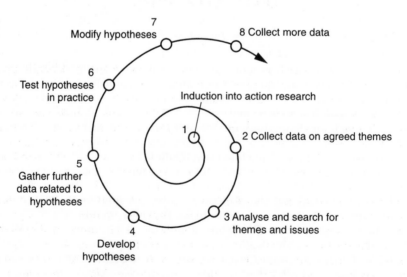

Figure 7.3   Action research model

Action research is essentially a problem-solving strategy. It approaches research situations through practitioners' eyes and uses problem-solving techniques familiar to managers wherever possible. A key benefit of the action research approach is that members of the organization itself are empowered to change and develop their own working culture. The research work of individuals and teams tends to produce a climate of open discourse, depersonalized debate and a resolution of conflict and tensions. The resulting participative environment facilitates frank exchanges of views, making it possible to bring different levels of organizational hierarchy together in a positive way. Thus learning, professional development, and cultural and behavioural change may all be outcomes of an action research project.

In practical terms, the facilitator role involves a mixture of administrative and research-related tasks, as follows:

1   The facilitator must plan the research carefully and integrate it into the organization's own schedule, so that it fits naturally. It may also be necessary to ensure that results are produced in a particular time-frame: so that they are available for a particular 'watershed' meeting, for example.

2   The research team must be identified, motivated and persuaded to participate. They should be individuals involved with parts of the organization where the research is particularly relevant: for example, key departments, key activities or key levels of management. Usually it is necessary to arrange this with senior managers in the organization, since the scheduling of meetings may have repercussions upon resources, timetabling or release from work.

3   A series of meetings must be arranged. At the first of these, the team is introduced to the concept and philosophy of action research. At subsequent meetings they identify suitable ways to proceed with data gathering and analysis, share findings, and analyse and reflect upon them.

4   The facilitator is responsible for reminding team members of meetings, minuting them and ensuring that each meeting has the information it needs. The facilitator may also need to steer the meetings to ensure that they stay on track and achieve their objectives.

5   The facilitator may also carry out some data collection if this is required by the team or by the research plan. The facilitator may also need to get data analysed, if this is beyond the team's means or skill.

In an 'ideal' action research model, the type of data collected depends upon the wishes of the team. They may include observations and recorded interviews, as well as minutes and documentation from the meetings themselves. The style of working means that an action research team cannot justifiably adopt a positivistic attitude to its work, although teams sometimes opt to carry out an informal survey. An inductive approach is usually the main basis for analysing the data. However, action research situations frequently deal with much-studied themes (for example, TQM and organizational culture), and quite often need to take account of existing theoretical constructs.

Action research usually adopts a case study approach to its work, so that there is a progressive focusing upon the research subject. However, in principle it is possible to develop action research investigations in other ways. The nature of the techniques used often reflects the interests and skills of the participant research team. On the other hand, this 'idealized model' is not the only way to conduct action research. The facilitator may take a more prominent role in choosing the team, setting the agenda or analysing the results. Alternatively, the research goals and techniques may be more or less imposed from outside the research team, by the organization's senior management or by a sponsoring funding body.

Thus, in methodological terms, the facilitator role may be a very complex one. It may have to concern itself with issues of language and communication, behaviour, status, power and communication. It may also have to reconcile quantitative and qualitative aspects of the work. Frequently, the action team's perceptions of what 'research' is about must be brought into line with case study philosophy. Eden and Huxham (1996) note that the action research model is a very attractive one for aspiring higher degree students in management. However, they caution against its use in such studies, suggesting that quantitative and traditional qualitative approaches are preferable, because their methodologies and analytical strategies are widely accepted and need little further justification.

ACADEMIC VERSUS PRACTICAL ACTION RESEARCH

Action research is difficult to justify in terms of rigour. It can certainly claim that it deals with problems as they are perceived by problem-owners. On the other hand, the fact that the research situation is seen through the eyes of people immersed within it may be a drawback. Their involvement may inhibit their wider perception, or they may concentrate upon desiderata (what might be) rather than the pre-assumed and therefore 'uninteresting' facts of the case. Besides this, action research shares with case study method problems of wider applicability and external validity.

Eden and Huxham (1996) propose twelve criteria to which action research should conform if it is to claim academic rigour and acceptability. They suggest that these should always be applied to action research projects undertaken in a business setting. The criteria neatly encapsulate the potential gulf that exists between academic and practical needs in vocational subjects such as service industry management, as discussed below.

1 There must be some implications beyond the findings and actions required by the project itself. However, the generalizability of findings may not be of interest to managers, who are usually not interested in situations outside their own sphere of activity.

2 Action research findings must be both usable in everyday life and explicitly concerned with theory. A theoretical context is ultimately of use to both practitioners and academics, but tends to be overlooked as such.

3 It is not enough to draw generality from the action research findings themselves. The basis upon which the action research project is planned and executed must also be explicitly related to theory. However, this restriction would seriously prejudice many practical research projects, because it would prevent all but academically research-trained individuals taking part in the research design. Relatively few managers are likely to fit into this category.

4 Theory should emerge from action research as a synthesis of the inductive findings with what has already been published on the research subject area. In principle it is valuable to both managers and academics to draw from and build on the academic knowledge base. The problem is that at the time of writing it is comparatively rare for practising managers to take an interest in published academic theory of this kind.

5 Theory building should be incremental, moving from the specific to the general in small steps. This is natural and reasonable in any research context.
6 Presenters of action research findings should be clear about the requirements of the research 'customer', and should present the findings in accordance with this aim. This item identifies the role of the facilitator/researcher as a consultant, outside the organization. Alternatively, the researcher might be working on behalf of a funding agency: for example, with a number of small businesses. It may be still more effective to use skills from within the organization itself if this is feasible.
7 Action research should be conducted with a high degree of method and orderliness, in which the phases of the work can be clearly perceived. This criterion is true of all research, and the only problem may be in reconciling the wishes of a team of individuals when identifying an acceptable methodology.
8 The process of exploring/analysing the data should be either replicable or demonstrable through argument or analysis. This is specifically an academic requirement, where self-consciousness of process is often a goal in itself.
9 The eight contentions outlined above are necessary, but not in themselves a sufficient condition for the validity of action research.
10 Data collection and reflection should be focused only upon research aspects which could not be captured by any means other than an action research model. This statement seems to demonstrate that the authors (Eden and Huxham, 1996) distrust action research as a model and would prefer it to be used only as a last resort.
11 Opportunities for triangulation which are not available through other research models should be exploited fully, but also used to enhance the incremental development of theory. This item restates the importance of theory to academic research, but not necessarily to practical action research.
12 The history and context of the action research project must be taken as critical for the likely range of validity and applicability of the findings.

In fact, action research is a very attractive management tool. It seems able to combine research with action, and hence to reduce costs. The empowerment aspect of action research, together with its open format, make it particularly appropriate for investigating 'organic' management initiatives that are typically used in service industries. For example, it is widely recognized that service quality improvement must come at the level of front-line staff, and that it must be flexibly and organically engineered. The operation of quality teams within a continuous quality improvement programme represents a highly appropriate subject for action research programmes.

PHILOSOPHICAL ISSUES OF CASE STUDIES AND ACTION RESEARCH

A considerable battery of research techniques can be brought to bear upon a case study, usually in such a way as to provide closer and closer focusing upon the research situation. This gives the researcher the feeling of being in control of the data, so that he or she seems to be seeing 'what is actually there'. Case studies may use both quantitative and qualitative techniques in the same project.

In the social sciences, quantitative research assumes that knowledge is objective, factual and waiting to be proved or disproved. It is also assumed that this knowledge can be used to explain events and generalized to make predictions. On the other hand, qualitative research provides a richness, colour and depth of description which quantitative research is obliged to ignore. As Withams (1992, p. 107) comments:

> Real people and their work settings cannot be explored and described solely in terms of objective data and associated statistics.

The case study method takes the pragmatic view that research problems should be approached using the best means available. Effective case study research models frequently draw upon several techniques, reflecting a range of methodological stances. The methodological domain of all research processes is characterized by a conflicting set of desiderata, as follows:

- generalizability with respect to the populations of individuals, situations or conditions to which the information applies;
- precision with respect to the measurement and control of the behavioural and situational variables that are involved;
- realism with respect to contexts, or behavioural systems, to which that information is intended to apply.

In principle, these criteria all demand to be maximized at the same time, but in real research situations this is impossible. Methodologies designed to maximize one aspect always diminish one or more of the others. No set of research procedures can optimize all criteria simultaneously. The researcher needs to adopt a research strategy which offers the best trade-off between the desired criteria, i.e. the most appropriate for the study situation.

Case study research restricts itself to a narrowly defined study situation, usually limited to a particular environment and geographical area and to the time-frame of the data-gathering process itself. Findings may be generalizable to other comparable situations or systems, but this is not a claim of the case study approach. Rather, it aims to provide a glimpse of how the wider picture might look, or possibly a reference frame from which researchers elsewhere might begin parallel studies, or benchmark their findings.

Thus, where quantitative and qualitative techniques are used to examine a case study, researchers are not really 'marrying' positivist and phenomenological stances. The use of quantitative and qualitative techniques can certainly provide a clearer picture of the research situation. However, the nature of case study situations means that the researcher's actual stance is unlikely to be anything but phenomenological. The way in which this is actually expressed will vary from situation to situation, but must be kept perpetually in mind as the research progresses.

Action research projects introduce further methodological and ethical problems. For instance, at least two levels of activity may be occurring in an action research project. In principle, the results of an action research project may be of interest in much the same way as a conventional case study. For example, they may represent a feasibility study or an evaluation of a management initiative. However, at the same time, the research process itself has an influence upon the organization, since part of its objective is to make active professionals reflect upon their practice. Thus not only the results of the nominal action research team, but also its effects, may be treated as research findings.

However, this leads to a confusion of research with action. Action researchers are by definition involved in the situation that they are attempting to research. This makes it impossible for them to claim objectivity or detachment, and this further detracts from the rigour of the research process. Moreover, the case itself may change as a direct result of the research, as the participants gain new skills or knowledge. Thus, in principle, what is being researched at the beginning of the programme may be different from what is being researched at the end. This must reduce the effect of any triangulation, since the two techniques used cannot generally be brought to bear upon the same problem at the same time.

In theory, an 'ideal' action research project looks at a research situation through the eyes of practitioners. However, to do so absolutely requires a situation where the practitioners themselves identify the need for the action research. In such a position, external intervention is minimal and restricted to the presence of the researcher/facilitator alone. In principle, researchers can be trained to work in ways which further reduce this intervention. However, this is by no means the usual picture in organizations. In such cases, research, including action research, is a management tool. Its objective is to identify problems in order to change situations, i.e. specifically to intervene. The action research format is usually chosen to reduce employees' resistance to the intervention by giving participants a sense of ownership of the research.

Thus there is generally a philosophical conflict of ownership with action research in business organizations. Top management pays for the research in the hope that it will change circumstances within the organization. Middle management and employees participate in it partly because they are instructed to do so, but also because it empowers them and gives a sense of ownership. Academic researchers may seek to 'own' certain aspects of the research, usually as data for thesis or project work. In this case, ownership is more subtle and often dependent upon the methodological rigour that has been used to carry out the work, and the philosophical rigour needed to defend it.

CONCLUSIONS

Integrative approaches use a variety of techniques in order to gain a clearer view of a research situation. Three main types – triangulation, case study and action research – have been discussed. All differ in terms of outcome and methodological stance. (See Figure 7.4.)

Triangulative methods compare results obtained by two different techniques. The two techniques are carefully chosen so that they overlap in a parallel way as far as possible. Their strengths are intended to be complementary, in order to reduce bias and error as much as possible. Triangulative methods may take a positivistic stance to research if they are based on a quantitative approach. They can also take a phenomenological viewpoint.

Case study research uses different techniques in order to focus progressively on to the research situation. The techniques used are generally chosen specifically for this purpose, but also usually overlap to some extent, so that some triangulation is possible. The case study method generally adopts a phenomenological stance and the results may not be truly generalizable outside the specific research situation. A strength of the method is its ability to uncover complexity within a research situation. Soft systems methodology may be appropriate as an analytical tool for managing this complexity.

In action research, teams composed of the research subjects themselves plan and carry out the research. The role of the 'researcher' may be far-reaching, or it may be

Triangulation: observer distanced from both the research situation
and any subsequent intervention

Case study: observer involved in the research situation but distanced
from any subsequent intervention

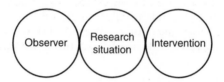

Action research: observer involved in the research situation and in
the intervention to some extent

Figure 7.4   Triangulation, case study and action research

restricted merely to facilitating the research process. The research situation can therefore be viewed through the eyes of the participants. Action research aims to encourage reflective professional practice among members of the research team, and therefore in principle the study situation is changed by the research.

Integrative methods are often very popular with service industry practitioners. Triangulation gives a clearer image of a research situation. Case study research focuses upon one specific situation or problem, rather than making 'irrelevant' generalizations. Action research offers an organic, empowering way to change organizational culture and modify work behaviour.

However, all integrative research approaches bring methodological problems of some kind. Those encountered with triangulation are the fewest, and relate to the differences of philosophical stance that exist between specific methodologies. More severe problems are found with the case study method, because considerable generalizability is also lost. The most severe difficulties are encountered with action research, where the researcher's own role must be identified, together with the 'boundary' between research and intervention.

Despite these problems, it seems likely that integrative methods hold the key to the development of research in service industries. It is up to researchers to strive continually for recognition for one of the most exciting areas in the world of research.

REFERENCES

Argyris, C.R. (1985) *Action Science*. Jossey-Bass, San Francisco.

Cronbach, L.J. *et al.* (1980) *Toward Reform of Program Evaluation: Aims, Methods and Institutional Arrangements*. Jossey-Bass, San Francisco.

Denzin, N.K. (1970) *The Research Act in Sociology*. Aldine, Chicago.

Eden, C. and Huxham, C. (1996) 'Action research for management research', *British Journal of Management*, 7, 75–80.

Hackman, J.R. and Oldham, G.R. (1980) *Work Design*. Addison-Wesley, Reading, MA.

Johns, N. and Chesterton, J. (1994) 'ICL Kidsgrove: snapshot of a changing culture', in R. Teare (ed.), *Achieving Quality Performance: Lessons from British Industry*. Cassell, London, pp. 79–110.

Johns, N. and Tyas, P. (1997) 'Customer perceptions of service operations: *Gestalt*, incident or mythology?' *Service Industries Journal*, 17(3), 474–88.

Lee-Ross, D. (1996) 'A study of attitudes and work motivation amongst seasonal hotel workers', PhD Thesis, Anglia Polytechnic University, Chelmsford.

Mars, G. and Nicod, M. (1984) *The World of Waiters*. Allen and Unwin, London.

Parasuraman, A., Zeithaml, V.A. and Berry, L.L. (1986) 'SERVQUAL: a multiple-item scale for measuring customer perceptions of service quality', Marketing Science Institute, *Working Paper Report No. 86–108* (August).

Sanger, J. (1989) *Teaching, Handling Information and Learning*. British Library Research and Development publications, Boston Spa.

Schon, D. (1983) *The Reflective Practitioner*. Basic Books, New York.

Silverman, D. (1993) *Interpreting Qualitative Data*. Sage, London.

Withams, S.C. (1992) 'The work of senior nurse managers: demands and conflicts', PhD Thesis, De Montfort University, Leicester.

Yin, R.K. (1989) *Case Study Research: Design and Methods*. Sage, London.

8

Writing, Reporting and Publishing

INTRODUCTION

Practically every research project is eventually expressed, discussed, justified and evaluated in a research report. Report writing is the most effective way to summarize and evaluate the methods, outcomes and significance of research projects. Underlying the production of a report is the process of communication between the writer and the reader, which always aims to transmit complex information as economically as possible. Report writing is not only an essential research skill, but also a life skill, because communication can be applied to a wide variety of practical situations. Reports may vary in function and structure, depending upon their purpose and intended readership. There is no single 'ideal' type of report, and different subject areas tend to favour particular styles. However, all reports can be regarded as possessing a number of common features. This chapter discusses the communication issues inherent in report writing and identifies the basic structural elements which make up an effective report.

Not all research reports are published, but publication is increasingly being recognized as a primary goal of academic research. Publication allows the sharing of research findings, and encourages peer group discussion, a cornerstone of the academic process. It also promotes subject development, by providing an inter-institutional forum in which research work can be constructively criticized. In addition, publication is one of the main ways in which research findings become incorporated into higher education curricula. For these reasons, this chapter also discusses the publication process in detail and makes recommendations for those who wish to put forward their work for inclusion in a book or journal.

THE COMMUNICATION PROCESS

A research report is a direct communication, which sets out to transmit ideas and data from the researcher to an audience. As with other forms of communication, successful

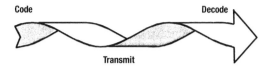

Code Decode Transmit

Figure 8.1   A simple model of the communication process

reporting depends upon three different activities, shown in Figure 8.1. The researcher *encodes* information and *transmits* it to members of the audience. These individuals must then *decode* the information (and to some extent tailor it to their own needs) in order to make use of it.

- *Encoding* must take account of the nature of the information and the nature of the code. This process assumes that the code is intelligible to the recipient (i.e. the recipient understands the ideas expressed in terms similar to those intended by the writer) and that the recipient is interested in the information.
- *Transmission* may just be a matter of photocopying, binding and posting off the report to a named list of individuals. This is usually the case with internal reports in business organizations. Publications, however, depend for their effectiveness upon a third party, the publisher or academic referee, who must be persuaded that the research results are likely to be interesting to readers and pitched in such a way that they can be decoded.
- *Decoding* is at the mercy of the recipient and involves a trade-off between the interest value and the way it is expressed. Recipients must find the contents of the report sufficiently interesting to make the arduous process of decoding worthwhile. Decoding is likely to be more difficult if words are used in an unaccustomed sense, or express very precise shades of meaning. Complicated diagrams and abstruse formulae also make the process difficult. Decoding is always a very subjective process and generally involves a certain amount of translation (i.e. reinterpretation of terms and meanings).

Thus, the objective of a research report is to present as much valuable information as possible in the form that is simplest to decode. In practice this may bring a variety of problems. Codes have to conform to certain rules. For example, an academic research paper must convince its readers that it has reviewed data objectively, and must summarize the work of others in an acceptable way. Simple, direct language is best – as close as possible to the spoken word – and diagrams should be made as familiar as possible. This can present problems, because a research paper cannot afford to be considered frivolous. In fact, many authors have a tendency to write research reports in rather formal, stilted English, which is often more complex than is necessary to avoid 'frivolity'. There seem to be three possible causes for this. For some writers, formality seems to equate almost to personal dignity. Others may be unsure of the appropriate level, and may be over-formal (and hence over-complicated) in order to err on the side of caution. Sometimes, too, formal language may be used to mask an underlying insecurity or confusion about the content or value of the work. The ideal English style is a simple direct one, phrased as closely as possible to natural spoken English, but lacking the hesitations, imprecisions and duplications which are common in everyday speech.

PRACTICAL COMMUNICATION

On the basis of the code–transmit–decode model it is possible to divide practical written communication into the following five basic steps:

1   Identify the intended recipient.
2   Identify what is to be communicated.
3   Encode the information.
4   Check the coding.
5   Check the decoding.

The Intended Recipient

Before any effective communication can begin, it is important to identify the audience to whom the communication is addressed. A research audience can best be identified by asking the questions: 'Who will want to know the results of the research?' and 'To whom might the results of the research be useful?' Researchers usually need to bear in mind that they themselves are much more committed to their research than any audience, and know much more about it. Audiences usually have specific interests which can be met by discussing the work from a particular standpoint. For example, an academic audience may prefer a theoretical stance, while an audience of industrialists usually likes a practical, businesslike one. Identifying the audience also makes it possible to choose a periodical in which to publish the research and to consider the style and language in which to couch the article.

The Substance of the Communication

Choosing an audience also makes it possible to choose the content of the article. This involves asking the questions: 'What interest will the audience have in the results?' and perhaps 'How might the audience use the information?' Writing up research may be likened to the 'artist's window' problem, i.e. which part of a view should be selected to form the subject of a painting. This involves choosing the scope and scale of the 'picture' (the angle of view, the size of the subject, the proportion of subject to background, etc.) and deciding where to put the 'frame' and form its boundary. Thus, the process of encoding information begins with identifying and rationalizing the ideas and data that are to be communicated. This varies with the nature of the audience, who must feel immediately that the discussion and results will be interesting enough to justify the work of decoding the article. This may be difficult, because most reports are completed at the end of research projects and the author has often been intimately immersed in the work for a long period. Thus, it is hard to get an outsider's perspective or to see which part of the research is most likely to appeal to an uninvolved spectator. This may make it particularly difficult to put the work into perspective or to identify the aspects which are most interesting to uninvolved spectators. There may also be a tension in considering the *report* as an entity rather than the research problem. This is even truer for a general publication than for a limited access report. A good way to manage this aspect of the communication process may be to regard the main research project as an unfolding series of subprojects, which can be published as a series of articles as work progresses. Authors can become practised at identifying subtopics in their work, and can exploit publishing opportunities as they crop up. This helps to overcome the 'artist's window' problem, helps to develop writing skills and also keeps the main project on track.

Example 8.1   A Series of Reports from One Project

Darren Lee-Ross was able to produce a number of related academic papers during the course of his six-year PhD study. His thesis was entitled 'A study of the work attitudes and behaviour of employees in seasonal seaside hotels'. It consisted of a case study of hotel employees in hotels in Great Yarmouth, UK. Several different techniques were used: a standardized questionnaire (the Job Diagnostic Survey), a biographical questionnaire, structured interviews and in-depth interviewing. It was possible to view each set of results as a potentially separate topic. In addition, new ideas cropped up which were generally related to the PhD study, but not positioned directly in its path. Darren identified a number of 'frames' within his work, each of which offered a publication opportunity. In this way he was able to produce the following list of articles and conference presentations, which supported the development of his thesis.

1   Lee-Ross, D. (1992) An investigation to test the validity of the job characteristics model, applied to a sample of workers in seasonal seaside hotels, *First CHME Research Conference*, Birmingham, April.

This paper argued the validity of using new moderators in the job characteristics model, in order to differentiate difference in the work attitudes of specific worker groups.

2   Lee-Ross, D. (1993) An investigation of core job dimensions amongst a sample of seasonal seaside workers in five hotels, *Second CHME Research Conference*, Manchester, April.

This paper reported the identification for groups of workers who differed in terms of job attitudes and behaviour.

3   Lee-Ross, D. (1993) An investigation of core job dimensions amongst seasonal seaside hotel workers, *International Journal of Hospitality Management*, 12(2), 121–6.

This paper summarized the previous two conference contributions in more detail, for a more formal publication.

4   Lee-Ross, D. (1993) Two styles of management, two styles of worker, *International Journal of Contemporary Hospitality Management*, 5(4), 20–4.

An offshoot suggested by the main project was the possibility that management style had an effect upon worker behaviour. This paper dealt with a survey which investigated this possibility.

5   Lee-Ross, D. and Ingold, A. (1994) Productivity: academic solution or industrial nuisance?, *Third CHME Research Conference*, Edinburgh, April.

Worker attitudes and behaviour also influenced perceptions of productivity, which were being studied in a different survey of this particular group of hotels. This paper resulted from a collaboration with the group carrying out the productivity survey.

6   Lee-Ross, D. and Johns, N. (1995) Identification of different seasonal hotel worker categories, using the job diagnostic survey, *Fourth CHME Research Conference*, Norwich, April.

Rigorous analysis of the Job Diagnostic Survey results necessitated far-ranging statistical treatment, including factor analysis. This paper described for the first time the factor structure of the most recent version of the Job Diagnostic Survey instrument.

7   Lee-Ross, D. (1995) Attitudes to work and motivation of sub-groups of seasonal hotel workers, *Service Industries' Journal*, 15(3), 295–313.

This paper discussed in depth the biographical and behavioural attributes of some members of the worker subgroups that had been identified using the Job Diagnostic Survey.

8   Lee-Ross, D. and Johns, N. (1995) Dimensionality of the job diagnostic survey among distinct subgroups of seasonal hotel workers, *Hospitality Research Journal*, 19(2), 31–42.

This paper expanded and formalized the factor analysis material which had been presented at the Fourth CHME Conference.

Encoding Information

Once the audience and the intended message have been decided, the encoding process can begin. This usually involves expressing the information in a variety of forms, including diagrams, illustrations and tables, as well as text. Each of these forms must be adapted to the style, depth and content most appropriate for the intended audience. For example, black-and-white line drawings and photographs are usually satisfactory for academic readers (and certainly for academic books and journals), but these diagrams may be quite subtle and complex. Industrialists and trade journals often prefer colour illustrations with simplified, 'see-at-a-glance' formats. A common problem with coding information is that research authors are very familiar with their subject. Thus they tend to take for granted ideas and information which may be unfamiliar to the target audience.

Checking

Coding information is a complex process and it is worth building some kind of check into the report-writing process. For example, the work can be discussed with people with a similar outlook to the expected target audience, e.g. colleagues in an academic institution, or in industry. It is also critically important to review and edit all text, diagrams, figures and tables before publication. As a general rule it is impossible to get the encoding right first time, and it usually takes several adjustments before the article is acceptable.

Successful communication depends ultimately upon the success of the decoding process. Research ideas are always complex, and the audience is never as knowledge-able about the subject as the researcher. Therefore, the research writer must always seek to convert complex ideas into simple terms. Even then, complex or novel material may be hard for the audience to grasp. Everyone uses words in an individual way, and this means that readers have to disentangle the report's message from the writer's language, and then make sense of it in their own words. In order to make this process as easy as possible, authors must express themselves simply and directly. The ideas expressed in the report must be easy to locate by means of headings and tables of contents. The text must be as close as possible in style to the spoken word, and the diagrams and tables must be user-friendly. While writing and (particularly) editing a report, the author should envisage the intended reader struggling to understand it, annotating it and converting into new expressions. Thus reports should be written with this process of disentanglement in mind.

REPORTING FORMATS

A research report should have a clear overall structure, which comes across quickly to the reader. In order to achieve this, the objectives must be clearly stated at the outset and the significance of important ideas, hypotheses and results should become clear to the reader as the report unfolds. A clear initial report design makes it possible to do this, by linking together the different sections and themes and integrating the report in a coherent way. A good basis for designing reports is to consider the following basic elements, which are required in most reports:

- title;
- author details;
- acknowledgements/dedication;
- abstract/summary/executive summary;
- table of contents;
- introduction;
- aims/objectives/terms of reference;
- methods and methodology;
- results;
- discussion;
- conclusions;
- recommendations;
- references, notes, bibliography;
- appendices.

These elements need not appear as separate sections; often two or more can be amalgamated together. Moreover, there is no absolute 'right' way of ordering them: there is generally a logical order, but this depends upon the author's taste, the style of the report, its content and its target readership. Some of these report elements have a similar purpose to their counterparts in the research proposal (discussed in Chapter 3). Their functions are discussed below.

Title

A report title must say concisely what the research is about. Depending upon the report's target audience it may be worthwhile increasing the title's impact with a topical phrase or slogan. Titles can also be divided into two parts (like a proposal title – see Chapter 3), so that an eye-catching phrase is followed by a more prosaic statement saying what the report is about, e.g. 'Employee attitudes in the banking industry: a quantitative study using the Job Diagnostic Survey'.

Author Details

A report should generally indicate the name and address of the author. It may be helpful to give some other author details: for example, field of expertise, qualifications, interests and recent publications. This information may interest readers and motivate them to read the report. Most generally available publications ask for authors' names and details, but these are sometimes omitted (for various reasons) from privately circulated reports. A completely anonymous report is usually unsatisfactory. Because its claims cannot be verified, it contributes little to knowledge and is unlikely to be taken seriously.

Acknowledgements and Dedication

In the process of gathering data, the researcher frequently incurs a heavy debt of gratitude. People often put themselves out to supply information, or may generously spend time helping with the gathering or analysis of data. Organizations may help by making their library or archives available. A report should acknowledge everyone who helps in its preparation. Gratitude should be expressed adequately, but the format nevertheless kept as brief as possible.

Abstract or Summary

An abstract provides a thorough overview of the report contents in the minimum possible space. Journals and conference proceedings sometimes specify the maximum length of an abstract, which in any case should never exceed 500 words. An abstract is always written in hindsight, because it has to encapsulate the contents of the report, but it usually appears at the beginning. Publications often ask for keywords as well as an abstract, and it is good practice to identify and list the keywords before compiling the abstract. Some journals give useful frameworks for doing this; a good example is that provided by the *International Journal of Contemporary Hospitality Management*. This requires the author to examine the article and list its keywords according to a series of different criteria:

- county, geographical area, e.g. Africa, Sweden, developing countries;
- industrial sector, e.g. hotels, contract catering;
- organization/organization-related, e.g. small business, multinational, corporate image;
- people, e.g. consultants, trainers, top management;
- broad functions, e.g. marketing, production management;
- specific functions, e.g. sales promotion, scheduling;
- management and managerial activities, e.g. matrix management, policy-making, decision-making;
- other processes and subject areas, e.g. industrial relations, market research, economic forecasting.

The next step in writing an abstract is to review the report, noting all the major points, which are then rationalized, so that only the most significant remain. Abstracts must be edited with great care so that they are as concise as possible, but the meaning is still clear.

A summary performs much the same function as an abstract. It is usually aimed at a non-academic audience and therefore found in commercial reports rather than academic ones. The best of such summaries outline all aspects of the reported research, but emphasize the persuasive aspects of the findings and the action which should be taken to deal with them. Such summaries are often headed 'executive summary', implying that they provide a quick overview of the practical aspects of the report. By their nature, executive summaries need to stress the outcomes, recommendations and practical implications of the research discussed in the report.

Table of Contents

Sections and subsections of the report should be listed clearly near the beginning of the document to make it easier for readers to navigate their way around it. Contents sections may be formatted in two basic ways. Each section or subsection may be shown against the page number on which it appears, as is done in many textbooks. This makes the contents easy to find in overview, but if there are many short subsections, several may end up listed on the same page, and the table of contents can look cluttered and clumsy. Alternatively, the sections, subsections and even the paragraphs can be numbered, for example in decimal point format: – 1.0, 1.1, 1.1.1, 1.1.2, 1.1.3, 2.0 and so on. However, this may clutter and complicate the text unnecessarily. It also has consequences for the style of the report overall, making it look formal, pedantic or to some readers even intimidating.

Introduction

The introduction to a report is similar in concept to that of a research proposal, discussed in Chapter 3. It should be structured like a funnel, beginning with an account of the broad subject area and narrowing in scope until it identifies the conspicuous gap which is to be filled by the results of the research. Introductions to academic research proposals should be heavily referenced, to indicate that the author understands the field well and/or has contributed substantially to it. Commercial reports do not usually need to be introduced with a review of background knowledge, but they should begin by placing the research in context and whetting the reader's interest.

It may well be appropriate to discuss the purpose of the research project in the introduction, rather than having a separate 'aims and objectives' section. An introduction may also have to absorb other essential material which is not sufficient in importance or volume to form a section of its own. For example, it may be a good idea to amalgamate methodological discussions with an account of the theoretical background (to which they are often relevant). It may also be possible to view the methods used, or the sample, as part of the background. One way to do this is to divide the introduction into two parts. The former should supply the background, including the theory and (if appropriate) the methodology. The second should lead into the main body of the report, by discussing the aims, objectives or terms of reference of the work, and the approach used (for example, the method and the sample).

Aims, Objectives and Terms of Reference

Aims, objectives and terms of reference are ways of expressing the original purpose of the research. Aims tend to be general statements, which can be considered to consist of a number of objectives: succinct, measurable goals. Terms of reference are general statements similar to aims, usually imposed on the work from an outside agency such as a commercial client. Aims, objectives and terms of reference have been discussed in Chapter 3, and in principle it is possible to copy them from the original research proposal into the final report. In practice, aims, objectives and even terms of reference may change in response to new research findings or to developments in the wider subject area. Moreover, research reports (and particularly published articles) tend to deal with a specific, restricted area of the overall project, which happens to be topical at the moment, or to tell a particular coherent story. This is related to the 'artist's window' problem discussed earlier, and the aims and objectives may shift as the 'window' is moved. It is often best to incorporate them in the introduction of a report; a separate aims/objectives section is more appropriate in a research proposal, where the emphasis is on making the purpose of the work accessible. In a report, the main concern is to make clear the relationship of the objectives to the research work and its outcomes.

Methods and Methodology

A methods section should describe what has been done in clear, practical terms. In principle, it should give sample sizes and details of the techniques used, and indicate time scales or other specific factors which affected the work. A thesis submitted for an MPhil or PhD degree must give this information in great detail to show that the candidate fully understands the research process. A report intended for publication or for a commercial client must say what was done, but can restrict itself to a concise account of the most important points. These almost always include details of the scenario and the sample, but may omit details of standard quantitative or qualitative techniques which readers might reasonably be expected to know. Such details of the method are only necessary if a novel technique has been used in the research. Sometimes it is possible to cut the 'methods' section right down and include it in the introduction as described above.

It is important to distinguish clearly between 'methods' (what was actually done) and 'methodology' (i.e. the justification and evaluation of the methods used). Methodology normally has no place in a 'methods' section, unless a novel technique is being evaluated. If it is necessary to discuss methodology, this should be done in the introduction (if the methodology forms part of the rationale of the research work) or in the discussion (if the results need to be evaluated in the light of the methodology). It is perhaps worth mentioning in passing that methodology may itself play a part in structuring a research report. Experimental methodologies make the assumption that the experiment could be repeated by another researcher, and confirmed or falsified. They are therefore philosophically bound to give the fullest possible details of method for the benefit of those who might want to repeat the work. This is a characteristic of scientific articles, which mostly follow the experimental model. Research which makes no positivistic assumptions does not expect to be rigorously duplicated. Methodical detail is not required for the purposes of repeating the work, but it may nevertheless be needed for the discussion, because methods are apt to influence the data that are produced.

Data, Results

Experimental work aims to falsify or confirm theory. Therefore, the observations from experiments can be considered the 'results' of the research. This is not the case with work that is not strictly falsifiable, and many authors therefore avoid the subtitle 'results', preferring to put this type of information into a section called 'data'. This emphasizes that the data are not the principal output of the research, but only the basis upon which the author's conclusions and recommendations (the true output) have been made. It represents yet another example of the way in which management studies are distancing themselves from the scientific, positivistic base which dominated during the earlier part of the twentieth century. 'Data' sections themselves appear mainly in reports of quantitative research. Qualitative data are often reported in an integrated format, together with the relevant discussion. This is a good thing to do if separating the results and discussion sections would mean repeating information twice. Sometimes the methods used to gather the data are also included in the 'data' section, rather than being put in a separate 'methods' section, or in the introduction.

The data section answers the question, 'What was observed, recorded or experienced as a result of the research work?' It must present all the relevant data that have been gathered in the most concise, coherent way. From the reader's point of view, the facts in this section must be (as far as possible) interesting, digestible and clearly relevant to the report. Academic dissertations may reasonably include all the data gathered (though they should give some thought to organizing them so that they are relevant and easy to read). Reports for publication or for practical action should present only the most relevant aspects of the collected data. Data must often be analysed in graphs or tables before they can be evaluated. It is often best to publish data in this form, so that they are ready for further discussion in the subsequent chapter. Data should only be included in a report if they are to be discussed in a later section, and should be presented in a way that indicates to the reader that they are significant.

Discussion

The discussion section addresses the question, 'Which issues emerged from carrying out the research?' As a general rule, discussion must relate directly to data produced by the research. It may draw upon previous published work, theory or methodology, but should avoid simply repeating existing knowledge. The best way to write the discussion is to decide what is new about the results. The discussion should also say what has gone as expected and highlight any surprises. It should prepare the reader for any conclusions or recommendations that seem to flow naturally from the research. As mentioned above, it may be appropriate to integrate discussion with the reporting of qualitative results. Alternatively, it may be possible to add the conclusions to the end of the discussion section, but this can also become an excuse for poor mental discipline. It is important that the nature and functions of these different sections are kept clearly in mind, even though in practice they may be amalgamated together.

Conclusions

The conclusions section answers the question, 'What did the research discover?' This is not the same as asking what was observed or recorded, since the observations are only a means to an end, and the conclusions are concerned with the interpreted data. Conclusions are related to aims and objectives and the outcome of research should always be evaluated in terms of the original purpose. Conclusions must also follow the reporting and discussion of results in a relevant way, so that they emerge as natural outcomes of the research. It is important to avoid repeating details given previously; the conclusions should just outline what has been discovered and what it means. Readers often look at the summary first and then turn straight to the conclusions, so these must be clear, uncluttered and informative, encapsulating the work in a simple form. A conclusions section differs from a summary because it deals only with the outcomes and significance of the research. In contrast, a summary should present a brief outline of all aspects of the work, including details of methods and sampling, but usually does not have space to deal with its significance.

Recommendations

Research reports in practical subjects such as service industry management are expected to make recommendations. Ideally these should be designed to help practising managers. However, it is often impossible to avoid calling for future research before practical recommendations can be made. Recommendations must be clear and concise and it is often worth numbering them and (if they are diverse, or very numerous) dividing them into logical subsections for easy reading. The section must make clear who is expected to carry out the recommendations and how he or she should go about doing so. Recommendations should be located conspicuously, where readers can easily find them. Good places for this are within (or immediately after) an executive summary, or within (or immediately after) the conclusions. In commercial research reports, the recommendations often form the most important section and should be highlighted accordingly: for example, by printing them on coloured paper.

References, Notes and Bibliography

'References' and 'bibliography' are often used synonymously, but for the purpose of reporting (and publishing) it is better to treat them as two different functions. It may even be worthwhile to have two separate sections with these headings. References are precise locations in the literature from which ideas discussed in the text have been drawn. They must be given accurately and unequivocally, so that readers and researchers can locate and use them. On the other hand, a bibliography is a list of books, articles and papers which form background reading for the study. Thus the scope of a bibliography is often wider than that of a reference section. Although the items in a bibliography must be relevant, not every one needs to be integrated into the text of a report. References, by contrast, must not be listed unless they have been specifically cited in the text. It is important to check both the text and reference list just before a report is finalized, to make sure that they tally with one another.

Notes are comments which the author wishes to make about a piece of text to which they are not directly relevant. Notes can appear at the bottom of each page (footnotes), at the ends of chapters or at the end of the whole report. References are sometimes also listed on the relevant page or at the end of the chapters, occasionally mixed together with the notes. Although this can be achieved by using a single numbering system for both, it makes a text complicated and ungainly. As a general practice, both notes and page-by-page referencing should be avoided. Notes are seldom strictly necessary. It is almost always better to integrate them into the text, or simply to rationalize them away. Many publishers will not accept footnotes because they cause pagination problems. In any case, references collected in a separate section at the end of the text tend to be more useful for the reader than those at the bottom of each page.

References may be given in one or other of two basic forms, the numbered referencing system and the Harvard (author–date) system. In the numbered system, a number is inserted into the text at the point where the author wishes to place a reference: for example, after a quotation, or where an idea has been expressed which is not the author's, but is relevant to the research. The number is usually in parentheses or brackets or appears as a superscript: for example, (1), [1] or [1]. Although the name of the reference's author may appear at this point, it does not necessarily have to. At the end of the report, all the references are listed in numerical order (i.e. against the numbers that have appeared in the text), so that they can be looked up easily. In the Harvard system, the author's name must appear in the text at the point where the reference is made. Each reference consists of the author's name plus the date of publication, and in the reference section the list of references is organized alphabetically, with the dates (usually in parentheses) against them. This makes them easy for readers to find.

Numbered referencing looks neater and is less distracting to readers. It also keeps the references in the order in which they appear in the text, and this is sometimes helpful in terms of finding them in the list. However, readers (particularly academic readers) may wish to know the authors and dates of references as they read the report. It is also relatively difficult to insert new references into a numbered system, because all subsequent numbers must be changed in the reference list as well as in the text. The Harvard system enables readers to see the authors and dates of references as they crop up in the text (albeit at the cost of a little clumsiness). The alphabetical listing makes inserting, or removing, references considerably easier. Sorting routines in modern word processing packages make it possible to add references as they are needed and then to sort them alphabetically at the touch of a button.

Unfortunately, there are no universal standards for referencing, and each publication has its own house style. As a result, there are almost as many minor variants as there are publications. For example, some publications put (Harvard style) dates in square brackets or between commas, rather than in standard parentheses. Some enter the volume and number (i.e. the issue of a journal) in the form 'Vol. 2, No. 3', while others may use a bold typeface for volumes and brackets for the number, e.g. '**2**(3)'. Yet others may put the volume number into Latin numerals and the number/issue into Arabic ones, e.g. II(3). Titles of books or journals are often (but not always) italicized or underlined. (Before the advent of computer printers which could produce italics, everything that would eventually be italicized in the printed text was underlined in the typescript.) The place of publication sometimes precedes the name of the publisher and sometimes follows it. Titles of articles are often (but not always) enclosed in single or double quotation marks. The possibilities for minor variation are enormous, and authors are expected to put their references into the correct form before publication. The format of the references gives away the author's knowledge of the targeted journal, and may be a source of comment by referees. It is worth carefully examining the publication in which a report or article is to be placed and adjusting the style of the referencing accordingly. This by no means guarantees acceptance, but it is likely to dispose editors and referees a little more favourably towards the author.

Example 8.2   Referencing Styles

A typical journal reference in the numbered style is as follows. A comment or quotation would appear in the text of the report against a numbered insert, like this:

> Operations management, which has increasingly emphasized strategic awareness over the past few years, has also identified a need to recognize the importance of the service economy (2).

The reference would then appear as follows in the reference section:

2.   Johnston, R., 'Operations: from factory to service management', *International Journal of Service Industry Management*, Vol. 5, No. 1, 1994, pp. 49–63.

The same reference would be given in Harvard style as follows:

> Operations management, which has increasingly emphasized strategic awareness over the past few years, has also identified a need to recognize the importance of the service economy (Johnston, 1994).

The Harvard system makes it possible to present the same reference in the text in a different way, like this:

> Johnston (1994) notes that operations management has increasingly emphasized strategic awareness over the past few years and has also identified a need to recognize the importance of the service economy.

In both these cases, the actual reference would appear at the end of the report in an alphabetical list, in the form:

Johnston, R. (1994) 'Operations: from factory to service management', *International Journal of Service Industry Management*, Vol. 5, No. 1, pp. 49–63.

Note that the title of the article is in plain type (and in this case enclosed in single quotation marks). The journal title is italicized.

If there are two authors, both should be included, e.g. Johnston and Bryan (1994); or Johnston, R. and Bryan, R. (1994). It is better to avoid the '&' sign, which most copy editors replace by the word 'and'. More than two authors are usually indicated by the Latin '*et al.*': for example, Johnson *et al.* (1993) indicates that the article was written by three or more authors. This abbreviation (for the Latin *et alii* 'and others') should strictly be in italics because it is in a language other than the normal English of the text.

A book is referenced in text just like an article (i.e. by a number, or a name and date). In the reference list, the book title should be italicized. In most cases there are no volume or issue numbers, but the number of the edition must be given, and so must the name of the publisher and date of publication. For example, a typical numbered reference to a book might be:

3.   Oakland, J., *Total Quality Management*. Heinemann, London, 1989.

The corresponding Harvard reference would be:

Oakland, J. (1989) *Total Quality Management*. Heinemann, London.

A page number must always be given if the reference is a table, an illustration or a direct quotation from the text of a book or article. Otherwise it is not generally required in the case of a book. Initial page numbers of articles are almost always required, and for most referencing systems so are final page numbers. It is best to include all this information in references.

Articles may also be published as items or chapters in a book. In this case the title of the item/chapter should be presented in the same way as titles of journal articles (in normal type and often enclosed in quotation marks). The book title itself should be italicized (or underlined) like that of any other book or journal. For example, a typical numbered reference might be:

4. Messenger, S. and Tanner, S., 'Prudential Assurance: the "Way of Life" Programme', in R. Teare, C. Atkinson and C. Westwood (eds), *Achieving Quality Performance: Lessons from British Industry*. Cassell, London, 1994, pp. 143–69.

The corresponding Harvard reference would be:

Messenger, S. and Tanner, S. (1994) 'Prudential Assurance: the "Way of Life" Programme', in R. Teare, C. Atkinson and C. Westwood (eds), *Achieving Quality Performance: Lessons from British Industry*. Cassell, London, pp. 143–69.

It is possible (and may become increasingly necessary) to use non-literature references. A numbered example is as follows:

5. Deming, W., *Road Map for Change: the Deming Approach*, video recording. Encyclopaedia Britannica Educational Corp., Chicago, Ill, 1984.

Or

Deming, W. (1984) *Road Map for Change: the Deming Approach*, video recording, Encyclopaedia Britannica Educational Corp., Chicago, Ill.

Appendices

An appendix is sometimes a valuable addition to a report. It offers a chance to provide readers with material which would otherwise clutter the main text. For example, raw data or certain aspects of the method can be presented in this way. In particular, an appendix is a good way to show the details of a questionnaire or of interview transcripts. However, appendices used in this way must be relevant and easy for the reader to find. This means they must be numbered logically and always referred to clearly in the text. Sorting what should and should not be included may be a difficult task. It is often heartbreaking to have to discard hard-won material, and there is a great temptation to abandon mental discipline and add appendices indiscriminately. However, an appendix should not normally be needed for the reader to make sense of a text, and it is better to reword material or to leave it out altogether than to include it as an appendix. Only three types of material are generally justifiable as appendices:

- maps, plans or large diagrams which apply to the whole report;

- chronologies, genealogies or large schedules which are needed to understand the content or sequence of the data or method;
- practical details (e.g. of experiments, survey questionnaires or interviews) which are not relevant to the whole readership, but which other researchers might need in order to repeat the work or comment on the value of the results.

STRUCTURING THE REPORT

Logical construction is probably the most important ingredient of report writing. The overall sequence, the structure of each section and the text itself must all be planned so that the message comes through clearly. However, custom and practice should also be taken into account. Different subject areas, different publications and even different methodological stances tend to use different structures. A report with discrete subsections, numbered in a legal style (e.g. 1.0, 1.1, 1.2, etc.) may be more acceptable to some audiences, by virtue of appearing more businesslike and objective. Other readerships might find such a style off-putting, preferring a more literary approach, with longer paragraphs interspersed with subheadings. The style and structure should also take into account the interests of elegance and expressiveness. It is wise to include (or at least consider) all the elements of a report discussed above. However, some of these can be amalgamated together, rather than broken down into short dedicated sections. This tends to make the style flow easily and to avoid repetitions. Table 8.1 summarizes various logical amalgamations which have already been discussed above.

Table 8.1 Possible combinations of elements of a research report

Element name	Can be amalgamated with	and/or with
Title	None	None
Author details	None	
Acknowledgements/ dedication	None	
Abstract/summary/executive summary	Recommendations	None
Contents	None	None
Introduction	Methodology	Aims/objectives, etc. Method (perhaps data)
Aims/objectives/terms of reference	Introduction	
Methods	Data/Results	Discussion
Data/results	Methods	Discussion
Discussion	Data/Results	Conclusions
Conclusions	Discussion	Recommendations
Recommendations	Conclusions	Abstract/summary/executive summary
References	None	None
Bibliography	None	None
Appendices	None	(Appendices must not be amalgamated with any other section)

STYLE

The essence of successful research communication is to convey complex ideas in simple terms, in a way that fits with readers' coding expectations. The level of language, for instance, must be chosen so that it is easy to read, but will not be regarded as patronizing. Sentences should be as short and simple and as close to natural speech as possible. The fact that a literary construction with long paragraphs is used does not excuse unwieldy sentences or ill-focused thoughts. Short numbered paragraphs tend to expose poor English and long-winded communication.

The 'Fog Factor'

Long sentences make reading unnecessarily difficult, and so do long words. It is possible to grade structural complexity precisely, by analysing a convenient passage of 100 to 200 words and calculating the 'fog factor' as follows

$$\text{Fog factor} = \frac{\text{Number of words of more than two syllables}}{\text{Number of sentences}}$$

The fog factor of the passage (196 words) immediately preceding this sentence, but not including the headings, table or equation is:

$$\frac{36}{11} = 3.3$$

It is worth calculating the fog factors of articles intended for publication and comparing them with those of target journals. Articles will have a better chance of acceptance if they are clearly expressed, i.e. it is better to have a slightly lower fog factor than competitors. Removing unnecessarily long words reduces the fog factor and improves the decodability. For example, academic articles quite often employ the word 'utilize' in place of 'use'. There is a fine shade of meaning here. 'Utilize' is more appropriate than 'use' for expressing exploitation of something, or the use of something for a purpose other than its intended one:

> Strategies are concerned with improving the utilization of employees and getting them to accept that their interests coincide with those of the organization.

Or:

> It is possible to utilize a standard questionnaire for this type of research, but this is not the preferred approach.

The long words in the first sentence make it unnecessarily heavy going, although it is grammatically correct. The best way of editing such a sentence is to change the wording substantially, to something like:

> Strategies aim to get the best from employees by persuading them that their interests coincide with those of the organization.

In the second sentence the word 'utilize' is quite redundant. 'Use' is more appropriate and reduces the fog factor a little.

Complicated phrases also render text difficult to read. Many authors find themselves producing this sort of construction when they first sit down to write:

> When considering productivity measurement within the hospitality industry, some writers have based their recommended approach on the original concept of Johnson *et al.* (1992).

The first part of this sentence ('When considering ...') is a sign that the author has been 'wool gathering' (thinking vaguely about the background, but not about the matter in hand). It sets a scenario which should have been made clear much earlier in the article, perhaps even in the title. All that is needed in the text is the statement itself:

> Some writers have based their approach to hospitality productivity on the original concept of Johnson *et al.* (1992).

Subject, Verb, Object

The natural structure of the English language has a subject (a person or thing who/which performs an action), followed by a verb (an action), followed by an object (a person or thing to whom/which the action is done). This arrangement (subject, verb, object) is typical of the *active mood*. A typical sentence of this kind is:

> A pilot study explored women's experiences of public houses, using a small sample of middle-class women.

Here the subject (a pilot study) precedes the verb (explored) and the object (women's experiences).

Report styles should avoid addressing the reader as 'you', because to the writer, the reader is unknown. This may make it difficult to find a suitable subject in some sentences. A way around the problem is to use 'it' as the subject, like this:

> It is worth calculating the fog factors of articles intended for publication and comparing them with those of target journals.

Many publications prefer their articles not to use the pronouns 'I' or 'we' in text, although this practice is becoming more and more acceptable. A way to deal with this problem is to use passive constructions, in which the object of the verb appears first in the sentence.

> The sample used for the present study consisted of eight small hotels and guest-houses in the casual/holiday/business market. Proprietors were contacted and the nature of the project explained.

These sentences begin with the objects: 'the sample' and 'proprietors' followed by the verbs 'used' and 'were contacted'. Passive constructions are always more ambiguous than active ones, which is why they are harder to read. Standard works on style (such as Bowker, 1989) recommend authors to avoid passive constructions, but this is often impossible. Removing all passive verbs would lead to very clumsy or over-familiar sentences (for example, try doing this in the example above). Besides, in this example it is not necessary to put the subject in, because it is assumed that the work was done by the authors of the research article from which it comes. (Of course, if this was not the intention, the sentence must be changed.)

Another situation where passive constructions come into their own is shown in the following example:

> Activities must be planned and coordinated to make the best use of resources, meet customer needs, compete effectively and permit an overview of performance.

This sentence is actually a recommendation to the reader to plan and coordinate activities. It gives the author an opportunity to say why this should be done and it is not necessary to specify the subject of the action. However, authors sometimes use passive constructions where they lose all sense of who the subject is. In particular, phrases such as 'it is suggested' or 'it is felt' should generally say who is doing the suggesting or feeling. In academic papers this is often achieved by providing a reference.

The style of a report must be constantly compared with the style of other articles with which it will be compared, i.e. the publication in which it will appear, or the other reports with which it must compete. The rule is that using pronouns such as 'I' or 'you' is acceptable if the others do it. It is a gamble if they do not, but sometimes such a gamble may pay off in the form of better communication. There is a growing tendency for academic papers in business subjects to use 'I' and 'we' in their reporting, to emphasize a break from a more 'scientific' style.

Example 8.3   Tenses of verbs

The tenses of verbs subtly influence the way readers understand text, and for this reason it is important not to jump back and forth between present, past and future when writing a report. A workable rule is that work that has been done by the author should be in the past tense, while tables, graphs and theories may be discussed in the present tense. The work of other researchers and authors may be reported in the present tense to distinguish it from work done by the author of the report and place it in the domain of 'theory', e.g.

> Parasuraman *et al.* (1985, 1986) identify ten attributes which they regard as essential to the quality of all services.

Alternatively it is acceptable to use the present perfect tense, like this:

> Fick and Ritchie (1991) have employed the SERVQUAL instrument to compare services provided by various types of organization within the travel and tourism industry.

The simple past tense, i.e. 'Fick and Ritchie (1991) employed ...' is to be avoided in this case. Otherwise, readers might confuse the quoted work with findings of the report itself (also reported in the simple past tense).

The future tense may be used in research proposals to say what the author is going to do. It is sometimes also used in research reports to mention some aspect which will be discussed again later in the document. However, this is bad practice as a general rule. It tends to confuse the reader and should be unnecessary if the report is well-structured.

Agreements

A common problem of style is caused by the need to make subjects (especially pronouns) and verbs agree in number. 'He' and 'she' cause particular difficulties, because the use of 'he' throughout for a third person subject is not politically correct. On the other hand, alternative pronouns such he/she or (s)he are clumsy, pedantic and generally unsatisfactory. For example:

> A job competency is an underlying characteristic of *a person* in that it may be a motive, skill, trait, aspect of *one's* self-image or social role, or a body of knowledge which *he or she* uses.

'He or she' is clumsy, and in this sentence it clashes both with 'a person' and with 'one's'. In normal speech, 'one's' sounds pompous and 'they' is often used, like this:

> A job competency is an underlying characteristic of *a person* in that it may be a motive, skill, trait, aspect of *their* self-image or social role, or a body of knowledge which *they* use.

This is less stilted, but it is nevertheless an example of careless writing, because 'a person' is singular and does not agree with the plural 'they' and 'their'. In both cases, the extract needs extensive editing. One way to do this is to rebuild it in the plural around the phrase *'which people use'*, so that it becomes:

> Job competencies are underlying characteristics of individuals. They may be motives, skills, traits, aspects of one's self or one's social role, or bodies of knowledge which people use.

The potential masculine/feminine problem is removed by converting the singular systematically to the plural. In addition, it has been possible to increase clarity further (and reduce the fog factor a little) by cutting the sentence into two.

Academic journals are comparatively forgiving in terms of style. They will accept long-winded, non-conversational English, large numbers of tables and fumbling attempts at expressing new and complex concepts. These would generally be unacceptable to trade journals or to publications aimed at the general public. Practising managers tend to dislike learned discussions, but are often happy to see ideas expressed in their particular jargon. Thus, expressions such as 'downsizing organizations' and 'the bottom line' may render an otherwise complicated text acceptable to them. Articles for the general public must avoid the style of 'learned discourse', and should carefully weigh the amount of information they contain and the obscurity of the jargon they use. Too little and the author might lose credibility, but too much may confuse and alienate readers. (The way to achieve the best balance is to follow the style of articles published in the target journal as closely as possible.) Trade journal articles should also ration the amount of information they express. The guiding principle is that readers do not feel overwhelmed.

THE MECHANICS OF WRITING

To write effectively it is important to have a system. Different individuals approach the problem of how to think creatively in different ways, but it is seldom effective to sit over a piece of paper (still less a word processor) for a long time in the hope that ideas will emerge. This is a stereotyped situation which used to produce waste paper baskets full of crumpled, partly written papers, and nowadays leaves files full of disconnected thought on a word processor. It is often a good idea to earmark a fairly long stretch of time: a morning or afternoon, or even a whole day. However, the actual writing should be tackled in fairly short bursts (an hour at a time, say) interspersed by clear breaks for cups of coffee or gentle physical exercises. Everything should be written down quickly and saved, with the express intention of coming back and editing it later. In fact, every piece should be edited *several times* before it is finished. It is best if there is also a lapse of time between writing and editing. It is not a good idea to break away completely to do something else between the actual writing sessions, as this is distracting. Periods between the one-hour writing sessions should be spent near paper and a pencil, as this is the time when new thoughts and ideas often occur. A reasonable target for a day's writing is 1000 words.

A good system for producing a (hand written) manuscript is to write double-spaced (i.e. on alternate lines) in pencil on one side only of ruled feint paper (preferably with widely spaced lines). Pencil script can be erased and rewritten as required. Double spacing allows work to be edited and annotated and pieces can be added if necessary by cutting and pasting. For word-processed work, editability is enhanced by using a non-proportional font such as Courier which spaces well along the line, and double line spacing, which spaces well down the page. These details make it easier to insert comments. Wide margins also make it easier to make notes about the text during editing, and the pages should always be numbered, so that particular items are easy to find. It is essential to make and keep several electronic backups, which should be managed carefully, so that more recent versions do not get over-written with older ones. Hard copies of work should be produced at regular intervals, both for security and for editing, and they should be kept until superseded. It is worth maintaining a good stock of used paper for this purpose.

EDITING

Good editing is the single most important factor in successful writing. Editing allows the writer to get an overview of a document, and perhaps to see it through the reader's eyes. The more a work is edited the better it becomes, and experienced writers frequently edit work three or four times. Editing is a subtle skill which takes time to learn, but it is also a valuable learning process, through which skills of writing and expression are gained. Editing needs concentration and a clear head. It is best to do it somewhere away from the place where the actual writing is done, and like writing it should be done systematically.

It is best to resist the temptation to edit directly on to a word processor screen or on to manuscript. The reader (and any prospective publisher or editor) will see the document in the 'cold light of type', and it is always best to edit in this form (i.e. hard copy). This makes it much easier to read the material quickly and to refer freely back and forth to different places in the text, as the eventual readers will probably do. It also tends to put the written words in a fresh light. Hard copy for editing is best made on the back of used sheets (previous edited work, page proofs, etc.) in order to save paper. Editing should aim to take words out rather than to put new ones in, so that the edited version is generally shorter than the original. Editing should also aim to weigh each word and to make the text easier to understand. Details of spelling, punctuation and grammar should be attended to, but the overall construction, meaning and content are even more important. Editing should also consider the consistency of the work. For example, it is unnecessarily confusing to give a list of items to be discussed, which are then dealt with in a different order, or under slightly different names. A report or article should tell a coherent story, in which facts, figures and observations agree with one another at different points in the text. Editing must also ensure the accuracy of references to literature sources, appendices, figures and tables.

DIAGRAMS

Diagrams and illustrations can perform the communication work of hundreds of words, and lighten the task of reading. They are much the best way to express any concept or idea that has a spatial, figurative basis, or to model abstract concepts. However, diagrams should not be included gratuitously. They must be relevant and appropriate, and their significance must be clearly stated in the text. Diagrams and illustrations must be clearly labelled, titled, numbered and referred to accurately in the text.

It is as difficult to encode information into diagrams as into text (and similarly difficult to decode them). Each diagram should therefore be worked and reworked to make it as comprehensible as possible, a process analogous to editing text. This ensures that the illustration expresses what the author intends in a way which is accessible and relevant to the reader. It may be necessary to try out several versions of diagrams and tables in order to get the clearest, most appropriate one. There are some subtle conventions: for example, graphs may be better turned on their side to match the 'expectations' of the reader. The human eye naturally expects to see measures and dimensions in particular positions on a graph. For example, sizes, volumes, numbers and quantities are perceived as 'rising and falling', and are therefore easier to comprehend if they are represented along the vertical axis. Time, distance and movement are perceived as 'progressing', and are therefore easier to interpret if they are represented on the horizontal axis (Figure 8.2). Vertical measures such as histograms must always measure upwards, never downwards, and bar charts must measure from left to right, never right to left. Some examples of good and bad charts are shown in Figure 8.3. As with text, the simpler the diagram, the more

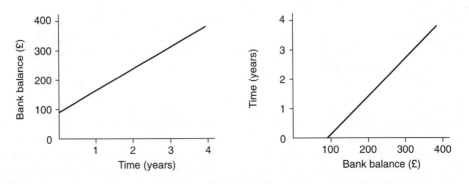

Figure 8.2   More and less acceptable forms of a graph

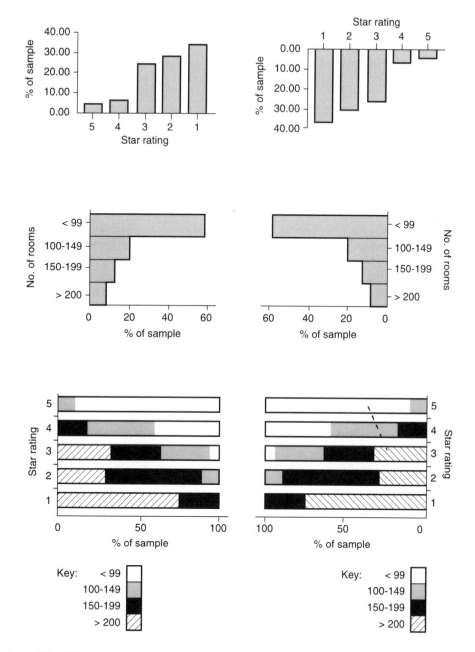

Figure 8.3 Different styles of histogram of different comprehensibility

accessible it is to the reader. Line diagrams representing relationships or models must also be developed very carefully. A good practice is to try new diagrams out on colleagues unfamiliar with the concepts they express. It is also worth questioning whether a diagram can be replaced by a table or vice versa. It is seldom necessary to include the same information in both forms, and a balance should be sought between tables and figures in terms of information density and comprehensibility.

TABLES

Tables can lighten text by putting lists or data into a readily accessible form. A table is sufficiently separate from the true text not to obstruct it, but is also available on the same page (or a nearby page) for reference. Tables can be divided into two categories: those which present information and those which simply store it. Tables designed to present (and clarify) information should be placed in the text in such a way that readers can refer to them as the discussion progresses. Tables which act as repositories simply store a mass of data. They are useful only as archives and should be strictly confined to an appendix. Such tables are included mainly for the benefit of other researchers who may wish to examine the work more closely and repeat it or compare it with their own. Whether tables are used depends on the target readership, since not all readers are accustomed to deciphering tables as part of their reading. Generally, however, readers of business- or management-oriented reports expect to find tabulated materials there.

Tables designed to clarify the text can make an important contribution to the communication process. As much care should be paid to encoding them as to text and illustrations. Tables should be simplified as much as possible. Every column, line and cell should be scrutinized to establish what, if anything, it contributes to the discussion. Those which seem to contribute nothing to the article should be removed. Tables, like diagrams, must be properly labelled, titled and numbered. As with graphs, it is sometimes possible to make tables more intelligible by turning them on their sides, so that rows become columns. Changing the order of the rows or columns may be helpful. It may also be worthwhile to split tables up into smaller sub-units and to spread them more thinly throughout the text. Tables can sometimes be lightened by including little diagrams or unexpected characters (Dingbats, Wingdings, etc.) within them, though this should not be overdone.

GETTING PUBLISHED

Getting published is an essential part of academic research. It enables individuals and institutions to establish their reputations, and frequently forms a basis for attracting research grants, better facilities or promotion. Researchers have a number of potential opportunities to get themselves into print, which can be summed up as follows:

- *Journals:* articles, review articles, conference proceedings, book reviews, trade contributions.
- *Books:* subject textbooks, contributions to edited collections, conference proceedings, research reports and other publications for official (e.g. government) bodies.

As already noted, the research process involves reading, abstracting and reviewing the work of others, as well as writing up the results of research work. The effective researcher is therefore in a good position to tackle all types of publications, as researcher/author, subject reviewer, book reviewer, editor, sole author or joint author. The implications of these different roles are discussed below.

GETTING PUBLISHED IN JOURNALS

Journal articles may be accounts of researchers' own work. Alternatively, they may be commentaries upon current trends, or upon the research of other authors. Subject reviews aim to provide an overview summarizing all work accomplished in the subject area in a concise form. A given journal may specialize in one particular type of material (for example, reviews). However, most prefer to accept quite a wide range of material, but to slant monthly issues towards particular aspects, concentrating upon a particular subject area or a particular type of article. Journals also usually have target readerships (e.g. mainly academic, or mainly industrial) and each therefore prefers its material to be written in a particular style.

For this reason, articles should never be sent out randomly for publication. They must be targeted at one specific journal. This increases their chance of being accepted, because it ensures that the style, structure and details such as referencing are correct for the intended publication. The discipline of getting articles right improves one's writing skills enormously and is never wasted, because the targeting becomes more and more accurate. Points to watch are correct style and language, correct length, and correct structure and format. For example, an abstract must be included for some journals but not for others. In order to make life easier for editors and referees, it is a good idea to use a fairly large font size, such as 12 point, leaving room for referees to make notes and comments. For the same reason, the text should be set out in double spacing, with wide margins at either side. Another way to help the editor of academic journals is to send enough copies of the article. Two are usually needed for the referees, and the editor may wish to keep one copy for reference. Many journals specify that they should be sent three copies of prospective articles, though some only require two. All this information can usually be found in 'notes for contributors' published within the journal itself, but editors will send copies out on request.

It may be worth contacting editors about an idea before writing the article. Most are willing to discuss a potential contribution, and can give useful insight into the sort of material that is likely to interest their readers and indicate the sort of changes which would adapt a piece of work to their journal. Editors generally plan journal issues well in advance and often centre them on particular themes. Thus, a little adaptation can make a proposed article more acceptable by fitting it more readily into a specific issue. Editors can often recommend other publications for which the article might be more suitable. Ambitious publication plans, such as a series of articles or a major subject review, should always be discussed with editors beforehand. As a general rule, they are less likely to be accepted 'out of the blue'.

Refereeing

Editorial policies of academic journals usually insist that all articles pass a peer review process before they can be published. This means that each article is sent anonymously to two members of the editorial review panel, termed the referees. A 'double blind' system is employed, so that neither the authors nor the referees know each others' identities. Referees either write a brief report or comment about the article on a standard form. They generally make one of three recommendations about it: it can be published as it stands, it may be published after specified modifications or it should not be published at all. Refereeing aims to maintain the editorial standards of the journal by weeding out work that is not novel or relevant and ensuring that articles are written as clearly and economically as possible. Although it sometimes seems to present an undesirable hurdle to publication, refereeing is usually very helpful for authors. It ensures that work is of a good standard, provides valuable advice on the presentation and content of research reports and helps to keep researchers in touch with new work. Some referees are extremely helpful, taking great pains with their analysis and providing detailed notes, references and comments. This aids the academic process considerably, and it is generally to the author's advantage to follow the referees' suggestions carefully. However, it is also important to remember that refereeing is in effect an academic discussion; it is quite legitimate to challenge the referees' comments.

Invited Contributions

Sometimes journal issues are put together from invited contributions. A designated editorial team invites well-known authors to contribute pieces on a particular topic. Such articles or chapters may not be subjected to the double blind refereeing process. Instead there is a dialogue between the editorial team and the authors, during which any questions or other points arising from the articles are sorted out. Invited articles may also start life as conference contributions, which will have already been refereed and discussed by an academic audience at the conference.

Textbook reviews are another way to 'get into print'. Book reviewers are usually invited to contribute by journal editors and a free copy of the book may be the 'reward' for submitting the review. Reviewing provides an opportunity to write a structured critique of an important academic work. The author of the book in turn benefits from the open discussion and constructive criticism which the process entails.

Editing and Proofreading

When an article has been revised along the lines suggested by editors or referees, it may be passed to a copy editor at the publisher's office. This individual reads through all the articles and deals with matters of style and detail. Copy editors are responsible for the consistency of spelling, grammar and English usage, and for accuracy of detail. They may also designate different subsections and headings, which may be negotiated with the author. The copy editing process usually gives rise to a number of queries which are sent to the author for clarification. Typical examples are references given in the text which do not appear in the reference list, inaccurate or incomplete references and apparent inconsistencies of fact or detail. Copy editing takes time, and editors are increasingly leaving this job to the authors themselves. The advent of the word processor means that text can be adjusted quickly in terms of both content and style, and can even be output in 'camera ready' typescript for direct incorporation into the printed work. The copy editor sends the finalized typescript to a typesetter, who produces a page proof. This is returned to the author for checking, and represents the last opportunity to correct mistakes before the work appears in print. It is worth making a note of the page numbers (if they are on the proof) before returning the corrected proof, so that one has an early indication of the exact reference of the article, but these can change.

GETTING PUBLISHED IN BOOKS

The needs of course curricula dictate the contents of most course textbooks, which usually consist of historical reviews of all major work in a particular field. Such texts are usually carefully market researched, by both the author and the publisher, to ensure that there is a suitable market niche. This is a far cry from the publication of a research-based textbook, which should not be undertaken unless it can present a substantial amount of novel material. Much of the material for a research-based text will generally have already been expressed in the form of articles, conference contributions, discussions or debates. Putting these ideas together in a more coherent and intellectually satisfying form is usually only possible after an extensive research career. Occasionally, however, a single major piece of research (e.g. a PhD thesis) is of such strong intrinsic interest that it is commercially feasible to publish it in its own right.

Co-authors and Edited Volumes

An alternative to authoring a whole book is to collaborate with others. It is important to agree the fine detail of structure and the book's philosophy, aims and objectives at the outset, and to maintain good contact between co-authors. If a large number of authors contribute to a book, a central group of individuals usually acts as an editorial board, taking overall responsibility for the coordination and style of the chapters. Books of this type include the proceedings of conferences and symposia, and also collections of current or previously existing works. They may be richer in terms of thought and approach than books by a few authors, but the coherency and coordination of the chapters may suffer unless there is efficient editorial control.

Commissioning Editors

Publishers employ individuals called commissioning editors, who are responsible for identifying new authors and potential new books. Commissioning editors attend specialist subject conferences, visit institutions and talk to faculty members in order to identify gaps in the market and line up potential authors. It is worth contacting a publisher and speaking directly to the commissioning editor in order to get a clearer idea about the likely market for a book. This in turn will provide valuable information about the appropriate subject material and the way it should be treated.

Proposals

Most publishers issue quite detailed guidelines as to what they expect a proposal for a new book to contain. The basic function of a proposal is to justify the idea and to structure it sufficiently to enable the publisher to see whether it is viable. A proposal for a new book should identify existing books in the same field, pinpoint the area not already covered by these volumes and explain why it is important. The target market for the book should also be clearly identified. It is usually desirable to give an idea of the overall structure by sketching out the contents of chapters and showing how they will contribute to the whole volume. Sections and subsections of chapters should also be indicated. Publishers often ask new authors to submit a specimen chapter. Book proposals are sent to subject specialists in universities and colleges, who give their opinion on the value of the proposed book for teaching or research and its likely market appeal. Book reviewers may suggest major changes in style and content, and the aspiring author usually has to negotiate with the publisher how these will be achieved.

Reviewing and Editing

Completed book typescripts are not reviewed in the same way as journal articles; in most cases, refereeing as such usually finishes at the proposal stage. However, books are such lengthy works that the potential for minor errors is much greater than in the case of articles. Copy editing of book typescripts covers the same issues as that of articles but usually produces far more corrections, problems and questions. When all of these have been resolved with the author, the publisher passes the finalized typescript to a typesetter, who produces page proofs. Checking these is a longer and more detailed task than checking the proofs of an article. Publishers often ask for an index to be compiled at the same time, because the page proofs should have the same pagination and numbering as the finalized book. Indexing helps the checking of proofs, because every page must be scrutinized for keywords.

CONCLUSIONS

All research must be communicated, usually in written form. All communication can be considered as consisting of three stages: encoding, transmission and decoding. Writing an effective research report means optimizing these processes by clearly identifying the intended audience and message, and by carefully checking the encoding and decoding of the work. It often is best to consider a project as containing a series of publication opportunities, rather than as one single, publishable event.

There is no standardized reporting format suitable for all kinds of research and all kinds of audiences. However, it is often helpful to think of a report as containing 14 potential sections or elements. It may be appropriate to omit some of these or to run them together in the interests of style, and to avoid repetition.

Good referencing is the hallmark of careful academic writing. There are two basic styles. Harvard referencing, the style used throughout this book, uses the author's name and the date of publication to indicate the reference in the text. Numbered referencing employs a bracketed or superscripted number for this purpose. Publications tend to have a house style based upon one or other of these two basic methods, but a large number of minor variations exist, based upon small differences of detail.

Style is very important in all forms of writing. Language must be as close as possible to the spoken word to make it easy to read. At the same time it must be precise and refrain from patronizing the reader. The complexity of a text can be measured by calculating the 'fog factor'. Authors should familiarize themselves with the rules of syntax and grammar.

Writing requires discipline but is also a creative process. Authors need to develop a system for producing written text, but should allow their own creativity to emerge. Editing is an essential skill to learn, and every piece of work should be edited at least three times before it is sent off. All work is copy edited before publication and this often produces questions which are referred to authors for comment or correction.

REFERENCES

Bowker, R.R. (1989) *Manual of Style*. US Government Printing Office, Washington, DC.
Pinker, S. (1994) *The Language Instinct*. Penguin Books, Harmondsworth.

Students may also find the following text useful: Poynter, J.M. (1993) *How to Research and Write a Thesis in Hospitality and Tourism*. John Wiley & Sons, Chichester.

Further Reading

MANAGEMENT AND PROBLEM-SOLVING

Allen, R.E. and Allen, S.D. (1997) *Winnie-the-Pooh on Problem Solving*. Methuen, London.

Management practice and problem-solving and research are closely interrelated. This book is easy to read and may provide 'leavening' among those recommended below. It will also help to keep the reader's mind lightheartedly on the underlying purpose of service industry research. In addition the problem-solving process discussed has striking similarities to qualitative analysis and to soft systems methodology.

Allen, G. and Skinner, C. (eds) (1991) *Handbook for Research Students in the Social Sciences*. The Falmer Press, London.
Bryman, A. (ed.) (1988) *Doing Research in Organisations*. London, Routledge and Kegan Paul, pp. 68–81.

These books in their different ways give valuable insights into the research process, from the soul-searching which accompanies it to the practical details of carrying it out.

Lashley, C. (1995) *Improving Study Skills*. Cassell, London.

This is a valuable book for anyone approaching research or study in the service industry vocational field.

RESEARCH PHILOSOPHY

Chalmers, A.F. (1982) *What Is This Thing Called Science?* Open University Press, Milton Keynes.

This is a readable book, which dicusses the development of philosophy in science in depth, with startling clarity. It is valuable as a comparison with the methodological views expressed in many social science texts.

188

SYSTEMS THEORY

Bertalanffi, L. von (1968) *General Systems Theory*. Braziller, New York.
Boulding, K.E. (1956) 'General systems theory; the skeleton of science', *Management Science*, 2(3), 56–68.

These are two of the classic works on general systems theory. Given the general interest in systems theory in management fields, they represent useful background reading for the research student.

Checkland, P. (1981) *Systems Theory, Systems Practice*. Wiley, New York.
Checkland, P. and Scholes, J. (1990) *Soft Systems Methodology in Action*. Wiley, New York.
Patching, D. (1990) *Practical Soft Systems Analysis*. Pitman, London.

Peter Checkland is perhaps the best known figure in soft systems methodology. David Patching's book places soft systems methodology in a simple, organizational framework, discussing it in an easily accessible way.

QUANTITATIVE TECHNIQUES

Ryan, C. (1995) *Researching Tourist Satisfaction: Issues, Concepts, Problems*. Routledge, London and New York.

This volume gives an account of research methods available for tourism research. The emphasis is mainly quantitative.

Lazarsfeld, P. (1955) *Survey Design and Analysis*. Hyman, Herbert, Free Press, New York.
Oppenheimer, A.N. (1992) *Questionnaire Design, Interviewing and Attitude Measurement*, 2nd edn. Pinter, London.

These two books provide a good grounding in the design of questionnaires and surveys.

STATISTICS

Miller, S. (1986) *Experimental Design and Statistics*, 2nd edn. Methuen, London and New York.
Ott, L. (1984) *An Introduction to Statistical Methods and Data Analysis*. Duxbury Press, Boston, pp. 549–57.

Both of these volumes discuss aspects of basic statistical analysis, providing details of testing, full formulae for calculations and so on.

MULTIVARIATE ANALYSIS

Malhotra, N.K. (1993) *Marketing Research*. Prentice Hall, Englewood Cliffs, NJ, pp. 589–611.

This is a good text for understanding multivariate analysis in a marketing context.

Nunnally, J.C. (1978) *Psychometric Theory*, 2nd edn. McGraw-Hill, New York, pp. 206–20.

This is one of the 'bibles' of quantitative psychological research, and provides a good understanding of the techniques and a detailed grounding in methodology and the philosophy of quantitative work.

QUALITATIVE TECHNIQUES

Glaser, B.G. and Strauss, A. (1967) *The Discovery of Grounded Theory: Strategies for Qualitative Research*. Aldine, Chicago.
Strauss, A. and Corbin, J. (1990) *Basics of Qualitative Research: Grounded Theory Procedures and Techniques*. Sage, London.
Gummesson, E. (1991) *Qualitative Methods in Management Research*. Sage, Newbury Park, CA.

As its name suggests, the volume by Glaser and Strauss is the classic text on grounded theory. The book by Corbin and Strauss is a shorter and simpler version, which provides a good way to get into the subject. Evert Gummesson's book discusses qualitative research methods in a business context, from the view of consultants as well as that of academic research.

Hamersley, M. and Atkinson, P. (1983) *Ethnography: Principles in Practice*. Tavistock, London.

This book provides details of ethnographic techniques, expanding on the outline given in Chapter 6.

OBSERVATION

Sanger, E.J. (1996) *The Compleat Observer*. The Falmer Press, London.

Jack Sanger's book is fast becoming the key work in observational research. It is written in an understandable style and contains a great deal of useful practical information about this type of qualitative research.

CASE STUDY METHOD

Patton, M.Q. (1980) *Qualitative Evaluation Methods*. Sage, Newbury Park, CA.
Yin, R.K. (1989) *Case Study Research: Design and Methods*. Sage, London.

Robert Yin's book is probably the most quoted text on case study method. He discusses all aspects of the subject in detail.

VALIDITY

Brinberg, D. and McGrath, J.E. (1988) *Validity and the Research Process*. Sage, London.
Bulmer, M. (1986) 'The value of qualitative methods', in M. Bulmer (ed.), *Social Science and Social Policy*. Allen and Unwin, London.

These texts discuss in detail the concerns that may be levelled at qualitative research. They analyse the underlying philosophical issues and provide independent views, against which readers can match their understanding of this complex area.

TRIANGULATION

Jick, T.J. (1979) 'Mixing quantitative and qualitative methods: triangulation in action', *Administrative Science Quarterly*, 24 (December), 602–11.

This is a seminal paper written on triangulation, which provides a more detailed look at the aspects discussed in Chapter 7.

WRITING

Pinker, S. (1994) *The Language Instinct*. Penguin, Harmondsworth.

This book contains a wealth of information about the way we communicate. It is well worth reading by anyone who wishes to design a questionnaire or interview research subjects.

Gowers, E., Greenbaum, S. and Whitcut, J. (1987) *The Complete Plain Words*. Penguin, Harmondsworth.

Plain Words is the 'bible' for anyone who wishes to reflect on written communication. It contains invaluable advice on expression and understanding in the written word. It also contains some amusing quotes and comments.

Poynter, J.M. (1993) *How to Research and Write a Thesis in Hospitality and Tourism*. John Wiley & Sons, Chichester.

This is a fairly basic book, designed for students on undergraduate programmes and below. However, it is useful because it breaks down thesis structure into its components and explains each one in detail.

Index

193